Alaska Memories

Alaska Memories

Adventure in the Wilds of Alaska

John McGoldrick

iUniverse, Inc.

New York Lincoln Shanghai

Alaska Memories
Adventure in the Wilds of Alaska

Copyright © 2007 by John McGoldrick

iUniverse books may be ordered through booksellers or by contacting:

iUniverse
2021 Pine Lake Road, Suite 100
Lincoln, NE 68512
www.iuniverse.com
1-800-Authors (1-800-288-4677)

Because of the dynamic nature of the Internet, any Web addresses or links contained in this book may have changed since publication and may no longer be valid.

ISBN: 978-0-595-41644-8 (pbk)
ISBN: 978-0-595-86111-8 (cloth)
ISBN: 978-0-595-85992-4 (ebk)

Printed in the United States of America

The events related in this work of creative nonfiction have been portrayed as accurately as the writer's memory permitted, but many of the names and identifying details of the characters have been altered to protect their privacy.

Cover photograph by Ningying Lou
Plates 1 through 22 by John McGoldrick
Plate 23: Photographer unknown. Photograph given to author in 1983.
Author photograph by David McGoldrick

For my children, David and Jessica.
And for my wife, Joan, who has done all the heavy lifting.

Contents

Acknowledgments

I would like to thank all those coconspirators who participated in my Alaskan adventures and generously gave of their help and friendship, thereby contributing to my survival. And, Alan Shavarsh Gardner, who loved these stories—teacher, mentor, musician, martial artist extraordinaire, and friend.

I would also like to thank Beth Wechsler, who provided me with invaluable advice and encouragement along the long road to publication.

Preface

As I look back over the years to the time that I, as a young man running wild, lived in Alaska, I feel a desire to commit to paper some of my experiences in order to provide a lasting memory for my children. I hope that in some fashion this book will help guide them along life's rocky course. I would like them to learn from my many mistakes and lapses in judgment, but I realize, as some wise man once said, that "wisdom comes from experience and experience comes from making mistakes." Mostly, I want to impart to them a sense of adventure, a love of wild places, and a realization that with determination, perseverance, self-reliance, and self-confidence you can do anything that you set your mind to. I want to point out to them, as well, that the bonds of special, lifelong friendships are forged during shared experiences, especially desperate, arduous ones.

I came of age in the 1970s, graduating from Bowdoin College in Brunswick, Maine, in 1977. I had no particular plan for the rest of my life but could not imagine inhabiting a nine-to-five world, and I certainly had had enough of formal schooling at that time. When my classmates had talked of business school, banking, or managing mutual funds, my eyes had glazed over. I had spent my free time then working in the woods of New Hampshire and camping, hiking, climbing, and kayaking throughout New England. Even these exploits seemed tame, and I was looking for something a little more adventurous. I often thought then that I should have been born a few hundred years earlier, when much of the Earth had been wild and still relatively unexplored. In retrospect, I now realize that there were still many wild places to explore, and of course, adventures could be had anywhere.

Chapter One:
On the Road

During the summer of 1975, at the end of my sophomore year in college, my friend Peter and I left Maine bound for Alaska in search of adventure and our fortune as Alaskan clam barons. We traveled by pickup truck, carrying an old Boston Whaler cantilevered out the back on a wooden cradle. That school year, Peter and I had lived in a weather-beaten house on an island off the coast of Maine, where we enjoyed exploring the rocky coast in our kayaks, paddling offshore to other islands, and surfing the winter waves.

"When I was in Alaska last summer, the crab fishermen were screaming for bait," Peter told me that winter. "They use clams for bait, and all we would need to do is find a way to get to the Alaskan clam flats," he said. "If only we could drag my old Whaler there, I know we could make a fortune digging clams."

Alaska. I conjured up images of glacier-encrusted mountains, miles upon miles of unpopulated wilderness, wild rivers teaming with salmon, and beaches littered with clams. The adventure of it all called seductively to me, and besides, I needed the money.

"Let's go, Pete," I said. "I'm sure I could rig up a cradle for the Whaler on the back of my pickup."

That summer found us rolling down the hard-packed dirt of the Alcan Highway on our way to the magical clam kingdom near the town of Cordova, Alaska. We were certain that millions of valuable clams were just waiting there for us to pluck them like juicy, ripe fruit, newly fallen from trees.

It was a long drive from the coast of Maine to Alaska—about five thousand miles—and one that I would eventually make many times. Peter was an affable sort who didn't let anything get him down for long and tended to look on the bright side. He wore wire-rimmed glasses and had an unruly mane of brown hair. In college, he had played lacrosse and hockey, while I had run cross-country and ski raced.

We couldn't afford to stay in hotels on the trip, so we slept in a tent beside the truck, usually cooking canned beef stew or ramen noodles on a small camp stove.

1

We occasionally varied our menu with stray ducks we shot from the cab of the truck in the wilds of Canada. In a hurry to make it to Alaska, we drove upward of eighteen hours a day. Our course took us through Canada, north of the Great Lakes, and the farther north we traveled, the longer the daylight hours became. The almost endless wheat fields of the Canadian Great Plains were dotted with small towns and a few larger cities. We traveled through Winnipeg, Manitoba, Regina, Saskatchewan, and Edmonton, Alberta, stopping every now and then to sample the products of the local breweries. The scenery changed as we reached Calgary, Alberta, and crossed the Rocky Mountains into British Columbia.

"We have to stop and spend a few days exploring here," Peter said, as we drove through Banff, British Columbia. "Look at those mountains and glaciers!"

"They're more rugged than the Rockies in Colorado and nothing like the mountains in Maine," I said. "But we can't stop, Pete. We're on our way to Alaska. These mountains will have to wait for another trip." Heeding the siren call of Alaska, we continued north to Fort Nelson and then to Dawson Creek, British Columbia, the start of the Alcan Highway.

The Alaska-Canadian Highway (known as the Alcan) was a 1,522-mile-long road originally carved out of the wilderness by the American military. During World War II, the U.S. Army had constructed a series of bases in Alaska, which were used to supply Russia by way of Alaska and the Russian Far East. As part of this project, roads had been built to support the bases. The most ambitious undertaking had been the plan to build the Alcan Highway through northwestern Canada to connect to existing roads in Alaska. After the Japanese invaded the Aleutian Islands, completing this road had become a high priority for the military. More than ten thousand U.S. troops, as well as Canadian troops and independent contractors, had completed the road in eight months. It had been an incredible engineering feat, given the wilderness terrain and the extreme weather conditions. The road had opened in November 1942, connecting Dawson Creek, British Columbia, to Fairbanks, Alaska.

The road we traveled in 1975 was unpaved and still had a wild reputation. There were roadhouses with gas pumps every few hundred miles; so semitrailers needed no extra gas tanks to travel the route. We crossed uneventfully from British Columbia into the Yukon and stopped for gas, food, and beer as needed—and not necessarily in that order. Gas stations in Dawson Creek did a brisk business selling headlight, radiator, and windshield protectors because of reports that passing semitrailers would spray oncoming cars with gravel shrapnel, resulting in broken headlights, smashed windshields, and leaking radiators. Along the road, our truck sustained a few minor wounds from passing trucks, but nothing similar to what had been advertised in Dawson Creek. We hit Swift River, Teslin, Johnson's Crossing, Jake's Corner, and then drove on into Whitehorse.

Whitehorse was the territorial capital of the Yukon and had a population of around nineteen thousand. It had received its name from the Whitehorse Rapids, which was by then submerged under Schwatka Lake behind a hydroelectric dam. The small town had grown after it became the terminal end of the White Pass and Yukon Railway, a narrow-gauge railroad, built between 1897 and 1900 at the time of the Klondike Gold Rush, which stretched from Skagway, Alaska, on the Pacific coast to Whitehorse. By the time the railroad had been completed, the Gold Rush was essentially over, but Whitehorse then had become an important staging and supply center for other mining operations because of its location at the head of the navigable portion of the Yukon River.

In 1975, Whitehorse was filled with dirt-encrusted pickup trucks whose drivers were either drinking from cans of beer, spiting chewing tobacco into them, or perhaps both. A large sign was planted by the highway reading: "Welcome to Whitehorse, Territorial Capital of the Yukon."

"Hey, are those people fighting under that sign?" Peter asked.

"Umm … no, Pete, they're not fighting," I said, when we got closer and could see clearly a man and a woman having sex under the welcome sign, just a few feet from the highway.

"You don't see that in Maine," Peter said with a laugh.

"Whitehorse must be an interesting place, Pete," I said. "Let's check it out."

With over nine hundred miles of the Alcan Highway behind us, we splurged and had a meal in town. "That looks like our kind of place," Peter said, pointing to the sign over a door proclaiming Scotty's Pizza.

The Scotty's Special had the usual "everything pizza" toppings and, in addition, was sprinkled with salmon, giving it a local culinary flourish. Driving that dusty road and then eating that salty pizza was thirsty business, so we located the closest bar. Up to then, all the bars we had visited in Canada seemed pretty much the same—dark and smoky with a pool table positioned centrally and inhabited by friendly Canadians whose every other word was "eh." This bar appeared to be no exception, so we walked up to the scarred wooden counter and ordered a couple of beers.

After our eyes adjusted to the dim light, I looked around and said to Peter, "Do you notice anything strange about this bar? We're the only non-Indians in the room, and everyone is staring at us."

Back in those politically incorrect days, the natives in Whitehorse referred to themselves as Indians—at least the gentleman drinking next to us at the bar did.

He turned to us and, looking us over said, or rather slurred, "I'm an Indian." Peter made some insightful comment about the weather. Then, the Indian looked us in the eyes and half-whispered in a perfectly sober voice, "What's it like to be responsible?"

We were nineteen years old, four thousand miles from home, driving a pickup truck with a Boston Whaler hanging out the back, on our way to dig clams in Alaska. Obviously, we didn't know what it was like to be responsible, but before we could muster a suitable response, something set off a bar fight all around us. As we watched in horror, a woman broke a pool cue over another woman's head. We ducked as glasses and beer bottles shattered against the bar counter and the floor, which was soon littered with overturned chairs and tables. The only two white boys in the room sensibly, and very quickly, retreated outside, unscathed.

"Wow, we're not even in Alaska yet, and we're having *way* too much fun," I said on our way out the door.

To this day, I wonder if that Indian was really a Zen master in disguise giving us a secret Zen koan—the kind of unanswerable puzzle that Zen Buddhist masters use to stimulate their students—to help us mediate on the meaning of life: "What's it like to be responsible?"

If we had been more experienced, we would have realized that that was enough excitement for one town, but being young and stupid, we moved on to the next bar. I'm sure I must have drunk more beer than I should have, because except for remembering some strange, flashing, psychedelic lights, the rest of the night is still a complete blank.

"You didn't drink any more than I did," Peter told me later on. "Someone must have spiked your drink."

"Or maybe the Scotty's Special was very special after all," I added.

In the morning I woke up in the cab of the truck, covered in Scotty's Special vomit, with Peter sleeping next to me, and a young Indian man snoring like a bear behind the wheel. The truck was parked beside a wide, slow-flowing river a short distance from the deserted dirt road.

"Peter, wake up!" I yelled, kicking him awake. "Hey, thanks for puking all over me," I grumbled, stumbling out of the truck to soak my head in the glacial river water.

"I didn't puke on you, you idiot," Peter pointed out. "You're the only one that ate the Scotty's Special."

"And just who is that?" I asked, pointing to the slowly stirring young man behind the steering wheel of the truck.

"That's your friend from last night," Peter replied. "Don't you remember offering to give him a ride home?" By this time our new friend was awake.

"Thanks for the ride," he said, climbing out of the truck and starting to amble away down the road as if this was what he did every day. "I never would have made it home otherwise, eh?"

"Hey, where are we?" Peter shouted after him.

"You're just outside of Carrmacks," he called back. "That's the Yukon River right there, eh."

"Carrmacks?" I muttered to Peter. "That doesn't sound familiar."

"Here it is," Peter said, pointing to a dot on the map. "And look, it's only 110 miles from Whitehorse."

"Yeah, but it's 110 miles in the wrong direction, Pete. You'll have to drive back to Whitehorse," I said, holding my pounding head. "I wonder if I'll ever feel well again," I whined, "or ever again eat salmon."

"Welcome to the Yukon," Peter said with a laugh and slapped me on the back.

We traveled back down the road, and this time, wiser from our recent experiences, we did not stop in Whitehorse, but headed directly toward the Alaskan border. Whitehorse was 290 miles by road from the border at Beaver Creek, and I was still feeling pretty miserable but hoped the restorative powers of youth would pull me through. As we headed west toward Haines Junction on the rutted and potholed highway, a beautiful, expansive, and unpopulated taiga landscape greeted us. The taiga is a subarctic, coniferous forest environment, located south of the tundra, and is dominated by fir and spruce trees but can also contain cedar, pine, larch, birch, and aspen. The area typically becomes swampy during the spring and looked quite wet when we passed through.

A few miles outside the small town of Haines Junction, the usual bumping, shaking, and rattling of the truck gave way to a sensation of freefall as Peter drove into a pothole big enough to swallow a semitrailer. The truck hit bottom and bounced out the other side with a sickening, loud cracking noise originating from somewhere in the back.

"What was that?" I asked, dismounting from the cab and fearing for the worst. "The rear axle?" Bending down to examine the undercarriage of the truck caused my head to ache twice as much as before.

"It's only this wooden brace," Peter said, pointing to the cradle supporting the boat. This was much preferable to a shattered axle, and we were soon able to make an adequate repair.

"Hey, Pete, watch out for the potholes," I mumbled, holding my pounding head as we continued down the highway.

At Haines Junction, the road jagged northwest to Kluane National Park. This park contained some of Canada's highest mountains, including the highest, Mount Logan at 19,524 feet and Mount Saint Elias at 18,008 feet, which straddled the border of southeast Alaska and the Yukon. The park also contained one of the world's largest systems of nonpolar ice fields. On the western shore of the turquoise-hued waters of Kluane Lake, surrounded by seven-thousand-foot mountains, lay the town of Destruction Bay. "Town" was too large a word, for what greeted us was a roadhouse with a gas pump and a few supporting buildings. "Destruction Bay … that has a nice ring to it," Peter said, pulling into the roadhouse for gas.

Destruction Bay had been established as a construction and maintenance station during the building of the Alcan Highway in the 1940s and received its name when a storm swept across the lake and destroyed most of the buildings.

"Just look at the color of that water," I said when I got a good view of Kluane Lake. "We have to take the kayaks out on this lake, Pete,"

"That shade of blue reminds me of the water in the Bahamas," Peter replied. "Let's go."

The turquoise lake water might have resembled Bahamian waters, but the glacier-fed lake certainly didn't feel tropical. We didn't dally too long out on the lake, because the Alaskan border was near and the clams were calling.

The border at Beaver Creek is only one hundred miles from Destruction Bay. In those days, there was a small customs house that was much like a weigh station on a modern highway. A large sign in front of the customs house read: "Welcome To Alaska" and below that were listed several exclusively Alaskan attributes, including the fact that Alaska had no snakes. Under this, someone had carved into the wooden sign, "until Jake arrived." Passing through customs was a breeze. The officials seemed mainly interested in what weapons we might be carrying. I had brought along my old lever-action Winchester .30–30 and a .22 rifle, which wasn't much firepower by Alaskan standards. The officials were unimpressed, took a brief look at the Whaler hanging out of the back of the truck, and waved us on across the border.

"Alaska at last," I said.

Chapter Two:
Cordova

Route One headed southwest to Tok, then on to Glennallen, and, eventually, to Anchorage. At Glennallen the highway split, and we took Route Four, the road that would take us to the coastal town of Valdez. It was 120 miles from Glennallen to Valdez, down a highway that initially followed the Copper River. It then became a twisting mountain road that crested over Thompson Pass. We were surrounded by waterfalls and glaciers as we finally glided downhill into the port of Valdez. In the early summer of 1975, Valdez was a beehive of activity connected with construction of the southern terminus of the Trans-Alaskan Oil Pipeline.

Valdez and Cordova did not sound like Alaskan names, and in fact, they had been named by a Spaniard, Don Salvador Fidalgo. In the late 1700s, the New World Empire of Spain had extended to the settlement of San Lorenzo de Nootha on the northwest coast of Vancouver Island. The Spanish, concerned about Russian fur traders establishing settlements in America, had dispatched the young Captain Fidalgo to sail north in 1790 to verify the extent of Russian encroachment. Sailing on the ship *San Carlos*, out of Nootha Bay, he had explored the area around Prince William Sound. He had found friendly native peoples living in the Cordova area and claimed the area for Spain, naming it Puerto Cordova after the captain general of Spain, Don Luis de Cordova y Cordova. Sailing north, the expedition had discovered an excellent harbor that Fidalgo had christened Puerto Valdez, for Don Antonio Valdez, minister of the Spanish Navy. Fidalgo continued north, finally encountering a Russian outpost on the Kenai Peninsula.

The town of Valdez was located at the head of a deep fjord surrounded by the snowcapped Chugach Mountains. The town had been initially a destination point for prospectors during the 1898 Klondike Gold Rush, and the Valdez Glacier Trail had been promoted as an alternate route to the goldfields for would-be prospectors sailing up from Seattle and California. After the gold petered out, the town's economy came to revolve around fishing. Valdez had been built on a foundation of glacial silt, and most of the town had been destroyed in the 1964 Alaskan Earthquake by a process known as liquefaction. The energy from the quake essentially had transformed the solid glacial silt into a liquid mass that led to a massive underwater landslide. Part of the town had sunk into the sea, and a thirty-foot tsunami had destroyed most of the rest. Thirty-two people had lost their lives in the quake. Valdez had been rebuilt subsequently on a more solid foundation at its present location.

Valdez had been used as a military base during World War II, and thirty years later, because of its excellent ice-free port, it had become the southern terminus of the Trans-Alaskan Oil Pipeline. The pipeline, completed in 1977, brings oil from Prudhoe Bay on the North Slope of Alaska to Valdez, where it is pumped into tankers and shipped around the world. The notorious oil tanker, the *Exxon Valdez*, struck a ledge not far from the port of Valdez in 1989, spilling eleven million gallons of its cargo and polluting a large area of the surrounding coastline. We arrived in Valdez on a bright summer day in 1975, two years before the Oil Pipeline was completed, and we spent only a few hours there because we were very close to our destination.

There were no roads to Cordova, and the only way to get there was by boat or small plane. The state of Alaska maintained an extensive ferry system, called the Alaska Marine Highway system, and we drove the truck onto the ferry for the five-and-a-half-hour, seventy-four-nautical-mile trip from Valdez to Cordova. The ferry ride was a welcome change from the long days of driving. Standing on the deck, we drank in the sea air, the blue water, and the forested mountains running right down to the shoreline.

"This is a little different from the coast of Maine, Pete," I said, taking in the scenery. I was used to jagged, rocky coastlines, having lived on the Maine coast, but this shore was wild, pristine, and uninhabited—and the snowcapped peaks gave it a much grander scale. We saw sea ducks, seals, porpoises, and a few orcas as the ferry wound its way through Prince William Sound, Orca Bay, around the Narrows by Hawkins Island, and into Orca Inlet. Finally, we sighted our destination—the fishing village of Cordova, which had been founded by prospectors around 1884 and named after Puerto Cordova, the legacy of Salvador Fidalgo.

The town had grown dramatically in the early 1900s, when copper, silver, and gold were discovered in the Copper River Valley area. A literal mountain of copper had been discovered by two prospectors, who selected a green, grassy appearing area on a hillside as a good grazing spot for their pack horses. The hill turned out to be a green-colored ore with the richest concentration of copper in the world. The prospectors staked their claim and formed the Chitna Mining and

Exploration Company. Following a typical historical sequence, wealthy eastern interests, including the Guggenheim family and J. P. Morgan, bought out the prospectors. They renamed the new company the Kennecott Copper Corporation and began development of the mine in earnest in 1903.

At first, ore had been packed out by horses on a trail to Valdez, but this was not very efficient, and in 1907, a survey was begun for a railroad to transport ore from the Kennecott mine to Cordova. Thousands of workers had flooded into the area, boosting the economy of Cordova. It took four years to build the 196-mile railroad, crossing canyons, skirting glaciers, and spanning rivers. One hundred and twenty-nine bridges had been built, the most expensive of which came to be known as the Million Dollar Bridge, spanning the Copper River near its mouth. This bridge has recently become something of a tourist attraction for Cordova and sparked political controversy in 2004, when the State of Alaska wanted to spend $17 million to repair the bridge. About 80 percent of the cost would have been covered by federal highway funds, giving critics a good example of political pork barreling: spending $17 million of tax payer money on a bridge that goes nowhere. The road deadends a few miles from the Copper River on the other side of the bridge, and no one lives within forty miles of it.

Cordova became the railroad terminus and port for shipping the ore by steamship to a smelter in Tacoma, Washington. The mines produced over $207 million worth of copper and silver (in early 1900s' dollars), with the peak production coming in 1916, when $32 million worth of ore was shipped from Cordova. The deposits were eventually depleted, and in 1938, the mines closed. Kennecott has been a ghost town ever since. When we arrived in 1975, the economy of Cordova revolved primarily around fishing and canning.

As the ferry rounded Hawkins Island and steamed into Orca Inlet, we could see Cordova across the sun-dappled blue waters, surrounded by the jagged, snow-clad mountains of the Chugach Range. The waterfront was dominated by a series of long, wooden, barnacle-encrusted wharfs, which were supported by pilings rising from the ocean. The wharfs were associated with the town's two canneries. The local fishing fleet was anchored behind the shelter of a rock causeway just southwest of the cannery docks, and several small, brightly painted houses formed the bulk of the town that nestled under the white peaks in a lush, wooded setting.

"Well, we made it to Cordova in one piece," Peter said. "Now we need to find a place to set up base camp."

In 1975, you could drive out of town a few miles, find a likely spot, set up a tent, and call it home without being bothered or raising anyone's concerns.

"This looks like a likely spot," I said, when we explored a secluded clearing in the woods by a small, crystal clear stream a few miles south of town, just past the local dirt landing strip out by Eyak Lake.

"Hey, look at these tracks," Peter said, pointing at large tracks in the mud that looked suspiciously like bear paw prints.

"Yeah, these aren't dog tracks," I said, kneeling down to study them. "You can fit your whole hand in one."

Sitting on the hood of the truck with my .30–30 in my hands, pondering our decision to set up camp by the creek, I noticed that Peter had his back to me while taking a leak, and I couldn't resist throwing a rock into the woods and shouting: "What was that, Pete?" In a blink of an eye he had leaped onto the hood in all his glory and started swearing at me.

"Oh great, Pete, first you puke on me, and now you're trying to pee on me. Where are you from … New Jersey?" I asked.

"That wasn't funny," Peter said. "There's no way we can camp here with all these bear tracks."

At least we hadn't unloaded every piece of gear yet, so it was back into the truck to search for another spot. This time, we tried a few miles west of town and settled into a wooded area. After pitching our oversized army-surplus tent and organizing the camp somewhat, we headed into town.

"Where are you guys staying?" one of the locals inquired, as we downed a couple of beers at one of the bars.

"Well, initially, we were going to set up camp out by Eyak Lake, but there were way too many bear tracks there," Peter replied.

"So, we moved camp just west of town were the road forks," I added, thinking he'd be impressed with our ability to avoid bear-infested spots.

"From what you're telling me, it sounds like you're only a few hundred yards from the dump. You might want to consider moving again. The bears enjoy dining there," he said with a laugh.

If only we had gone a little further down the road before setting up camp, we might have realized this error on our own. We soon sheepishly left the bar, resigned to having to move camp yet again. I'm sure the whole bar crowd had a good laugh over the stupidity of the two *cheechakos* from the lower forty-eight, as they refer to new arrivals from out of state.

"Let's check out the dump," I suggested on the drive back to the campsite.

"Look, there they are!" Peter whispered excitedly, when we got to the dump. He pointed at two huge brown bears that were foraging in the garbage.

"I didn't think they would be so big," I whispered back.

We finally resettled on a terraced hillside, midway between the other two locations, and made our summer home, such as it was, on a flat, mossy shelf surrounded by fir trees, just uphill from a small stream. It was a quiet, green, somewhat wet Pacific Northwest rainforest habitat, and as we settled in, it began to rain softly.

After getting organized and exploring the immediate area for a day or two, it was time to launch the Whaler and prepare to go clamming. There was a boat launch at the harbor, where we muscled the Whaler out of the truck and into the water. Once we secured our thirty-horsepower outboard motor, we were almost ready to make our clamming fortunes.

"We need to buy a couple of shovels," I said. "I'll go to the hardware store while you ask around as to where the best clam flats might be, Pete."

Early the next morning, we cruised north across Orca Inlet, heading for the appropriately named Mud Bay on Hawkins Island, about two and a half miles from Cordova. The summer sun reflected brightly off the cold water, and before long, we arrived at the island around mid-ebb tide.

"That's a lot of mud flat," Peter said, gazing at the extensive muck already exposed by the receding tide.

"Why don't we just beach the Whaler here, Pete?" I suggested. We had dug clams in Maine using small clam rakes on a recreational basis, but we had never dug for clams commercially.

"Let's start with clam rakes and see what we find," suggested Peter. As we scratched away at the mud, we were immediately rewarded with the sight of hundreds of small, quarter to half-dollar sized clams.

"Look at all these clams!" I exclaimed. "We're going to be rich!"

Swapping the rakes for shovels, we began harvesting clams with every shovelful of mud. The tide flowed out, leaving the Whaler high and dry, and we dug trench after backbreaking trench in the mud under the bright Alaskan sun. The day wore on, and eventually, the tide flooded back in and refloated the Whaler. We were covered in mud and exhausted from the digging but elated at our good fortune.

"Man, first day out and we harvested thousands of clams," I said, gazing at our catch, which weighed down the Whaler. "How much do you think they're worth?" I wondered.

"I don't know," Peter replied. "Let's head back to the docks and find out."

We motored slowly back across the inlet to Cordova, weary but excited at the prospect of selling our clams at the dock. "With all the cash we'll make from these clams, we'll be able to enjoy a good meal in town tonight," I said.

"It's about time we had a good meal," Peter agreed. "What a perfect Alaskan day."

Soon we tied off at the cannery pier and went looking for a buyer for the fruits of our day's labor. A crab fisherman ambled by and perused the catch with a quizzical look. "What are you going to do with all those clams?" he asked us.

"We're selling them for crab bait," Peter replied. "Interested?"

"There was a time when razor clams were used for bait," he informed us, "but not this type of clam. Besides, no one uses bait clams anymore; we use fish instead."

"Well, what can we do with them?" we pleaded.

"Might as well throw them back into the water, because no one will eat them either," he said.

Peter and I stared at each other as our dreams of a profitable summer clamming were crushed. Without speaking a word, we both bent down and started shoveling our hard-won clams back into the sea. Peter, being the irrepressible optimist that he was, started smiling, and soon we were laughing at ourselves. As the last clam plopped overboard, the late evening Alaskan sun set on our short careers as Alaskan clam barons.

"We need to find a job if we want to continue to eat," I told Peter. "I'm almost out of money."

"Me too," Peter replied. "The commercial salmon season will be starting soon. We might be able to sign on as crew on a gill-net or purse-seine boat."

"Okay, let's check the docks tomorrow," I said.

Cordova had a relatively large commercial fishing fleet at that time. We spent days walking the docks searching for work, but no one needed more help or didn't want to take on inexperienced crew members. Though disappointed at our lack of success, we didn't let these days go to waste. After an unsuccessful morning of pounding the docks, we went off in the Whaler to explore the surrounding coastline. After touring most of the southern edge of Hawkins Island, we took the Whaler out to Hinchinbrook Island, which lay about fifteen miles west of Cordova. We spent hours beachcombing the rocky shores and poking around its bays and inlets. Hinchinbrook was a fairly large island at 165 square miles and was said by the locals to have the highest density of brown bears of any of the islands in Prince William Sound.

Investigating the outlying islands wasn't the only exploring we did around the Cordova area. "Do you think we'll die if we slip and fall?" Peter asked, after we had scrambled our way up the beginning slopes of the Sherman Glacier.

"Well, we probably should have ice axes and crampons instead of sneakers," I agreed, staring back down the steep snow-ice slope. "Let's stop and eat here."

We had bought the largest watermelon we could find in town and had passed it back and forth like a medicine ball during the couple of hours it took us to muck our way through the glacial outwash plain and ascend to a point where we could look out over the delta area toward the waters of the Gulf of Alaska.

"Do you have a knife?" Peter asked.

"Of course," I said, stabbing the watermelon and splitting it in two. The glacier soon became littered with black seeds, and the sweet juice ran down our chins. It was a rare, crystal clear day, and the warm sun reflected off the silver water of the Copper River Delta in the distance.

"We need to take the kayaks and explore the delta," Peter suggested.

"Yes, that looks like fun," I agreed. "Maybe, if we don't find work, we can come back in a few days."

"I'll race you to the bottom!" Peter shouted, starting a glissade toward the snout of the glacier.

A few days later, we drove out to the Million Dollar Bridge that spanned the mouth of the Copper River, fifty miles south of Cordova on the road that went to nowhere. We intended to launch our kayaks from there. "I hope we don't get lost in this maze of channels," I said, gazing at the broad expanse of the delta through which the river braided.

"Let's paddle upstream first," Peter suggested, as we put the kayaks in the water. "That way, the road and the bridge will always be downstream, and we can stay oriented."

The Copper River was a glacial river, and the water was laden with glacial silt, the product of glaciers slowly crushing bedrock as they grind their way downhill, giving the water a slivery gray hue and making it hard to determine how deep the river was. I noticed something frequently jolting my kayak as I paddled through the icy, murky water. At first, I thought I was just grounding the boat on rocks or sandbanks, but it soon became clear that the river was full of salmon swimming upstream on their last journey to spawn. The fish were running into the kayak, and I was hitting a fish with almost every stroke of my paddle.

"Pete, I just saw a black head poke out of the water over there," I said. "Do you think there are bears swimming in here eating the salmon?"

"They're not bears," Peter replied. "Look again. They're seals!" And sure enough, a colony of seals was swimming up and down the river, chasing salmon and feasting on the Alaskan bounty.

That night, after enjoying a long, sunny day on the river with no one else in sight, except for the seals and the salmon, we camped beside the Million Dollar Bridge with a view of the Child's Glacier that emptied into the Copper River to the west.

"Look at that glacier," Peter said. "You don't see that in Maine."

"I never saw this many mosquitoes in Maine, either," I said. "Let's get the tent set up before we die of blood loss. We can heat up water for dinner in the tent." After a midnight meal of ramen noodles, we were lulled to sleep by the roar of millions of mosquitoes attacking the netting. The next day, we headed back to our base camp in Cordova to face the reality of our dwindling financial resources.

"Well, it looks like we have only one choice if we're going to stay in Cordova," Peter said. "We're going to have to find a job at one of the canneries."

I imagine that from the time shortly after humans first crossed the Bering Land Bridge, following migrating animal herds tens of thousands of years ago, they depended on the abundance of fish in southeast Alaska for their survival. Over the ensuing thousands of years, local native peoples built a rich culture based on the wealth of ocean resources, especially salmon. The geography of southeast Alaska, with its mountainous coastline and glaciers, mandated that travel along the coast be primarily by boat. This was true for the native peoples of the past, the Europeans who arrived in the 1700s, and remains true today, even with an abundance of bush planes.

The first European expedition to visit Alaska had been Russian: Vitus Bering, his second in command, Alexei Chirikov, and their crews. Bering was actually a Danish navigator and explorer hired by Russian Tsar Peter I to explore far northeast Siberia. Wandering in an extensive coastal fog, Bering had failed to find any landmass east of Russia during his first voyage in 1728. He had made a second attempt in 1741 on the *St. Peter*, and this time made landfall at Kayak Island in the Copper River Delta. He had explored the area and had established trade with the natives before sailing north to the Aleutian Islands. In December 1741, Bering fell ill during the voyage home and had to give up command. The *St. Peter* had then lost its way in a storm and wrecked on an island several miles off the coast of Russia. Bering, along with half his crew, had died on the island during the bitter winter. In the spring, the surviving crew had managed to build a longboat of sorts from the material salvaged from the *St. Peter* and had sailed home to Russia with a cargo of over nine hundred sea otter pelts. The furs had brought a great profit and had provoked much excitement in Russia for Alaskan furs. The Russians eventually had developed a lucrative Alaskan fur trade, and the first permanent Russian settlement had been founded on Kodiak Island in 1784.

In 1776, at the time of the American Revolution, Captain James Cook of Great Britain had explored the Alaskan coast while searching for a northwest passage. He named many coastal geographic features, such as Prince William Sound, Hinchinbrook Island, and Cook Inlet. By the early 1800s, the Russians were competing with the British, Spanish, and Americans for control of the fur trade and other rich natural resources of the area, including fish. In 1867, Russia, needing money, sold 375 million acres of Alaska to the United States for $7.2 million. That worked out to less than two cents an acre. At the time, the deal was called Seward's Folly, after Secretary of State William Seward who negotiated the purchase. Of course, he had the last laugh—the beauty and the abundant wealth of its natural resources made Alaska priceless.

In the early 1880s, the first canneries had been constructed to exploit the rich fishing resources, and between 1878 and 1949, over 130 canneries had been built in southeast Alaska. The first canneries had actually been salteries, where fish were split in two, gutted, washed, salted, and packed in huge barrels. These barrels sat for a week and were then drained, repacked with more salt, and shipped to Russia and Europe. In the late 1880s, a new method of preserving fish by canning was developed, and a new industry was born that continues to this day. Initially, the canning process had been very labor intensive, requiring each individual can to be cut from tin with shears, hand soldered, hand packed with fish, and then topped with a soldered lid. As new methods had been developed during the Industrial Revolution, more and more of the process had become automated. Canneries typically had employed Chinese, Filipino, Japanese, and Native American workers to man the cannery line, and Filipino workers still dominate the work force of some canneries today.

"Pete, I don't know about our diet," I said, rummaging through our diminishing supplies. "Eating nothing but rice and ramen noodles can't be any good for you."

"Well, I read somewhere that Indian warriors could exist on nothing but ground corn for months," he replied.

"Okay, let's give it a try," I said. Cornmeal porridge with raisins became at first our staple, but we degenerated to swallowing dry cornmeal and washing it down with cold water.

"Hey, this isn't that bad," Peter said. "The cornmeal expands in your stomach and makes you feel full."

"Yeah, but the full feeling just doesn't last that long," I replied.

On Sundays, we spent a few of our remaining dollars on a ham, egg, and hash-brown breakfast at the Frontier Café. We greedily looked forward to that meal as the culinary high point of the week.

The first cannery we visited was not hiring. "Well, the Morpac Cannery is our last hope," Peter said. When we got there, we asked around for the supervisor. After finally locating someone who could speak English, we were pointed toward a lanky, weathered man in a red baseball cap with MORPAC emblazoned above the visor.

"Are you hiring?" I enquired.

After looking us up and down, he said, "This is your lucky day, boys. I just lost two workers. When can you start?"

"How about right now?" Peter said.

The going rate in those days was somewhere between $4 and $5 an hour, with time and a half for overtime (over eight hours a day), and double time for more than sixteen hours a day. We weren't considered part of the regular cannery work force that got room and board as part of their compensation, and except for a few locals living in town, we were the only workers that did not live in the cannery barracks. We started in that day, but would not receive a paycheck for two weeks. Fortunately, we were saved from starvation by a care package that arrived from home the next day.

"That's the heaviest box I've had at this post office in a long time," the woman behind the counter said, as we picked up our mail.

"It's from my grandmother," I told Peter, placing it on the tailgate of the truck and slitting the cardboard top open with my knife.

"Look at all that food!" Peter yelled. The box was full of canned food, including canned sausages, canned Spam, canned chicken, and canned fruits.

"We're rich, Pete," I said, popping open a can of Vienna sausages. "Look at all that Spam."

There was also a letter from our mutual friend and college roommate, Ned, containing a golden, Bruce Lee good-luck medal to ward off bears or any other evil creatures that may be lurking in Alaska. "That might come in handy at the cannery," Peter said.

In the 1970s, the Morpac Cannery processed mostly salmon but sometimes crab as well. There are five types of wild Pacific salmon that are caught commercially in Alaskan waters: Chinook (kings), Sockeye (reds), Coho (silvers), Chum (dogs), and Humpies (pinks). Most years kings account for about 1 percent of the commercial catch; reds 25 to 30 percent; silvers 5 percent; and pinks make up the balance. Dog salmon is of lesser value because its meat is a pale, yellowish-red color.

The cannery was built on a pier so boats could dock up and offload their catch. It was the same pier from which we had shoveled our clams back into the sea just a few weeks before. The Morpac Cannery followed the general layout of most canneries. It consisted of a large processing house, built on the pier structure that extended onto shore. The fish were processed and then canned in the main building. There was a separate area known as the egg house, where salmon roe was processed and boxed for shipment overseas. This cannery also had a dormitory for the workers, complete with a kitchen and dining room. Salmon were off-loaded at the pier from the cannery-owned and operated tenders, boats that traveled to the fishing grounds with supplies for the fishing boats and ice for preserving the catch. The tenders returned with fish purchased from the fishing fleet. Individual fishing boats also occasionally pulled up to the pier, offloaded, and sold their fish.

The salmon, mostly reds and pinks, were transferred to the processing room where a machine called the "Iron Chink" cut off the head, tail, and fins. This machine also crudely gutted the fish and separated the egg sacs. The derogatory name was a holdover from earlier days, when Chinese workers preformed these unpleasant tasks. The salmon were then fed to the sliming line, where workers cleaned out the remaining entrails and washed and sorted the fish into different grades. Oversized and undersized fish were sent to the patch table and cut into small pieces that could be added to cans that needed extra fish to bring them up to weight. From the slime line, fish were fed into the filler machine, which sliced and diced the fish and filled the cans. The fish-laden cans traveled on a conveyor belt past workers who removed any excess fish or added more fish where needed. The cans flowed into a machine that fitted them with lids, sealed them, and then spit them back out onto the conveyor belt. The cans then traveled toward the end of the line, similar in layout to the checkout counter at a grocery store, where they landed on a narrow table, the top of which was made of rolling metal wheels. The cans were pushed into neat rows in a large rolling metal bin with a wooden-handled squeegee-like tool. Each bin, hydraulically controlled by the worker at the end of the line, had approximately twenty layers, with around a hundred cans per layer. When full, the bin was rolled into a walk-in retort cooker where the canned fish was cooked. The retort cookers had doors at each end and were located in the wall that separated the processing room from the warehouse. Once the cooking process was complete, the warehouse end door was opened and the bins were rolled into the cooling room. After cooling, the cans were loaded into yet another machine that applied labels, and then finally, they were boxed for shipment.

I guess we didn't appear smart enough for the slime line, because our first job at the cannery was manning the "grocery store checkout" counter, loading cans into bins and then rolling the bins into the ovens.

"Even you two will be able to do this," the supervisor informed us. "You just have to keep the cans moving."

It was a two-person job, and those two people needed to work cooperatively and quickly. The machine that sealed the cans spit them out at warp speed, and if you didn't keep up with the flow of the cans, they would back up into the machine. An ear splitting screech would then usher from the machine as it shut down, cans were crushed, and salmon splattered all over the line. The engineer would then have to come, give us a dirty look, heave a deep sigh, open the machine, and clean it out. The supervisor would also arrive, give us a dirtier look, and yell, "Either speed it up or get the hell out!" The other workers enjoyed this show almost as much as the fifteen-minute break they received while the machine was repaired. So there we were, hour after hour, day after day, pushing cans, loading bins, and rolling bins into the retort ovens.

"Peter, this is really mind-numbing work," I complained. "I'm getting hypnotized by all the cans."

"Well, look on the bright side," Peter replied, rolling out another loaded bin, "the meals and the coffee breaks."

We were not part of the regular work force, which was made up mostly of Filipinos, so we couldn't eat in the cannery dining room. However, we were allowed to enjoy the morning coffee break, which always included homemade donuts, as well as the afternoon break consisting of small sandwiches. If we worked till 9:00 PM, we could eat at another break, but the best of all was if we worked till midnight, when a hot meal was served.

"You're right, Pete," I agreed. "This is quite an improvement over dry cornmeal."

During the scheduled lunch and dinner breaks, we retreated to our truck to grab a quick bite. We must have looked pitiful sitting on the tailgate, staring into the dining room and drooling as the other workers enjoyed their meals, because the cook—bless her kind soul—would sometimes call us over to the back door and give us "scraps for our dog." Everyone knew we didn't have a dog, and the scraps were always a couple of whole steaks or similar delicious fare. On the nights that we were not working late, we scrounged salmon cheeks from the discarded heads, which we added to our rice or potatoes. Overall, our diet had improved tremendously.

Fortunately, we didn't spend the whole summer chained to the can counter. After a few weeks, we were rotated to other spots on the line, as well as the warehouse and the dock. We made some friends in the cannery crew, despite the language barrier, and early on in the season, when we were not working most of the night, we spent time with them in the local bars.

One night, we had an encounter with a notorious, extra-large Indian known as Raging Bear. He carried a bowie knife that could have passed for a short sword. For some reason, he took a dislike to one of our Filipino friends, who was minding his own business, quietly sipping a beer. Raging Bear ambled over to our table and began screaming at our small friend, who of course did not speak English. I didn't catch all the words, but they mostly revolved around some mishap that had occurred to Raging Bear at the cannery sometime in the distant past.

"This is getting out of hand, Pete," I whispered to Peter. "I can't understand what he's yelling about, and now he's fingering his knife handle. Remember what happened in Whitehorse?"

"Oh yeah, Whitehorse," Peter replied, "but no one else at the bar seems that concerned. I bet he puts on this show every night."

Now I'm not a particularly large person, but at least I was a lot larger than our Filipino friend, and I was also armed with my secret weapon, the golden, Bruce Lee good-luck charm. When I stood up and stepped between Raging Bear and our friend and brandished the shiny coin, everyone at the table burst into laughter, including Raging Bear.

"Let us buy you a beer, Big Bear, and we can forget all about this misunderstanding," I said.

"You really are crazy," Peter whispered, as the sumo-wrestler-sized Indian sat down at the table. We bought him a beer, and the night ended peacefully.

A week later, Peter hired on as crew on a seining boat and shipped out with the rest of the fishing fleet. Before he left, we loaded the Whaler back onto the truck in case he didn't return before I had to leave for Maine at the end of the summer.

The salmon season swung into high gear, and work at the cannery became busier, and the hours grew longer and longer. I worked from 6:00 AM until past midnight most days, and I soon gave up driving back to the tent in the midnight dusk, opting instead to sleep in the cab of the truck parked in the cannery lot. I spent a lot more quality time at the canning station, loading bins at breakneck speed, but this was frequently broken up by other interesting jobs.

My favorite job was unloading salmon with my Filipino friends from the holds of boats. The tenders were set up to make offloading fish from their decks easy, but regular fishing boats had traditional holds where the fish were packed in ice below decks. Three of us went below, and a basket attached to a winch was lowered through a hatch to where we waited in the half-dark hold. Digging through the blood-tinged ice with our hands, we loaded the basket with cold, slimy, half-frozen fish. As the bucket was hauled up and we were waiting for it to return, someone inevitably slapped me in the face with a slimy salmon, and a full-fledged fish-fight erupted. When the hold was unloaded, we emerged laughing, covered in silver scales, blood, and slime. After hosing off on the dock with cold sea water, it was back into the processing house.

One job I was barred from was working in the egg house. In fact, I never saw anyone in the egg house, except for the one Japanese worker who either didn't know any English or just never bothered to speak it. The Japanese importers were fastidious about their salmon caviar and didn't want anyone to prepare it except another Japanese. The skeins of eggs were taken out of the processing house in baskets, washed, weighed, and soaked in a large stainless steel vat containing a brine solution. The Japanese worker took the baskets out of the vat, and graded and sorted the eggs by size and quality. He then packed them meticulously into handmade wooden boxes, arranging the eggs artistically and giving them just the right dusting of salt. He personally nailed the lids onto the finished boxes and stacked them in the egg house for shipment to Japan. I never did acquire a taste for salted salmon eggs, preferring instead to use them for bait. I'm sure it's my loss.

And so, my first Alaskan summer neared its end. The fishing season started to wind down, and the hours at the cannery were not as long. The hours of daylight were becoming shorter as well. It actually became more or less dark for a few hours at night. As the last week of August approached, I needed to pack up and hit the road for the long journey in order to make it home before Bowdoin started the fall semester. Peter was still stuck out on the fishing boat and was not going to make it back to Cordova in time to drive with me. I said my farewells to my new Alaskan friends, drove the truck onto the ferry, and prepared for the solo transcontinental drive back to Maine.

I had discovered a new level of freedom in Alaska. The scope of the Alaskan landscape seemed almost limitless, and the people seemed far less judgmental and more tolerant, adventurous, and generous than I was used to on the East Coast. As I began my long trek home, I promised myself that I would return to Alaska at the next opportunity.

Chapter Three:
The Matanuska-Susitna
Valley

My first chance to return to Alaska came when I completed college in May 1977. Since I had no master plan for the rest of my life, I lit out (as Mark Twain would have said) for Alaska within a week of finishing school. The pickup truck was loaded with my worldly possessions: kayak, climbing gear, .30–30 and .22 rifles, and my two dogs. The older dog, Nancy, was a ten-year-old Black Lab-Weimararner mix, and the younger one, Denali, was a three-year-old husky mix that I had picked up at the local dog pound two years before. She resembled a wolf and had come from the pound with the name Denali. "Her owner just left the country for Asia," the woman at the animal shelter had informed me.

"Where does the name Denali come from?" I asked.

"Oh, she's named after some mountain in India," she said.

Later I learned that Denali is the Native American name for Mount McKinley, the highest peak in Alaska and North America. Denali translates as "The High One" or "The Great One" in the Athabascan language and is now the preferred name for the mountain, but Mount McKinley remains the official federal name and is retained on all United States Geological Survey maps, although the park itself is called Denali National Park.

After finishing my last semester in college, I had only a vague plan to drive to Wasilla, Alaska, where Todd, a friend I had worked for in New Hampshire, had recently moved. A college roommate and kindred spirit, Gig, had a similar plan to travel to Alaska after graduation. Gig had been raised in northern Vermont and had spent his formative years tramping through the Green Mountains. We shared a common interest in ski racing, and he had also been a track star in college, specializing in the pole vault. He was handsome, muscular, and much more outgoing than I was.

When Gig and I graduated, we planned a tentative rendezvous for later in the summer, somewhere around Wasilla, Alaska. So, armed with my liberal arts college degree and a full tank of gas in the Jeep pickup truck, I headed out with my two canine copilots on the road again to the freedom of Alaska.

Instead of driving all the way through Canada and over the Alcan Highway again, I drove directly across the United States to Seattle and caught a ferry. From Seattle, it was a three-day ferry ride to Haines, Alaska. The ferry had staterooms for sleeping, but like many young vagabonds, I chose to camp out on the deck to save money. There was a cafeteria amidships, and forward, near the bow, was an enclosed room, lined with rows of chairs, that was available on a first-come, first-served basis, where you could get out of the weather if needed. The dogs were not allowed up on deck, but I could go down to the car deck twice a day to walk and feed them. I was also able to take the dogs ashore at the various ports of call and give them a quick break from confinement in the truck. The ferry stopped only long enough to unload cargo and then load passengers and cars, so we made a series of short visits to the various harbors of southeast Alaska.

The most comfortable way to spend the night on deck was to claim a place sheltered from the wind and rain by an overhang of the superstructure and crawl into your sleeping bag. There were not too many of these desirable locations, and experienced deck travelers staked their claims early in the voyage. From the comfort of your deck campsite you could make friends with fellow travelers as you spotted whales and watched the southeast Alaska scenery slip by.

From Seattle, the ferry headed to Prince Rupert, British Columbia, a former tent camp for the Canadian National Railway that subsequently had become a major port for exporting Canadian products, such as fish and lumber. Outbound from Prince Rupert, the ferry crossed Dixon Entrance, open to the Gulf of Alaska and its sometimes huge Pacific swells, and then on into the relatively protected inside passage of the Alaskan Panhandle.

The inside passage wound its way through the Alexander Archipelago, made up of more than a thousand islands off southeast Alaska. These islands were the exposed peaks of the submerged coastal mountains that rise from the floor of the Pacific Ocean. They formed a maze of deep, fjord-like channels between mountainous, heavily wooded islands that were capped by jagged, snow-covered peaks with glaciers visible down many of the channels. In this northern rainforest lay the Tongass National Forest, which at seventeen million acres, was the largest national forest in the United States.

The next port of call was the town of Ketchikan, Alaska, on Revillagigedo Island along the Tongass Narrows. Ketchikan had been a supply point for miners during the Gold Rush of 1887, but when I got there in the 1970s, its economy was focused on fishing and logging. Ketchikan had an excellent harbor and was a distribution and supply point for a large area of southeast Alaska.

The town of Sitka, located on the western coast of Baronof Island, was the next stop. Sitka had been established by Russian fur traders in 1799 and had been the capital of Russian America—some of the Russian architecture was still preserved. When Alaska was purchased from Russia, Sitka had become the capital of Alaska, but in 1906, the capital had been moved to Juneau, where we headed next.

"We will be docking in Juneau in one hour," a voice from the ferry's loudspeaker informed everyone.

"I hope this mist and the clouds lift so we can get a view of the area," I said to a fellow deck traveler.

"I've been living in Juneau for five years now, and it's almost always cloudy and wet," he said, "but when the clouds lift, it makes it all worthwhile."

Juneau lay along the Gastineau Channel at the feet of Mount Juneau and Mount Nugget. In 1880, Joseph Juneau had discovered gold in a nearby stream, and a gold rush town was born. As was the case in all the other similar towns, when the gold had run out, fishing became the predominant activity. Juneau, however, was also the seat of the state government and had thousands of government employees living and working there.

As the ferry rounded a bend in the channel, the clouds lifted, and there before us lay Juneau, nestled on the shore of the channel, surrounded by snowcapped peaks to the north, south, and east, and with a view of the Mendenhall Glacier up the channel.

After a brief stop in Juneau, the ferry sailed on to my destination port, Haines, which was located on the northwest shore of Chilkoot Inlet, at the mouth of the Chilkat River. Unlike the other towns of the southeast panhandle, Haines was connected by a road to the Yukon, and thus to the rest of Alaska. Haines had also been developed as a supply point for the would-be miners during the Gold Rush. From Skagway, the miners had lined up in their thousands to climb over White Pass to Lake Bennet, where they had built rafts and floated down the Yukon River to the gold fields around Dawson City.

Haines was famous for having the world's largest concentration of bald eagles, and between October and January, more than three thousand eagles descended on a five-mile patch of the Chilkat River. This section of the river remained ice free during the late fall and early winter because of a geological formation known as an alluvial fan reservoir, which allowed relatively warm water to percolate up into the river and keep it from freezing. A late run of salmon spawned in this section of the river, and the eagles feasted on the dead and dying salmon until the river froze over. That May in 1977, the dogs and I saw a few dozen eagles soaring over the river as we drove north, following the Chilkat upstream into the Yukon.

"The ferry ride was a nice break," I said to my two canine copilots, as we headed north, "but I'm happy to be back driving into the Yukon Territory."

We traveled up the Haines Highway to Haines Junction. From there, it was on to the familiar landmarks of Kluane Lake, Destruction Bay, and across the border at Beaver Creek back into Alaska. At Glennallen, we headed down the Glenn Highway toward Anchorage.

I first caught sight of the Matanuska River as it trickled out from the terminus of the Matanuska Glacier, just south of the road. The terminal moraines of the glacier were clearly visible from the road, and the dogs and I took a break from driving and explored a bit. We clambered over several rocky moraines—the gravel leavings at the tail end of a glacier—and discovered a constituent stream of the silt-laden Matanuska River where it issued from the mouth of a large ice cave. Many such small tributaries of gray, mud-colored water coalesced at the foot of the glacier to form the beginnings of the river itself. We scrambled a little ways up some snow-ice banks, but didn't try to walk out on the glacier proper because of the danger of hidden crevasses.

The Glenn Highway followed the river as it cut a valley between the Talkeetna Mountains on the north and the Chugach Mountains to the south. There were a few roadhouses along the way, but no major towns until we reached Palmer, where the valley widened to form the beginnings of the Matanuska-Susitna Valley (called the Mat-Su Valley for short).

Palmer had been developed as a railway station in 1916 on the Matanuska branch of the Alaska Railroad. In 1935, during the Great Depression, the federal government had created an experimental agricultural colony in the Palmer area by transplanting 200 families from elsewhere in the United States to start farms. Under the Homestead Act of 1862, a person could claim up to 160 acres of land, and if they worked the land for five years and made improvements, the home-steader would receive title to the land from the government. The Mat-Su Valley was one of the few good areas for farming in Alaska, and many homesteaders were able to survive and even thrive.

The valley encompassed twenty-three thousand square miles and was located south of the Alaska Range, with the Talkeetna Mountains soaring to the north and east and the Chugach Mountains to the south. Glaciers had carved out the valley during the last ice age. Today, the glacial Matanuska and Susitna Rivers flow through the valley: both rivers are major waterways for salmon traveling upstream to their spawning grounds, and the rivers have given the valley a rich covering of glacial slit that supports farming. During the long days of the Alaskan summer, huge vegetables grow there, as well as hay for horses and dairy cows. The dogs and I made our way through this beautiful valley to the town of Wasilla and then on to the homestead, high on a bluff overlooking the Knik Arm portion of Cook Inlet, where my New Hampshire friend, Todd, was living.

The farm belonged to the Justin family, who had immigrated to Alaska in the 1950s from Oklahoma and homesteaded 160 acres on the outskirts of Wasilla. They had built themselves a beautiful log home on the edge of a bluff, with expansive views south across the Knik Arm Duck Flats to the snow-covered Chugach Mountain Range in the distance, with Pioneer Peak dominating the foreground, and they had raised their children there. Todd had recently taken up residence in a trailer on the homestead and had invited me to stop by when I made it to Alaska.

The dogs and I were immediately befriended by the Justin household, which included Bill Justin, his wife, Sally, and his son Bill Jr. The trailer where my friend Todd lived was in the front yard of the homestead, about a hundred yards from the main house. There was a small barn with enclosed pastures for their horses, a number of barking dogs, and a flock of Guinea hens running around loose.

"Welcome to Alaska," they all greeted me.

"Feel free to stay here for a few weeks until you get your feet on the ground," Todd added.

However, I soon learned that jobs were hard to come by that year around Wasilla. Construction on the Alaska Oil Pipeline had just ended, and many of the workers from that massive project had flooded into the Wasilla area, making jobs and rental housing scarce. The heavy equipment operators and laborers who had worked on the pipeline were flush with cash. Fancy new pickup trucks were evident everywhere. I was able to work for Bill Justin clearing land for a while, but more permanent employment was elusive.

Gig and John, another childhood friend who had migrated to Alaska, caught up with me in June, and we banded together. John and I had grown up together, ski racing and kayaking all over New England. We had spent the summers together since we were both thirteen, working for Todd in the woods of New Hampshire and generally being crazy, irresponsible teenagers. John was larger than either Gig or me, and strong, with a mop of long, shaggy, brown hair and a ready smile. He had a playful, outgoing, easy-to-get-along-with disposition and was just the type of person you would want to have with you in a tight situation.

Between the three of us we had four dogs, which meant we took up a lot of space and poured out a lot of energy. Not surprisingly, we soon outgrew our welcome at the Justins' homestead. In spite of much searching, we didn't find a place to rent with our canine menagerie, so we decided we would try to buy a place instead.

"Look at this ad for forty acres up in Sutton," I said, looking at the real estate section of the local paper.

Sutton lay eleven miles northeast of Palmer, up the Glenn Highway, hard by the Matanuska River, and was a legacy of the Matanuska coal mining boom of the early 1900s. Gold and copper were not the only important minerals to be found in Alaska. The state also contains about half of the usable coal deposits in the United States, and as the first prospectors had spread out searching for gold in the late 1880s, they soon discovered the Matanuska Coal Field, estimated to contain two hundred million tons of bituminous grade coal. Sutton had been founded in 1918 as a station on the Matanuska Branch of the Alaska Railroad that was built for coal export. Both underground and strip mines had been developed just north of Sutton, including the Evan Jones Mine, Jonesville Mine, and the Eska Mine. At that time, the railroad locomotives were powered by coal-fired engines, and the majority of the coal had gone to the railroad or to the two military bases near Anchorage that used coal-fired steam power plants. By mid-century, when the railroads had converted to diesel engines and the military bases had converted to natural-gas fired plants, coal mining ceased to be economically viable in the Sutton area and had petered out completely by 1960.

Our prospective forty-acre slice of the former Alaskan coalfields lay about a half mile up the Jonesville Road from the main highway. It really was a beautiful spot, if you didn't travel too far up the road to where the old coal mines were. The strip mines were ugly, black gouges in the earth. Here and there, remaining underground coal had ignited and continued to smolder, issuing foul vapors into the air. It would have made a good setting for the Land of Mordor in J.R. Tolkien's *The Lord of the Rings*.

The piece of property we were interested in lay in a wooded valley, overlooking the snow-covered Chugach Mountains to the south, and had a small, clear creek flowing through it. The house was a 1920s-vintage log cabin, built originally at the time of the coal boom. Ramshackle additions had been tacked onto the original small log house, and a freestanding barn, now used as a garage and storage shed, stood near by. The house was run-down, but it had a large, comfortable kitchen, leading out onto a screened-in porch, and enough room for all of us and the dogs. The owners were two older brothers, who lived there together and had been miners. They now wanted to cash out their Alaskan holdings and retire elsewhere. They also wanted to sell two horses along with the property, and the farmstead included a rocky pasture, with a small corral and lean-to barn for the livestock. All in all, it seemed like the perfect place for us to settle into. However, we hadn't thought through how we were going to pay for it, especially since none of us had a job yet.

"Well, if you have the cash for the horses now and can put another $300 down, we'll give you six months to come up with the financing for the place while you rent the house," one brother said, giving us a toothless grin.

"We'll even apply the monthly rent toward the purchase price," chimed in the other, staring at us with one eye as the other gazed off spookily into space.

I parted with most of my meager savings and became the proud owner of a decrepit-looking, twenty-five-year-old gelding named Charcoal and a much younger, fifteen-hand quarter horse mare named Janie. As a bonus, we now had a place for the dogs and us to call our own, at least for the time being. Our pet menagerie grew again with the addition of a Great Dane mix puppy that Gig picked up on the side of the road from a girl giving away puppies. He named the dog Rask, after a character in a book.

We spent part of an idyllic summer working on the property and riding the horses, while exploring our forty acres of half pasture and half forest. Eska Creek wound through the western section of the property, and its waters were cold, clear, and inviting, but it seemed devoid of any life. Certainly, there were no fish in it that we could find. The stream originated up in the mountains, where the coal mines had formerly operated, and the water was most likely contaminated with toxic wastes from the mines. I think we must have overlooked that fact, because we constructed a small dam out of rocks, behind which enough water collected to form a summer swimming hole. From the backs of the horses we hunted ptarmigan (a northern grouse) and squirrels in our wooded area. The ptarmigan were delicious, and the squirrel pies were at least edible.

"We need to find jobs soon, or we won't be able to come up with next month's rent," I said to my roommates.

"Not to mention the rest of the money to buy the place," John added.

At that time, Sutton was no more than a loose collection of houses, with a roadhouse-gas station located just off the main highway, so there were no jobs to be had in Sutton. As the summer wore on, we became more desperate and started looking for work in the Anchorage area. John was able to find a temporary job with the giant oil company Atlantic Richfield (known as ARCO) at one of their exploration camps, and he was soon gone. Gig and I had a harder time finding work, but we finally had luck—of a sort—when I called to ask about a classified ad in the Anchorage paper.

"Do you have any experience hanging sheetrock?" asked the voice on the other end of the line, who turned out to be a guy named Richard.

"Of course we're experienced," I said. "We used to hang sheetrock back east." I had only a vague memory of helping a friend hang a couple of sheets of gypsum board a few years previously, but at least I had seen sheetrock before and knew what it was, and I wasn't about to let ignorance stand in the way of gainful employment.

"I'm paying four cents a square foot and another penny to stock," Richard said.

I had no idea what he was talking about, but said, "That sounds fair," not wanting to give away our lack of experience.

"Meet me at my house here in Anchorage in the morning, and I'll give you directions to the jobsite," he finished.

"All right, Gig, now we only need to figure out how to hang sheetrock and come up with a few tools," I said.

Early the next morning, on our way to the rendezvous, Gig and I stopped at a hardware store to buy what tools we needed. "Can I help you guys find something?" the clerk asked us as we perused the tool section.

"We need some basic sheetrocking tools," I said.

"Both of you?" he asked.

"Well, yes," Gig said. "We were just hired to hang sheetrock."

"Do you know which tools you need?" he inquired.

"Not really," I said, "we're kind of new at sheetrocking."

"Well, you'll both need tool belts and sheetrock hammers," he said, putting two wooden-handled hammers that resembled small hatchets into our basket. "And let's see, a couple of razor knives, measuring tapes, two circular compasses, sheetrock saws, and, oh yes, some pencils. That should get you started."

"Do you know much about hanging sheetrock?" Gig asked.

"Oh, it's easy. You just put it up against the studs and nail it in place," he answered. "The only hard part is cutting out the holes for the electrical boxes," he continued. "Experienced sheetrockers coat the boxes with lipstick and then press the sheetrock up against them to outline their location. Then, you just cut out the hole with your saw."

"Thanks for the tip," I said, as we forked over most of our dwindling cash reserves for the new tools.

"We'll have to stop at a drugstore," Gig said, jumping in the truck.

Gig must have lost the toss, or more likely, he was just braver than me, and he went in to buy a few tubes of red lipstick while I waited in the truck with the dogs.

"Gig, that shade of red really matches your outfit nicely," I complimented him upon his return.

"Shut up," he replied. "Let's go meet Richard."

Richard hailed from Arkansas and had recently arrived in Alaska to start a dry-walling business in Anchorage. He took us at face value and gave us directions to the house we were to sheetrock.

"I couldn't find anyone to stock the house, so I'll pay you an extra cent a foot to carry the sheetrock in," Richard said. "I'll stop by later in the day to see how you're getting along." Fortunately, he was a dog lover and spent the time patting our dogs instead of examining our shiny new tool belts, sparkling new tools, and tubes of red lipstick.

We found the newly constructed house in the foothills of the Chugach Mountains, overlooking Anchorage, without incident and surveyed our project. On the ground outside the house lay two large stacks of sheetrock. Sheetrock—also known as wallboard, plasterboard, drywall, and gypsum board—is used for the surface of most interior walls in buildings. It is essentially gypsum plaster, sandwiched between two layers of strong paper. You cut it with a razor knife to fit, and then nail or screw it to the room's wooden studs. It comes in various sizes and thicknesses, but we used four-by-twelve-foot sheets of one-half or five-eighths-inch thick sheetrock exclusively. A sheet of half-inch rock weighs about ninety pounds, and a five-eighths-inch sheet weighs around 115 pounds. They come taped together in pairs, so two half-inch sheets weigh 180 pounds, and two five-eighths-inch sheets weigh 230 pounds. Anyway you look at it, they're heavy. There is an art to carrying, never mind hanging, sheetrock, but we had no clue how to do either, so we just jumped right in and started carrying the sheets.

"Gig, these things are really heavy," I complained.

"I know, but don't drop it," he said, as we muscled a 230-pound bundle into the house.

An hour later, exhausted from fighting the awkward sheets through the door and up the stairs, we gave up trying to carry in all the rock and decided to try our hand at hanging a few sheets. This went about as well as carrying the stuff in. Anything that could possibly be done wrong, we did wrong. We put the five-eighths-inch sheets on the walls, straight up and down. It was meant for the ceiling, and the sheets should have been hung crossways to the studs and joists. We hung the walls first instead of the ceiling, which would have been the correct way to do it. Hardly any of our nails were properly driven into the sheetrock so that they could be covered with mud compound later. Our only real talent seemed to be putting lipstick on the electrical boxes, but of course, it turned out that no sheetrock hangers really use lipstick. The only good thing that could be said for us was that we only managed to mangle and tack to the walls four or five sheets in the six hours we were there, before Richard showed up to inspect our progress.

Richard took a quick look around at our handiwork while we stood proudly, decked out in our new tool belts, shiny new tools, and tubes of lipstick conspicuously on display. He had only one question. "What's the lipstick for?" he inquired curiously.

"It's to mark the electrical boxes," we knowledgably answered.

Any half-decent sheetrock team would have been at least halfway done with the whole house by this time. He stared at us in amazement as we stood next to our pitifully few, improperly hung sheets, but Richard handled the situation calmly.

"I think you guys should take a break," he said. "Wait here until I come back, and please, don't hang any more sheets."

He soon returned with a rough-looking, muscular, forty-something man, who he introduced as Jake. Jake didn't have much to say at first as he looked around at the sloppily hung sheets on the wall, the untidy pile of sheetrock lying on the floor, and the red lipstick-coated electrical boxes in the room. Richard came right to the point.

"It's obvious that you guys don't know how to hang sheetrock," he said with a smirk. "Now, I can either let you go and pay you for today's work, or you can talk with Jake about working with him. He needs a partner. Now let's see ... you hung five sheets at four cents a square foot. That's $9.60, but you also managed to carry in twenty sheets at one cent a foot for another $9.60. That makes a grand total of $19.20 for the day," Richard said with a smile.

"What will it be?" he asked, peeling $20 off the top of a wad of bills.

Gig and I had a very short conference and decided we didn't have much to lose by working with Jake. We had just about killed ourselves for less than $10 each and figured it couldn't get much worse. "We'll work with Jake; if he'll have us," we said.

"Well, we can give it a try," Jake said, staring at us doubtfully. "But we split the money fifty-fifty; 50 percent for me and 50 percent for you two." Having no leverage for negotiating, we agreed to this apprentice arrangement.

"We need to carry the rest of the rock into the house before we leave," Jake added.

"Oh, great," I groaned, staring at those heavy stacks.

"Look, if it's too heavy for you, just pull the paper tape off and carry one sheet at a time," he instructed us.

"Why didn't we think of that before?" Gig asked, rolling his eyes at me.

Jake also showed us the proper way to pick up and carry the sheets and where to strategically place them throughout the house in preparation for tomorrow's work. It still wasn't easy, but it was a lot easier than the struggle we'd had before. After another hour or so, all the rock was stacked inside, and we agreed to meet back at the house early the next morning.

Exhausted, Gig and I loaded up the dogs and began the hour-and-a-half drive back to Sutton. "Well, that went well, Gig," I said.

"Yeah, what a great day," he sneered.

Rask, the puppy, was riding in the cab of the truck with us as we drove through Anchorage. Rolling to a stop at a red light, Gig stared at Rask and said, "Rask, you don't look well." Rask looked at Gig and promptly vomited a black, foul liquid all over him. "Ahh, what the …!" Gig screamed. "Hey, wait a minute. Didn't you take a dump in the woods behind the house before we left?" he asked, looking disbelievingly at his soiled clothes and grabbing his dog. Apparently, Rask had been dining in the woods while we had been working.

"Well, yeah. There are no port-a-potties at the jobsite," I admitted.

Gig leapt out of the truck screaming, tearing his clothes off in the middle of Spenard Boulevard. Naked, he dragged his dog around to the back and threw both the dog and his dirty clothes into the bed of the truck. He jumped back into the cab just as the light was turning green, still swearing and stinking.

"Now that is a perfect ending to our first day as Alaskan sheetrockers," I said with a laugh.

Chapter Four:
Jake

Gig and I ended up working with Jake for over a year. He lived in the Chickaloon area, eleven miles up river from Sutton. Chickaloon was just a dot on the map; there was no actual town, only a collection of a few scattered houses off the highway on the few hundred yards of buildable land between the Matanuska River and the Talkeetna Mountains. Before migrating to Alaska in the early 1970s, Jake had wandered the United States, working construction jobs—mainly hanging sheetrock. He had problems dealing with authority and putting up with routine daily hassles, and like a lot of people before him, he gravitated to Alaska, where he could keep these encounters to a minimum.

Chickaloon seemed to fit Jake just fine, and he had built himself a house off the Glenn Highway on a gravel shelf below a bluff leading into the foothills of the Talkeetna Mountains. If you stepped out his back door and walked north into the mountains, and could make it over the peaks, glaciers, and rivers, you wouldn't hit another road for over 250 miles. His nearest neighbor was miles away, and that was just how Jake liked it. What he lacked in formal education he made up for with native intelligence and street smarts. He liked to present himself as a tough, no-nonsense bad ass, which he certainly was, but he was also exceptionally well read, surprisingly articulate, and turned out to be an excellent teacher. He was patient with us and was able to transform Gig and me from a couple of bumbling klutzes into decent sheetrock hangers in a relatively short period of time.

With Jake living in Chickaloon and us in Sutton, we were able to commute together into Anchorage on our work days. Since we were paid by the square foot of sheetrock hung, the secret to making any money was speed and accuracy. Our days started early, 4:30 AM with the drive into Anchorage, and after a long day's work, we got back home around 9:00 or 10:00 PM. In the Alaskan summer, this was not much of a problem, given the twenty hours of daylight, but winter was a different story, when we had, at the most, only four or five hours of light. Our work schedules fluctuated throughout the year, depending on how much new construction there was. Richard kept us fairly busy that year, and we eventually became one of his steadiest and best teams of hangers.

That summer we also worked on the farmstead in Sutton and spent a lot of time riding and caring for the horses. Both horses had good temperaments and were easy-going, but Charcoal was an old, swaybacked horse and required more attention than the frisky, much younger, mare, Janie.

Before heading off for retirement in Texas, the wall-eyed brother had told us, "I don't know why, but old Charcoal will get these festering sores on his penis if you don't clean it once a week."

"You're kidding," I said, staring under the horse.

"No, it's not that bad," he continued. "You just grab it out of the sac and scrub it with warm, soapy water and then rinse it off."

"I think old Charcoal likes it," the other brother giggled with his toothless grin.

"Well, that's your job, Gig," I said.

"Yeah, right," he answered.

We more or less took turns each week and before long it became just another chore that needed to be done.

By the end of September, it was obvious to us that we were not going to be able to finance the purchase of the house and land. The two brothers had already departed Alaska and had left their elderly mother in charge of this real estate deal. She was none too pleased when we informed her in October that we wouldn't be able to buy the place.

"I told those two idiots not to sell it to you youngsters," she cackled at me over the phone. "Now I'll have to take care of it for them."

"I'm sorry, ma'am, but we have paid through the end of the month, so I think we're entitled to stay till then," I said.

"Not a minute more than that," she screeched.

"That went well," I said to Gig.

John had returned from his summer job with the mining company, so now we were once again the three musketeers, with five dogs and two horses, looking for a place to live on short notice.

"We're never going to find a place with all these dogs and the horses," I said.

"You're right. You need to sell the horses," Gig replied.

"I'll put an ad in the paper tomorrow," I decided. "Charcoal has been looking a bit poorly lately. I should really have a vet come out and look him over."

I was finally able to arrange for a vet to come out to see him in mid-October. The vet drew some blood from Charcoal for testing on the same day that a person called about buying a pack horse for hunting. I remembered the brothers had told me that Charcoal had been a great pack horse and had been on many hunting trips, but Janie had never carried a pack. The caller only wanted one horse to round out his pack train and opted for the experienced one. The next day he arrived with cash in hand and a horse trailer. He plopped down $600, and I gave him a bill of sale.

"Where are you going hunting with the horses?" I asked.

"My buddies and I are headed into the Talkeetna Mountains for three weeks," he replied. "We try to do this every year at this time."

As Charcoal disappeared down the road in the horse trailer, I turned to Gig and said, "At least we won't have to clean the gelding any more." Now we were down to one horse with only two weeks left to stay in the house.

A few days later, the official Alaska state veterinarian called to inform me that Charcoal's blood work had tested positive for equine infectious anemia. "That horse will have to be destroyed," he said. "There's no treatment for EIA, and it could spread to other horses in the area."

"I'm sorry, but I just sold that horse a few days ago," I replied.

He let out a long sigh and said, "Okay, where is the horse now?"

"Well, I sold him to a hunter from Anchorage who took him into the Talkeetna Mountains for a three-week hunting trip a few days ago," I responded.

"What!" he yelled down the phone line, following with a string of expletives. "How am I going to get a hold of that horse?"

"I don't know," I said sheepishly. "I don't even have the guy's name or address."

"I'm coming out there tomorrow and you better be there," he spat. "I understand there's another horse that needs to be tested as well. Don't sell that horse before I get there."

The disease was uncommon in Alaska and could have led to a serious epidemic. The next day, the state vet arrived and drew blood from Janie. He also quarantined her to the farm until her results came back. "If by any chance you hear from the person who bought the other horse, call me immediately," he said, as he departed. "And don't forget," he continued, pointing at Janie, "that horse there is quarantined."

Equine infectious anemia (EIA), also known as swamp fever, is a viral disease that can be transmitted from horse to horse by bloodsucking horseflies, deerflies, and mosquitoes. The EIA virus can only be transmitted by a fly or mosquito that has been interrupted while feeding on an infected horse and then feeds on another horse within thirty minutes. Flies and mosquitoes are frequently interrupted while feeding, so it is not hard to imagine how the virus could quickly infect a whole herd. Once a horse gets the virus, it is infected for life. The virus is fairly slow growing and usually causes intermittent symptoms, followed by normal periods. Horses develop a progressive anemia leading to tiredness, a staggering gait, and fever. To complicate matters, there are some horses that show no symptoms and are just carriers of the virus.

How Charcoal became infected was a mystery, but he could have been carrying the virus for years without displaying any signs. In retrospect, I could see that he had exhibited some of the classic signs of the intermittent fever that summer. There is no treatment or vaccine for the disease, so there are only two options for infected horses: to be euthanized or to be put under complete, permanent quarantine in a fly-proof building. The second option was not a realistic one for us or for 1970s Alaska.

We spent the next day hanging sheetrock in Anchorage, and when we returned home that night, were surprised to see a black horse illuminated in the headlight beams as we drove up to the house.

"Hey, there's Charcoal," I said happily.

"Yeah, but where's Janie?" Gig asked. "She's usually right here when we drive up."

"There's a note tacked on the door," John said, walking up the porch steps.

The note was short and sweet and to the point: "The black horse was no good for packing, so I took the other horse. I'll return the horse when I'm done hunting. You can consider the $600 as rent and you can have the other horse back."

"Oh, that's just great," I said. "Now I have a horse that needs to be destroyed, and the horse that was under quarantine has gone missing."

"The state vet is going to like this," Gig said.

The next morning I made the call. "Well, I have some good news and some bad news," I began. "The hunter dropped Charcoal off at the house last night so I have him right here."

"That's great," he said pleasantly. "I've been worried about an epidemic."

"Well, that's not all," I continued. "He also took the other horse with him."

"What!" he yelled, now sounding like his old self. "That goes against my quarantine order. I'm sending the state police out there tomorrow to sort this out," he finished, as the phone clicked in my ear.

"I think he took that pretty well," I said to Gig and John.

I didn't know if I could let them destroy Charcoal, since technically I didn't own him anymore, and I considered the other horse to have been stolen. In the morning, a state police officer arrived as promised, but he wasn't very interested in the problem.

"Look, the state vet can do whatever he deems appropriate; no matter whose horse it is," he said. "And the other horse wasn't really stolen," he continued. "Since a note was left, it's more like borrowing." Apparently having better things to do than look for horse thieves, the officer washed his hands of the whole matter.

"Give me a call if the other horse hasn't been returned in a month or two," he said, and he climbed into his patrol car and left us in a cloud of dust and flying gravel.

Janie ended up testing negative for the EIA virus, and the vet came back to collect Charcoal before he could disappear again. As he left with Charcoal, the vet turned and said to me with a smile, "I don't ever want to hear from you again."

October came and went without Janie being returned, but fortunately for us Jake was nice enough to let us move onto his property and live in an old broken-down school bus while we looked for another place to rent. His property was just off the main road, down a fifty-yard-long dirt driveway. Trees screened his house and two-acre gravel yard from the highway. The sign at the entrance to his property read: "No Trespassing On Pain Of Death." Like any Alaskan worth his salt, Jake had several junk cars, old washing machines, and assorted other broken and battered pieces of machinery scattered over his land. Among the debris was a school bus with flat tires and most of its windows shot out. It rested a couple hundred feet from his house in the middle of his collection of spare parts and assorted lawn ornaments. After evicting the mice and sweeping out the broken glass, we covered the shot-out windows with visqueen (clear plastic), moved in, and called it home.

"Don't forget about the two-by-fours," Jake warned us.

He had partially buried two rows of two-by-fours with spikes sticking out in his driveway to discourage any visitors.

"Did I ever tell you about the visiting Mormons?" he asked.

The Mormons had disregarded his warning sign and driven up to his house, dressed in their usual uniforms of black pants, white shirts, and ties. Before they could get out of the car, Jake had tapped on the driver's window with the butt of his shotgun. When the driver had rolled down the window, Jake had said in his nicest voice, "Do you hear that sound?" Apparently there had been an audible "shhh" as air had escaped from the four punctured tires. "That's the sound of all your tires going flat," Jake had said. "If you leave right now, you might make it a few miles down the road before you're driving on the rims. I'll even give you thirty seconds to get out of shotgun range." They wisely left in a screech of flying gravel. I wondered if this was how Jake came by all the junked cars littering his yard. Every time we drove in or out, we had to stop in the driveway, get out, move the two-by-fours, drive onward, and then go back and replace them.

Periodically, we drove to our old rental place near Sutton to see if Janie had been returned. Sure enough, about a week after we had left, we found her in front of the house. She seemed happy to see us, but we couldn't take her with us because she was chained with a hobble to the metal hitching post in front of the house. It was about nine o'clock at night, and there was no one home other than the horse. After giving her some hay and water from the barn, we returned to Jake's house to devise a plan to set her free.

"I don't want to talk with the state police again, and I'm sure they don't want to talk to me," I said.

"We could attach the winch cable onto the railing and pull it out of the ground with the truck," Gig suggested.

"Why don't you just cut the padlock?" Jake concluded. "You can use my bolt cutter. It will be easier and a lot less noisy."

"The voice of experience," I said.

Around midnight, Gig dropped me off on the road below the house. There was no sign that anyone nearby was awake, so I cut the padlock holding the chain together, and freed Janie. Slinging the bolt cutter and my .30–30 over my shoulder, I mounted the horse and rode her bareback down the road using a rope as a halter. The two of us escaped from Sutton without incident and crossed the highway to the bank of the Matanuska River. A full moon illuminated our way as Janie's shod hoofs clicked on the stones of the riverbank. Staying off the road as much as possible, I rode her through the chilly night for eleven miles, until we arrived safely at Jake's property. I tethered Janie to a telephone pole near the school bus and retired for a few hours of well-deserved sleep.

Stealing back my own horse in the middle of the night was not the only animal adventure we had. Soon after we had moved to Jake's place near Chickaloon, John's dog was run over and killed on the highway in front of the house. It was a sad day, and the event seemed to underscore the precariousness of our current living situation, but Jake tried to make the best of things.

"No sense letting that dog go to waste," Jake said. "I'll use it for bear bait."

He put the dog's body in a burlap sack and hung it from a tree about a mile from the house up in the foothills of the mountains. We checked the bait off and on for a week, but there was no sign of any bear activity. During one of these forays into the hills, Jake turned to us and said, "Have I told you I'm having a feud with my former brother-in-law? He drove out a couple of months ago and shot at the house from his car." Jake was vague on the details of what started the feud, and we didn't know if we should believe this story about Alaskan drive-by shootings. However, so far none of his stories had proven false, and this gave us pause as we considered how close we were living to his house.

"Do you think he'll show up again?" I asked.

"Don't worry," Jake said with a laugh. "I don't think he would bother shooting at the school bus, and besides, he's a piss-poor shot anyway."

We had promised Jake that we would try to shoot a moose to supply him with meat for the winter as a way to thank him for letting us stay in the bus, so on the days we were not hanging sheetrock in Anchorage, we were up early to hunt moose in the Talkeetna foothills above his house. There was plenty of moose sign around, but so far no moose. One cold, dark dawn, Gig and John crawled out of their sleeping bags and prepared to make another hunting pilgrimage into the bush.

"Come on you slug, let's get going," Gig said to me.

"Not today, man. I'm going to stay in my nice warm sleeping bag and get some more sleep," I muttered and rolled back over.

Two hours later, Gig woke me up with a yell, "I just shot a bear!" He was visibly trembling from adrenaline rush as he related his tale. "It almost killed me!" he shouted.

"Slow down, Gig," I said. "Where's John?"

He and John had split up, John going one direction around a small lake and Gig the other, with plans to meet at the opposite end. About halfway around the lake, Gig had been startled by noisy grunts and the snapping of twigs and branches behind him. He turned and faced a nightmare.

"It was less than twenty yards away, grunting and charging full speed through the brush," he said.

There was no time to weigh the options of what to do when facing a charging grizzly bear. Without further thought, Gig raised his Ruger .300 rifle and fired once at the galloping bear. "It dropped like a stone not ten feet from where I stood," he said, wide eyed. "I haven't been able to stop shaking since."

He had just taken the luckiest shot of his life. The bullet entered through the bear's right eye and exploded into its brain. A fraction of an inch one way or the other, and the outcome of the encounter would have been totally different. A grizzly bear's skull is extremely thick, and bullets have been known to ricochet off the sloping forehead. John had heard the shot and made his way over to where Gig was counting his lucky stars, expecting to see a moose. What he saw instead was a seven-hundred-pound grizzly, sprawled out in front of Gig, who was still staring in disbelief at the bear. John made sure that Gig was not injured and checked to make sure the bear was truly dead.

"What's that rustling noise?" John whispered to Gig.

The last thing they wanted to see was another bear, but to their dismay, they found two bear cubs a short distance away. Gig had unwittingly walked between the mother and her cubs.

"How old do you think they are?" Gig asked.

"About two years I'd say," John replied. "Most cubs leave their mothers at that age, so these two are probably old enough to survive on their own. You're lucky she didn't make a Gig sandwich out of you for their breakfast." The cubs soon wandered off, and Gig went back to fetch Jake and me while John stayed with the dead mother bear.

A full-grown Alaskan brown bear is an impressive, powerful animal—a true force of nature. There are three species of North American bears living in Alaska: the polar bear, the black bear, and the brown or grizzly bear. Alaskan brown and grizzly bears are classified as the same species scientifically. Bears found in coastal areas, where salmon is their predominant food, are usually referred to as brown bears, while bears found inland and in more northern habitats are often called grizzlies. Like people and pigs, bears are omnivores, meaning they can and will eat just about anything. Grizzly bears eat roots, berries, grasses, and small mammals such as ground squirrels. They can be opportunistic predators of newborn moose and caribou and are capable of killing full-grown animals, but they rarely spend time and energy on hunting large game, preferring to scavenge instead. Fully grown brown bears can range in weight from five hundred to over fourteen hundred pounds and may stand up to nine feet tall. Coastal brown bears are usually larger than the inland grizzlies, probably because of their access to a readily available supply of protein, namely salmon. The famed Kodiak bear is a separate subspecies found on Kodiak Island and can be much larger than the other brown bears, standing up to fourteen feet tall.

There is a wide range of opinions about what to do if you encounter a bear in the wild. It is generally accepted that you should try to not surprise bears. People are encouraged to make noise while hiking by singing, banging pots, or using a bell. This is not particularly useful advice if you are trying to be quiet while moose hunting. One should try to avoid thick brush, and if a bear is encountered, don't crowd it. Bears, like people, have a "personal space," an area that, when violated, makes the bear feel threatened. It seems only reasonable to grant a huge bear an extra-large space. Most bears would prefer to avoid people, and if given the opportunity to avoid an encounter, they generally will.

Bear attacks are rare, but what should you do if a bear does attack? All experts agree that you should not run. Bears can reach speeds of over thirty-five miles per hour in short bursts, much faster than a person, and running may make you look like food and trigger a chase response. Letting the bear know you are human by talking to it and waving your arms is considered a good idea. Imitating bear sounds and squealing like a pig is considered a bad idea. Bears have been known to make bluff charges, sometimes to within ten feet without making contact, but how you would be able to tell a bluff charge from a real one is not clear to me. If you are attacked, you are encouraged by the experts to surrender by falling to the ground, curling up in a ball, and playing dead. If the bear backs off the attack, remain motionless on the ground, because movement may bring the bear back for another attack. My favorite bit of advice from the State of Alaska is if the bear continues to bite you, he probably thinks you are food, and you might as well fight back as best you can, or, as Jake would say, "Just bend over and kiss your ass good-bye."

One thing everyone agrees on is that you should never, ever, get between a mother and her cubs. Female bears are fierce defenders of their young. Finally, if you are going to shoot a bear, you should have adequate firepower—at least a .300 magnum rifle or a twelve-gauge shotgun loaded with slugs for close encounters. Gig, obviously, had broken several of the recommended rules of engagement: but it's better to be lucky than good.

Jake and I went with Gig to the site of the encounter to help gut and carry out the bear.

"I'm going to make a rug out of this hide," Gig said, taking pains in skinning the bear and trying not to puncture the hide. He managed to do a decent job with the head and the rest of the body, but he couldn't negotiate the paws and had to just cut them off. After skinning and cleaning the carcass, we split it into quarters and packed the meat out of the bush the two miles back to Jake's place. We wrapped the quarters in cheesecloth and hung them in a shed to age for a week or so. Gig took the hide to a taxidermist in Eagle River to have it made into his rug.

All in all, we counted it a successful hunt. We butchered three of the quarters and wrapped up a good supply of bear meat for Jake's freezer. "Let's have a barbeque with the last quarter and invite some friends over," Jake suggested.

The next evening, we lit a large bonfire in the front yard by the house and improvised a spit for the bear quarter. We roasted it for several hours, taking care to thoroughly cook the meat in order to prevent the possibility of catching trichinosis, a roundworm parasite that can live in the muscle tissue of bears.

"This is great," Gig said through a mouthful of bear meat.

"This is the best meat I've ever tasted," I agreed, slicing myself another succulent piece.

We were all standing around the spit, slicing off chunks of steaming, hot bear meat with our knives, with grease running down our chins, and drinking beer, when an uninvited guest showed up to ruin the party. Fortunately, Jake had removed the spiked two-by-fours from the driveway, so when the game warden arrived in his truck there was no sound of air escaping from his tires.

I suppose we should not have been surprised to see the game warden, because news of a bear being shot did tend to travel fast. The warden, it seemed, was tipped off by the taxidermist that Gig had entrusted the hide to. State law allowed a bear to be shot in self-defense if you had not provoked it and there is no alternative, but the hide and skull were salvage and had to be turned over to the state. We were ignorant of these small details at that time.

"I was able to track you down from the address you gave the taxidermist," the warden informed Gig. "I've confiscated the hide and skull," he continued, "but I also need the paws and all the meat."

Now there were six or seven of us bearded, long-haired, dirty, rough-looking desperados standing around the fire with knives drawn and a profusion of guns lying close to hand. Jake, who doesn't typically respond well to demands, grinned at the warden viciously, spat in his direction, and pointing to the scrapes of meat lying in the dirt said, "Help yourself to the meat, that's all that's left."

The warden looked dubious and said, "Well, what about the paws?"

Without missing a beat, Jake stared him in the eye and said, "The dogs must have carried them off into the woods, and we haven't seen them since." Turning his back to the warden, Jake continued to slice bear meat off the spit and stuff it into his mouth.

You could tell the warden was debating with himself if it was worth pursuing this any further. He had already confiscated the hide, he was all alone, there was not going to be any bear meat. And, the ragged group of mean-looking bear eaters emanated nothing but hostility. I believe he made a good decision when he glanced at us one more time and, without saying a word, climbed back into his truck and drove out the driveway. Jake replaced his two-by-fours in case the warden decided to return, but that was the last we ever heard of the bear fiasco. I'm sure the bear skin rug looked great decorating the warden's floor.

Winter was beginning to settle in, and the school bus seemed less and less like a desirable spot to spend the winter. There was no shelter or pasturage for Janie anywhere on Jake's property, so I needed to bring in bales of hay from Palmer to feed her. So far, I had not been able to sell her, and she was looking pitiful staked out in the frozen gravel among the junked cars. We had been actively searching for another place to live but had no success.

One night, soon after bedding down and drifting off to sleep, we were rudely awakened by a series of gunshots that seemed to be coming from the direction of the highway.

"That must be the brother-in-law!" I whispered, peeking through one of the few unbroken windows of the bus.

"Look, Jake's returning fire," Gig said, as the flash of gunfire briefly illuminated one of Jake's windows. The whole episode lasted only a few seconds, and then we heard a car screech off into the night.

"Let's go check on him," John said.

Jake was standing in his doorway with his pistol, glaring toward the road.

"Are you all right?" I asked.

"Yeah, he's such a poor shot he missed me as usual," he said.

"There's no sign of any bullet holes in the house, Jake," John said, shining his flashlight up and down the front of the house. Jake was convinced his brother-in-law had paid him a visit again, but it's also possible some drunken idiot had been shooting at highway signs, a moose, or just shooting into the air.

"Well, he won't be back tonight," Jake said. "Go back to bed."

Walking back across the frozen gravel to the school bus, I said, "Using the dog for bear bait I could live with. Antagonizing the game warden was acceptable, but living next to the OK Corral is just too much. We need to find another place to live." The next day, I called Bill Justin in Wasilla to see if he had any leads for us.

"Well, Todd just left the state, so the trailer is for rent," Bill said.

"That's great, Bill. Can the three of us rent it?" I asked.

"Sure, there's plenty of room for three," he replied.

"Ah, Bill, we have four dogs also," I added.

"Well, as long as they stay outside the dogs will be okay," he said after a short hesitation.

"And, Bill, I have a horse as well," I finished. Only silence on the phone. "Bill … are you still there?"

"A horse, you say," he answered.

"Well, I'm actually in the process of selling her, and I'm sure she will be sold very soon," I added hopefully.

"Okay. Come on down then," he said finally.

The next day we packed our gear, borrowed a horse trailer, and moved on down the road to Wasilla. We thanked Jake for helping us in our time of need and continued to work with him hanging sheetrock from our new base in Wasilla.

Chapter Five:
Wasilla

The next day, we were ensconced in our new home and congratulating ourselves at having escaped from the school bus unharmed.

"Look at this," I said. "Heat, hot running water, an indoor bathroom, and a kitchen complete with a refrigerator and a stove."

"Yeah, what an improvement over the bus," John agreed.

As winter closed in, we were happy to once again become acquainted with modern conveniences. Janie enjoyed her new fenced-in pasture, where she was free to run, and she now had the shelter of a small barn in bad weather. The dogs, however, were probably disappointed with our new living situation. Bill Justin had a different outlook on dogs than we did. To us, the dogs were part of our family, with whom we shared our lives, and they were accustomed to having free rein wherever we lived. To Bill, dogs were more work animals than pets. Like his two dogs, our dogs were supposed to be outside animals that were there to guard the house, not to live in it. He had let us move in only with the understanding that our four dogs would be staying outside.

Our new home was in the front yard of the 160-acre homestead the Justins had staked out for themselves after Bill had finished his military duty in the early 1950s. "When my military stint in Anchorage was over, Sally and I decided to stay and homestead here on this bluff," Bill told us over dinner one evening. "There wasn't much back in Oklahoma for us, and I found plenty of construction work as Anchorage grew from a small town to what it is today."

"We built this log house ourselves, piece by piece, over the years and enlarged it as needed," his wife added. "In the early days, we lived mostly off the land, eating whatever we could grow or shoot."

He was soft-spoken, tall, thin, and tough. He looked exactly like the weathered Oklahoma cowboy that he was. She was more rounded than Bill—friendly, warm, and kind, and always working in the garden or canning vegetables, fish, or meat.

"Yup, the kids grew up eating moose, bear, and salmon," Bill chimed in.

"Bill shot that bear as it was ambling toward the kids playing in the backyard," Sally added, pointing to the stuffed black bear standing in a corner of the living room, just under a moose head mounted on the wall.

Wild game and salmon still made a large contribution to their diet. They always had moose and king salmon in the freezer or canned and stockpiled in the root cellar. They had one son still living at home, Bill Jr., who had recently graduated from high school and had just finished working on the Alaska pipeline as a union laborer. He was built like his father and had been a wrestler in school.

"Bill Jr. still keeps the larder well supplied with his hunting and fishing," Sally put in. "I'm sure he would love to take you all to his special spots. Isn't that right, Bill Jr."

"Of course, Ma. Anytime you want to go just let me know," Bill Jr. offered. He and a few of his Wasilla friends ended up sharing with us many of their secret hunting and fishing spots, and he became our guide, teaching us the Alaskan way to hunt and fish.

In the 1970s, Wasilla had a population of a few thousand people. Before the Europeans arrived, there had been several Athabascan villages dotted around the head of Cook Inlet. Around 1898, a supply station had grown into the tiny town of Knik, located at the mouth of the Knik River as it flowed into the Knik Arm portion of Cook Inlet. The Iditarod trail had run through here to supply miners working the interior gold fields in the Iditarod area. Supplies had arrived by boat or dog sled in Knik and then were transported to the gold fields by pack horse or dog sled, depending on the season. In 1917, with the construction of the Alaska Railroad, Wasilla had become the first boom town in the Mat-Su Valley, and the town of Knik had died out. Wasilla also had functioned as the entry point for the gold mines in the Hatcher Pass area of the Talkeetna Mountains just east of the town.

We continued working with Jake hanging sheetrock in Anchorage and had cut about forty-five minutes off our commuting time by moving to Wasilla. A week or so after moving in, we returned one day to find Gig's dog, Kiya, missing. Kiya was a beautiful, long-haired Siberian husky, which, unfortunately, had proven to be untrainable. Even Gig admitted she was the stupidest dog he had ever known and chalked it up to too much inbreeding. After she had been gone a day, we searched for her, driving around the area, calling her name, and asking neighbors if they had seen her.

The homestead was isolated on a steep bluff overlooking the Knik Duck Flats at the end of a long dirt road. Only a few other people lived along the road and in the general area. One of the neighbors happened to be Bill's son-in-law, Ernie, who lived about a half mile up the dirt road. Gig was driving by Ernie's ram-shackle place, when, to his amazement, he saw a hide hanging on the fence out front that looked just like his Kiya. He stopped his truck and made his way through the jumble of junked cars that had been reincarnated as chicken coops and tried to avoid the flock of squawking chickens that ran wild through the yard. Ernie, sporting a scraggly beard and dressed in greasy overalls, appeared with gun in hand.

"That looks like my dog hanging on your fence," Gig commented in a neighborly fashion.

"That is your stupid dog," declared Ernie. "I shot it while it was chasing my chickens, and I hung it up there so you would see it and know who shot it."

Gig really didn't know how to respond to this, but demonstrating wisdom beyond his years, walked away realizing that there was nothing to be gained by further antagonizing a person that seemed so unstable and confrontational. There was a lot of friction between Ernie and Bill Sr., who had a habit of spitting on the ground after speaking his name, but Bill never enlightened us as to the cause of their differences. Did everyone in Alaska feud with their in-laws?

"Sorry about your dog, Gig," I said. "This seems to verify Bill's opinion of Ernie's character."

"Yeah, we need to stay away from him," Gig concluded.

Janie was next to depart from our lives. As promised, I continued to try to sell her, and one night, a man from the Willow area called interested in the horse. The next day, he drove out to the homestead with his thirteen-year-old daughter in tow. "I'm looking for a nice gentle horse that she can ride," he said, pointing to his daughter, who was stroking Janie's neck.

"She's big, but she's about as gentle as they come," I said. "Go ahead and ride her around the pasture bareback if you want."

His daughter fell instantly in love with the horse, as young girls are wont to do. She brushed Janie, fed her apples, and rode her up and down the pasture. It seemed like a perfect match, the father had even brought a horse trailer so they could take her home with them that day.

"She really likes that horse," I pointed out to the father.

"She sure does," he agreed. "And I would surely like to take the horse home with us today, but I'm a little short on cash right now. Would you consider making a trade for the horse?"

"Trade? What kind of trade?" I replied dubiously.

"Well, I just happen to have a shotgun here in the truck that I'd be willing to let go for the horse," he said, reaching into the cab.

I don't know if they had perfected this negotiating technique in the past, but as the man gave the gun one final polish on his jacket and handed it over for inspection, his daughter continued to stare at me with a pleading look in her eyes while softly stroking Janie's neck. There was really nothing special about the gun, a twenty-gauge Remington pump action that appeared to be in reasonably good condition. I went through the motions of inspecting the gun while glancing back and forth between the horse and the girl. I realized the gun was probably worth about one third of what I was asking for the horse, but I said "yes" after only a few moments of considering my options. I needed to get rid of the horse to stay in Bill's good graces, and I had been trying to sell her unsuccessfully for months. I didn't have a shotgun at the time, and I would certainly be able to put the gun to good use. Besides, the girl and the horse seemed to be meant for each other.

"You're the worst negotiator I've ever seen," Gig told me, shaking his head afterward. "Just pathetic. I can't believe you traded your horse for that gun."

I still have that shotgun and congratulate myself for having the foresight to make such a great trade. Not only did Janie go to a girl who obviously would give her love and a great home, but every time I hold that gun I relive my furtive midnight escape with Janie from Sutton to Chickaloon and can hear the echoes of her shod hoofs clicking along the rocky banks of the moonlit Matanuska River as the white smoke of our combined breaths rose into the Alaskan night.

After Janie departed, I began to explore some of the interesting places and opportunities nearby our new home. My new mountain playground of Hatcher Pass lay in the Talkeetna Mountains just east of Wasilla, an easy half-hour drive away. It was a former gold-mining area, and I found it to be perfect for both winter and summer mountain activities. The pass area was surrounded by four-thousand- to five-thousand-foot peaks in a high alpine meadow environment. At this latitude, the tree line ended at around twenty-five hundred feet in elevation. The peaks were mostly granite, with crystal clear mountain steams running through steep valleys with alpine meadows. Many of the steams originated from tarns, small lakes formed in the bottom of a cirque after a valley glacier had melted. "Cirque" was the name given to a bowl-shaped valley on the side of a mountain where a glacier once sat.

In the winter, Hatcher Pass made for great telemark skiing, winter mountaineering, and ice climbing on the many frozen waterfalls that were just off the road leading up to the pass. We put skins on the bottoms of our mountaineering skis (a synthetic strip of material that is glued to the bottom of skis enabling a skier to ski straight uphill without slipping backward), then skied up gullies and along ridges, and telemark skied down through virgin powder. On our way home after skiing, we turned aside to hike a short distance to the base of a frozen waterfall and climbed the ice for an hour or two. We could still make it home in time for dinner.

In the summer, the granite cliffs beckoned us to climb them. In the 1970s, the area had not yet been discovered by many climbers, and Gig and I put up a few first routes among those crags. It was here in Hatcher Pass that I honed my mountaineering skills and met my good Alaskan friend, Harry, with whom I would climb many of Alaska's tallest peaks. In the relative safety of the Hatcher Pass Mountains, with instruction from Harry, I became familiar with avalanche safety techniques, crevasse rescue methods, igloo and snow cave construction, and other essential mountaineering skills that would help me to stay alive in the future.

In addition to its draw as a backcountry skier's and climber's paradise, the Hatcher Pass area was loaded with dilapidated mining buildings, perched precariously on the sides of the steep mountain slopes. Most of them had already disintegrated into piles of kindling, but there were a few buildings lower down the slopes that were still in decent condition. The area was riddled with old mining tunnels, some of which extend from one side of a mountain through to the other. I spent many days exploring the tumbled-down mining ruins and wondering at the ingenuity of the miners, who were able to delve through mountains and hang thick wire cables across valleys to transport their mine carts through the air. The tunnels still had rail tracks, old rail cars, and rusted mining paraphernalia scattered throughout them. Most tunnels were fairly short, but some stretched for a quarter of a mile or more. Once inside beyond the entrance, they became pitch black, requiring flashlights or headlamps to negotiate. A few had side caverns branching off the main tunnel where ice crystals hung from the ceilings and walls, glittering like a thousand diamonds in the beam of your headlamp. I explored one tunnel that went completely through a mountain, opening out in the middle of a thousand-foot cliff face with a rusty metal cable still arcing across the valley to another tunnel in the opposite cliff a half mile away.

Gold had been discovered in 1886 in the Anchorage area, and prospectors had spread into the Susitna and Matanuska river basins, testing the creeks in the nearby mountains for evidence of placer gold. There was a zone of mineralization running through the Talkeetna Mountains, where the granite had gold-bearing quartz veins scattered throughout it. Over tens of millions of years, the forces of weathering eventually had loosened flakes of gold from the quartz veins, and flowing water had washed some of the gold into streams and rivers. Gold, being one of the heavier elements, tended to settle out in pockets in a river where the current slowed down.

Placer mining involved finding and separating this eroded gold from the surrounding mud and gravel. Hard rock or lode mining entailed directly mining the gold-bearing ore from the rock in which it lay. The early prospectors were looking for rough-textured placer gold in the streams that would indicate a nearby gold-bearing source: the elusive mother lode. Smooth, well-worn gold signified that the gold had been eroded in the very distant past, and the source had probably been completely eroded away.

In 1906, Robert Lee Hatcher had been led by coarse-textured placer gold up the Willow Creek Valley to the gold-bearing source in the Talkeetna Mountains that now carries his name, and where he staked the first lode claim in the area. By 1941, there had been over two hundred miners, working twelve miles of tunnels and producing over thirty-four thousand ounces of gold a year. After America entered World War II, the War Production Board had declared gold mining was not essential to the war effort, and gold mining stopped throughout the United States. The Independence Mine in the Hatcher Pass area, however, had been allowed to continue operations, because the ore from the mine also contained scheelite, a mineral that yielded tungsten that was needed for wartime steel production. Unfortunately for the Independence Mine, its yield of scheelite had proved to be low, and the mine had been closed in 1943. When the war ended in 1945, the wartime ban had been lifted, but gold mining was slow to recover. The price of gold was then fixed at the rate of $35 per ounce by the U.S. government, and mines with marginal ore had become unprofitable. Independence Mine closed for good in 1951. Hatcher Pass became a state historical park, and some of the old mining-era buildings have since been preserved.

Proximity to Hatcher Pass was not the only benefit of living in the Justin's trailer. We lived in Bill Sr.'s trailer for over a year, and during that time, Bill Jr. introduced us to many of his favorite fishing and hunting spots. He had grown up fishing and hunting with his father as a way to provide the family with food, and outdoor life was more than recreation for him. When the king salmon were running, he could usually be found up some secret slough on the Susitna River, fishing in the wee hours of the morning. We spent many early mornings with him, learning how he and his Alaskan friends caught their kings. His fishing spots were always way off the beaten track. He drove his brand-new Chevy pickup truck, which had all the fancy extras and was a legacy of his recent well-paid job on the Alaska pipeline, down a maze of dirt roads and muddy trails, barely wide enough for the truck, eventually ending up on the banks of the Susitna or Little Susitna River.

"King salmon stop feeding once they start to run upstream to spawn," Bill Jr. informed us. "So you have to snag them."

"What do you mean 'snag them'?" I asked.

"Well, you put a treble hook on hundred-pound test line, cast it out, and jerk it hard as you reel it in," he explained. The idea was to set the big hook in the salmons' bodies and drag them to shore by brute force: there was not much angling prowess involved.

The silt in glacial rivers effectively hid the fish from view, so Bill Jr. picked a likely spot, where kings might be lurking, based on the current, the lay of the land, and his experience. On some casts, the line stopped suddenly as he was reeling it in. Most times, his treble hook had snagged a submerged log or branch, and he often lost his hook. But sometimes, the line stopped and then rapidly started winding off the spool of his reel as a snagged king salmon took off down the river.

"Bill, is it legal to fish this way?" Gig asked.

"Of course," he answered, "I've been doing this all my life."

"Then why do we have to fish at three in the morning if the fish don't feed anyway?" I asked.

In fact, snagging for salmon had been legal up until the early 1970s, but had since been declared illegal. That didn't matter much to Bill Jr. and his friends, and it became a contest of wits between them and the game wardens. They picked their spots carefully, snagged only in the early morning hours, and dragged any fish they caught a hundred yards or more into the woods, hiding them under leaves and brush until it was time to head home.

On the first king-fishing expedition, we watched him tirelessly throw cast after blind cast until he finally hooked a fish.

"I got one!" Bill Jr. said.

I had seen large king salmon before in the cannery at Cordova, but I was amazed at the size of the fish he had on the end of his line. "That fish has to be at least five feet long," I said, as the fish broke the surface of the water close to the bank.

"The tricky part to landing a king is getting it close enough to shore to grab it before the line snaps," he said. "If the fish makes it into the strong current, it will just snap the line," he continued. "You have to be patient and slowly play the fish to shore."

"How do you get it up onto the bank?" I asked him, after watching him slowly play the fish toward shore for half an hour.

"Well, I usually have a gaff, but I guess I forgot it this morning," he replied. "Just get into the water and grab it by the gills, the next time I bring it close."

"Okay, great, we're gaffless. Yeah, just grab a five-foot fish with a treble hook sticking out of it somewhere," I muttered. "Sure, I can do that."

We lost more fish than we landed that morning, but eventually Gig and I were swept up in the excitement of the hunt and developed a technique that we thought improved our odds of success. As one of us reeled a snagged king close to the steep bank, the other intrepid fisherman jumped into the water on top of the fish and tried to pin it to the bank by stabbing it through the head with a knife. A seventy-pound, five-foot-long fish was a worthy adversary when it was in its own element, so the fish won the wrestling contests more often than not.

"Flop it up on the bank so it doesn't get away, Gig!" I yelled, reeling my first king close to shore.

"I'm trying," he replied, slipping back under water. The fish and Gig thrashed about in the dirty water until with a satisfying "thunk," he pinned the king against the muddy river bank and drove his knife through its head.

As he emerged victorious from the cold mud, covered with silver scales and blood, I said, "Gig, I hope most of that blood belonged to the fish."

We managed to land three large kings that morning without stabbing ourselves and provided Bill Jr. with hours of entertainment. "Only a couple of idiot cheechakos would do that," he laughed. "Wait till I tell my friends about fish wrestling."

Splitting the catch between us, we cut one king into thick salmon steaks for the freezer, smoked another in Bill's homemade smoker, and gave one to his mother for canning. Three of those huge kings made a good beginning to a winter food supply.

In addition to teaching us his unconventional methods for catching king salmon, Bill Jr. also took us fishing for silver and red salmon. The reds and silvers were still feeding in the beginning of their spawning run and so were more easily caught on traditional gear, such as bait, lures, or flies. Fishing for these fish usually involved a float trip down the Susitna River to near its mouth, where it emptied into Cook Inlet.

"I can borrow a lightweight aluminum skiff," Bill Jr. said. "We'll float down the river, fishing the whole way, and at the end of the day, we'll use the outboard to power back upstream to the boat launch."

The Susitna River was a large, powerful glacial river that wound its way through the roadless, mosquito-infested Susitna flats, and as it approached the ocean, the river divided into numerous confusing channels, most of which seemed to deadend in a mudflat. Most of the fish were found down these dead-end sloughs. Navigating on a glacial river was a tricky business at best, because the depth of the water was hard to judge, and you had to avoid invisible sunken logs, especially on the trip back up river using the engine.

"Bill, if you don't know how to swim, why don't you wear a life jacket?" I asked as we floated downstream. Like most of his Alaskan friends, he never learned to swim, even though he spent a considerable amount of time on or near the water. Most of the high schools had indoor pools and kids could have learned to swim, so it was more of a cultural issue than a lack of opportunity.

"Learning to swim just didn't seem important to me or my parents when I was in school and a life jacket would just get in my way fishing," he replied. "Besides, I've never fallen overboard."

"There's always a first time, Bill," Gig said.

"Well, I do wear one waterskiing," Bill said. Waterskiing in the many lakes around Wasilla was a favorite summer pastime for Bill and his friends, and they relied completely on life jackets to prevent them from drowning.

"I'm going to teach you how to swim this summer," I promised.

"Thanks. I'd like that," he said. "Hey, do you guys want to go down to the Kenai to dig razor clams next week?"

"Why do you want to dig clams?" I asked. "I think I had enough clam digging in Cordova."

"No, razor clams are great," he answered. "They're huge and easy to dig. In a day, we could get a freezer full. We cut them into clam steaks and eat them all winter."

"Yeah, right, clam steaks," Gig said, rolling his eyes.

"No, it's true," Bill responded. "My mother rolls them in cornmeal batter and fries them up. Besides, it's a fun road trip down to Homer."

I had seen no razor clams during my clamming days in Cordova and doubted whether they really existed, but one late summer day, we found ourselves and the dogs riding in the back of Bill's pickup, heading down to Homer at the tip of the Kenai Peninsula. This peninsula was 150 miles long, and jutted into the Gulf of Alaska between Prince William Sound to the south and Cook Inlet to the north. The Kenai Mountains rose to seven thousand feet, and the road from Anchorage hugged the Turnagain Arm portion of Cook Inlet before heading down the peninsula to Homer.

On his third voyage of discovery, in May 1778, while searching for the elusive Northwest Passage along the Alaskan coast, the English explorer, Captain James Cook, had sailed his two ships, *Resolution* and *Discovery*, into a huge inlet that ran off to the northeast. He had spent two weeks exploring this inlet, hoping that it would be a river or sea passage connecting with the Atlantic Ocean. He had to turn around again at the head of one inlet, which he named Turn Again River. This had been later renamed Turnagain Arm by the British explorer, George Vancouver, who, along with William Bligh of *Mutiny of the Bounty* fame, had been a crew member aboard Cook's ship during the expedition. The larger inlet had been named Cook Inlet after its European discoverer.

In August of that year, the expedition had continued northward, but had been stopped by pack ice in the Artic Ocean off the coast of Siberia. Cook had made his way back south, past the Aleutian Islands into the Pacific Ocean, and in November, had sighted Maui in the Hawaiian Islands. Earlier that year, in January 1778, on his way to Alaska, he had become the first European voyager to touch on the Hawaiian Islands since the Spanaird, Juan Gaetano had landed there in 1555. Of course, the Polynesians had found the islands hundreds, if not thousands, of years before the Europeans. Cook had named the islands the Sandwich Islands after his English sponsor, the Earl of Sandwich. On this second visit, he and his crew wintered in the islands, and on February 14, 1779, Cook was killed at Kealakekua Bay on the island of Hawaii, during a fight with the Hawaiians over the theft of a small boat.

Once around Turnagain Arm, the modern road climbed over Turnagain Pass and headed down the length of the Kenai Peninsula to Homer. The town was the self-proclaimed halibut capital of the world, as well as being the western-most end of the paved highway system in North America. The road deadended at the Homer Spit, a narrow four-and-a-half-mile long, sand-and-gravel bar that extended into the bay. The spit was a submarine terminal moraine from the glacier that covered Kachemak Bay at the end of the last ice age, somewhere around fifteen thousand years ago. In the 1970s, Homer was a small, picturesque fishing village, overlooking the shores of Kachemak Bay with snow-clad peaks and glaciers visible all around the horizon.

When we got to Homer, Bill Jr. drove his truck down onto the deserted beach north of town, and we set up camp above the high-tide mark. After putting up our tents, it was time to dig for razor clams.

"See these small holes in the sand at the edge of the water?" Bill Jr. asked us, pointing to the sand in the intertidal zone. "That's where the clams are. They're very fast, so you need to dig quickly."

The holes indicated the presence of clams close to the surface. By using their powerful foot muscle, they were able to disappear deeper into the sand beyond our reach in a matter of seconds. Razor clams derived their name from the way the narrow, elongated, oblong shells resembled a folded, old-fashioned straight razor, but I think they could be called razor clams after the way their sharp shell edges sliced your finger open as you blindly dug through the sand chasing them.

"Why do it by hand, Bill?" I asked, watching my finger pattern the sand with red drops of blood. "Wouldn't a shovel be better?"

"Shovels just crush the clams, and then they're worthless," he answered, pulling clam after clam from the sand and piling them in his bucket. "You just need to get the hang of it." And he was right. After protecting our fingers with tape, we, too, were able to catch clams before they disappeared deep into the beach. Over a period of a few hours, a couple hundred five- to six-inch razor clams lay in a tub, waiting to be cleaned.

"There you go, Gig. There's your clam steak," Bill Jr. said, cutting strips of clam flesh from the large muscular foot and siphon of a clam.

We cleaned and sliced the clams there on the beach and packed the meat into a large cooler filled with ice. When we returned to Wasilla, we would repack the clam meat into bags and freeze them for use in the winter. That night, we enjoyed a bonfire on the beach next to the truck and tents, and as we watched the late evening Alaskan sun sink toward the pink mountainous horizon, we feasted on cornmeal-breaded clam steaks, fried over the fire.

Clams were only one of the food sources that Bill Jr. pursued for the family larder. He was happy to take on much bigger and more challenging hunts than digging in the mud on the beach at Homer.

"My friend, Roy, told me he spotted a huge black bear from his Cessna over by the Knik Glacier yesterday," Bill Jr. informed us over dinner one autumn evening. "Y'all want to go bear hunting?"

For some reason that now escapes me, we decided to take the dogs with us. Gig, John, and I, along with the dogs, piled into Bill's pickup with enough food and water for a short day of hiking and drove across the valley to Palmer. A winding dirt road led up into the Chugach Mountains and followed along side the Knik River for a few miles before petering out.

"We'll have to walk the rest of the way," Bill Jr. said.

"How far is it to the glacier?" I asked.

"Oh, about twelve miles, I guess," he replied, as we organized ourselves beside the river. Here the Knik River had divided itself into multiple braided channels of dark silver glacial water that flowed through a broad, alluvial, silt-laden valley about a mile wide.

Shouldering our rifles and slinging our small packs, we headed up a game trail that snaked along the northern edge of the valley, following the course of the river. The trail hugged the bottom of a wooded mountain, angling up and down steep gullies and wandering in and out of dense conifer tree stands that alternated with scrub willow and cottonwood closer to the river. The dogs had a great time running on ahead and then charging back to us, covering four times the distance we did.

After an hour of relatively easy walking, we were startled by loud, excited barking, growling, and squeals of panic from around the corner of the trail, where the dogs had just disappeared. I sprinted around the corner, rifle at the ready, with visions of a bear tearing the dogs apart, and saw, to my dismay, both my dogs struggling to take down a young moose calf. Denali had the calf by the throat, and Nancy had one hind leg.

"Get away from that moose!" I yelled at them, kicking them off the calf.

Holding the calf in my arms and checking it for damage, I felt its heart racing and listened to its mournful, baying call. Besides the panicked look in its eyes, there didn't seem to be any signs of significant trauma. "I think it will be okay," I said to the gathering onlookers.

"Oops," Gig whispered, as the sound of breaking branches in the brush signaled the presence of the mother moose close by.

After releasing the calf, we watched it take a few unsteady, wobbly steps. The gangly calf then ran straight to its mother, and they both crashed off through the underbrush.

"That's enough running loose for the dogs," I said, waiting for my own racing heart to calm down.

The day wore on without any further wildlife encounters or any sign of bears, and toward the late afternoon, we sighted the glacier around a bend in the steep valley wall. The foot of the glacier appeared to be another mile or two away, when a strong wind began blowing down the valley toward us.

"It's the Chinook wind," Bill Jr. said, turning his back to the windblown glacial silt.

I didn't want to quibble about what to call the wind, but this was no warm Chinook wind blowing off the Knik Glacier. It was a cold wind that was getting stronger by the minute, and soon the glacial silt was blowing in earnest off the valley floor, and we were in the midst of a dust storm that would have done the Sahara Desert proud.

"Let's get out of here," John called over the shrill whistling of the wind.

This was a katabatic wind, the result of a cold, dense air mass flowing down off the glacier that was accelerated by the force of gravity. It took its name from a Greek word meaning "going downhill." The upper glacier most likely had become shaded by the valley wall in the late afternoon, and that caused the air mass above the glacier to cool. Cold air, being denser than warm air, will slide downhill as far as the local topography will allow. The famous European Mistral wind, which can reach speeds of up to eighty miles per hour, is a katabatic wind that blows down the Rhone Valley and out over the Mediterranean Sea. One of the strongest katabatic winds on the planet is found in Antarctica. There, air sitting on top of ice plateaus is cooled by the ice and flows down over ridges, reaching speeds of up to two hundred miles per hour.

In contrast to katabatic winds, a Chinook wind is a warm wind pattern that results from the interaction of high and low pressure systems moving over mountainous regions. It is well known in the Rocky Mountains, particularly in winter. As a wind moves over and through mountains passes, the air is warmed through the release of latent heat energy when moisture in the air condenses. Colder, denser air above moves downhill and presses down on the warmer air mass, which causes further warming by direct physical compression. In the Cook Inlet area of Alaska, a similar phenomenon can occur as air moves over the Chugach Mountains between Prince William Sound and Portage Glacier, causing a warm wind to blow into Anchorage that the locals call a Chinook wind.

In our predicament, we didn't care too much what the wind was called. All thoughts of bear hunting disappeared, and we turned around to start the long trip back to the truck. We had hiked in about ten miles, so we had a long trek ahead of us.

"At least we're going downwind," John pointed out.

"That's the only good thing that can be said for it," I responded.

Windblown glacial silt is extremely fine and insinuates itself into every crease of your clothes and every orifice of your body.

"Wrap your shirt around your head and face," Gig yelled. "It will keep some of the dust out of your nose and mouth."

It was a long, cold, dusty walk back to the truck, but three hours later, as we turned the corner of the valley, we were out of the wind and dust. The evening was warm and sunny, and it was as if the cold dust storm had never happened, but everything we had been carrying or wearing was clogged or coated with glacial silt.

"Well, that was a pleasant twenty-mile jaunt," Gig said.

"I'm tired, dirty, and thirsty," I put in, "and I just want to go home and take a shower."

"Oh no, we can't go home," Bill Jr. said. "We're going to the festival in Palmer now."

"What festival?" I asked.

"They have it every fall. Bands from Anchorage will be playing for free and there'll be kegs of beer. Besides, all my friends will be there," Bill Jr. replied with enthusiasm.

"Sounds great," John said with doubt in his voice, peering out at Bill Jr. from a dirt-encrusted face with red-rimmed eyes.

We wiped the dirt off ourselves as best we could and agreed to accompany Bill to the party. Even back then, I must have realized that you should not use beer as a rehydration fluid, so I had no excuse for what happened at the big bash. I must have done something socially unacceptable or perhaps was just unlucky, being in the wrong place at the wrong time, and I found myself in the middle of a brawl. I went home that night with a big old black eye and have my friend John to thank for escaping with only that as a souvenir. If I ever have to be in another brawl or a knife fight, he's the one I want by my side.

Back at home the next day, we had to completely disassemble our rifles and clean out the glacial slit, and we coughed and spit silt out of our lungs for the next few days. I had learned an interesting lesson about the weather patterns of the local glacial valleys and reconfirmed the dangers of drinking too much beer after twenty-mile hikes.

During the time we lived in Bill's trailer, we did our best not to antagonize his son-in-law, Ernie, and tried to avoid him altogether. Bill never explained to us the basis for his deep dislike of the man, but any mention of his name would bring about a fit of cursing on Bill's part. The fact that Ernie lived only a half mile up the road and Bill had to drive past his house, coming or going, only made matters worse. Things came to a head one evening as we were dining at the Justins' house. Bill had done his share of drinking that evening and was going on and on about something Ernie had done that week to piss him off.

"I'm going to call that bastard up," Bill muttered to no one in particular after dinner.

For the next five minutes, he screamed and cursed at Ernie over the phone, while intermittently downing shots of whisky. "You're not man enough to meet me in the road!" we heard him yell. "All right, I'll be there in five minutes!" he shouted next. "And remember, no weapons!"

"Bill, you're all liquored up," his wife began. "You're not going anywhere."

"Yeah, Bill, you don't need to go see that idiot, Ernie," I added.

"Don't tell me what to do, Sally," he said. "I'm going to take care of him once and for all."

"Please go with him boys," Sally asked us. "I can't reason with him when he's like this."

After patting Bill down for weapons as best we could without being too obvious, Bill Jr., Gig, John, and I all started walking with Bill Sr. down the road toward Ernie's place for the big mano-a-mano showdown. It was late at night, but since it was the end of summer; a soft light still illuminated the distant mountains and silhouetted two approaching men. Ernie and someone we didn't know were striding toward us from the opposite direction. In a scene that might have been from a bad western movie, the two groups stopped ten yards apart and eyed each other. We were hoping that our superior numbers would convince the other side of the stupidity of the whole encounter and that we could keep Bill from getting hurt, as he was having trouble putting one foot in front of the other.

"I'm going to take care of you once and for all!" Bill yelled, swaying back and forth.

"You can't even walk," Ernie said, laughing at him.

For the next five minutes, they cursed each other soundly, and just as I thought that might be the end of it, Bill started stumbling toward Ernie. Why was I not surprised when Ernie drew a large knife from behind his back and started for Bill?

"Knife!" John yelled.

Not to be out done, Bill bent over and drew a .25 caliber revolver from an ankle holster, and Gig yelled, "Gun!"

Now this came as quite a surprise, because I had thought we had searched Bill fairly well, but he had fooled us. The situation was deteriorating quickly. I was the closest one to Ernie, and without really thinking, I grabbed his knife arm, twisted it, and swept him to the ground, disarming him. John and Gig were next to Bill and took his gun away before he could shoot himself or someone else.

"That's enough fun and games for the evening," John said, confiscating the weapons.

With curses from both antagonists in our ears, we hustled Bill back home, where he could simmer down and sleep it off.

"Well, that was really stupid," I concluded, once the three of us were safely back at the trailer.

"Yeah, that could have been a complete disaster," Gig added.

John started singing, "Demon alcohol …"

The next day, Bill thanked us a little sheepishly, and we never spoke of the matter again.

Chapter Six:
Hunting and Fishing

Over the years that I lived in Alaska, I spent a considerable amount of time hunting and fishing. It seems to me that for a lot of people, hunting and fishing are good excuses to spend time wandering in the forest or floating down a river in order to get away from the drudgery of their daily routine. These outdoor activities enable people to connect with nature and feel the rhythm of the seasons as once their ancestors did out of necessity. Some people seem to enjoy the thrill of stalking and shooting game, but I never did understand or relate to the trophy aspect of hunting. I never needed an excuse to disappear down a river, into a forest, or up a mountain, so to me hunting and fishing were more like work than recreation. It was a way to acquire food, and if I wasn't going to eat an animal or a fish, I would never kill it.

In Alaska, we were able to feed ourselves with fish and game almost all year round, but it did involve a lot of work. Every fall, we shot at least one moose. We had to field dress it, carry all the meat out on our backs, butcher it ourselves, and then smoke, can, and/or freeze it. This was time- and labor-intensive activity, but it paid dividends in the winter, when we could sit back and feast in the knowledge that we had an adequate store of food. Having a good supply of wild game on hand was also a useful commodity in Alaska, since game could be used to barter for services, such as electrical work, plumbing, or car repairs. Bringing wild game to a friend's house for dinner was also considered proper Alaskan etiquette. Of course, there were some hunting and fishing trips that stood apart from others as adventures in their own right.

Duck Hunting

"My friend, Davis, and I are going duck hunting for a few days," Jake said to Gig and me after we had worked with him for about a year. "Want to go with us?"

"Where to?" Gig asked.

"Up to the end of Cook Inlet," Jake said. "Davis has a large inflatable raft with an outboard that we use to cross the inlet to the Knik Duck Flats. Thousands of birds migrate through that area of Knik Arm each fall."

"How long will we go for?" I asked.

"Three days," Jake replied. "We can find some high ground above the tides at the end of the flats and set up a couple of tents."

The area Jake was talking about sat on the Pacific Flyway migration path for ducks, geese, and swans. Countless ducks of every kind flew through, including Harlequin, Mallard, Widgeon, Pintail, Teal, Scooter, Scaup, Canvasback, Ring Neck, Bufflehead, and Golden Eye. There were five species of geese: Canada, Emperor, Greater White-Footed, Brant, and Lesser Snow geese. Two species of swans could also be found, the Trumpeter and the Tundra swan.

The Tundra swan was formerly known as the Whistling swan for the distinctive sound of its wings in flight. The Trumpeter swan was the world's largest waterfowl, with males averaging twenty-eight pounds. Two distinct populations of Tundra Swans were found in Alaska. The Eastern Tundra swan breeding grounds ranged from northwest Alaska to the Canadian artic, and in late September, the birds migrated for the winter to the Atlantic coast. Formerly, they wintered primarily in the Chesapeake Bay area, but due to pollution and increased human pressure on the bay, most of the birds now winter in North Carolina. The western population of swans nested on the west coast of Alaska from Kotzabue Sound to the Alaska Peninsula and migrated through Cook Inlet. The rest traveled through inland Canada to winter anywhere from British Columbia to California.

Cook Inlet stretched 195 miles from southeast to northeast, and separated the Kenai Peninsula from mainland Alaska. At the city of Anchorage, Cook Inlet branched into Knik Arm (where the Susitna, Matanuska, and Knik Rivers all emptied into it) and Turnagain Arm, the place Captain Cook had to turn around. The tidal range in this part of Cook Inlet could be greater than thirty feet, and because of the local topography, this area was also susceptible to tidal bores. The term "bore" derived from the Old Norse word for wave, *bara*. A tidal bore occurs when the leading edge of an incoming tide forms a wave of water that is funneled up a broad, shallow bay into a narrow area against a current. Both Knik Arm and Turnagain Arm had the topography to produce tidal bores, and Turnagain Arm had an additional feature that increased its tidal bore potential: the natural resonant frequency of this shallow bay was similar to the ocean's natural tidal cycle of twelve hours and twenty-five minutes, so water ended up sloshing around Turnagain Arm, much like water sloshing in a bucket, thereby augmenting the power and height of the bore. The bore in Turnagain Arm could tower more than six feet high and travel at speeds greater than fifteen miles per hour. It was interesting to watch the bore from a safe distance on shore, but you would not want to see it if you were stuck in the quicksand-like silt mud of the bay as the bore roared toward you.

We headed for the Knik Arm portion of Cook Inlet and drove my truck, loaded with all our gear and the inflatable raft, down a dusty dirt road that dead-ended on the southern shore of Knik Arm, just south of the small town of Eklutna. The road snaked down a shallow gully that looked like it might flood at high tide and continued up a small hill through a copse of trees and down again to the shore.

"We can unload the gear here, and while Davis and I inflate the boat, you two drive the truck back up the road above that salt marsh," Jake said.

Gig and I parked the truck off the road about a mile away, well beyond the reach of any thirty-foot tides. The sun was shining brightly in a cloudless, crystal blue, autumn sky. As we jogged back to the water, we looked out across the inlet to the Susitna Flats six miles away on the far shore, and in the distance, we saw the snow-clad peaks of the Alaska Range glittering in the sun, fifty miles to the north. It was mid-ebb tide when we piled into the inflatable and began motoring through the dirty, gray ocean water, steering for the head of the bay.

"We'll have to fight the tide to get up to the flats," Davis said.

By the time we reached the Knik Duck Flats area, it was close to low tide, and we were gazing at miles of extensive mudflats, cut by a maze of twisting channels, all leading into the coastal marsh at the head of the bay.

"How do you know which channel to take?" I asked. "They all look pretty much the same to me."

"The biggest one should be Palmer Slough," Jake said.

"This should be the one," Davis said confidently, pointing the boat into a muddy channel entrance that, at least to me, was indistinguishable from all the rest. "This should bring us close to the mouth of the Matanuska River and a grassy marsh where we can camp."

At low tide, the channels cut through the mud about ten feet below the level of the marsh area, and it was impossible to see over the banks once you started into the canyon-like channels.

"Nice view," I commented, staring at the mud banks now surrounding us.

We traveled up the channel as it meandered its way into the salt marsh, and soon we saw tufts of grasses and reeds above us as they poked out beyond the edge of the steep channel banks.

"It's too shallow to safely use the outboard here," Davis said. "We'll have to paddle and pole against the current."

"The tide will be coming in soon," Jake added. "That should help carry us upstream."

It was impossible to see exactly where in the flats we were—our world was limited to views of the mud-silted water that flowed sinuously between the banks of glacial mud. We could never see farther than twenty yards up or down the channel. No one thought it would be wise to try to muck their way up a slippery mud bank to get a bearing.

"What's that noise?" I asked, as a low rumbling quickly became a roar approaching us from astern.

"Tide's coming," Jake said.

"Sounds like it will be a tidal bore," Davis added. "That should give us a nice push." Gig and I stared nervously at the curve in the channel bank behind us, trying to imagine what the tidal bore would look like from boat level as it materialized around the bend.

"Sure is loud," I mumbled. "I hope it's not like the bores in Turnagain Arm."

"That's it?" Gig said with a laugh when a wave of water no more than six inches high advanced from around the last turn in the channel and started to push the boat upstream. It was somewhat of a letdown, given the thunderous noise of its approach, but I was, however, very impressed at the speed with which the tide now filled up the channel and floated us high enough to see over the banks.

"I thought we had paddled for miles up the channel," I said, "but the ocean is only a few short turns away."

The tide had raised the water level enough to obliterate most of the seaward channels that had been cut into the previously exposed mudflats. Only a huge volume of water could have accomplished that in such a short period of time. Looking toward the head of the bay, we could now make out miles of marsh grass, sequined with small pools of water that glittered in the cold sunlight, and innumerable channels leading toward the snowcapped Chugach Mountains in the distance. I didn't know if we were actually in Palmer Slough, but the channel we had picked continued to meander into the marshland. We motored onward until a grassy hillock met the channel, and we could step out of the boat onto solid ground instead of slippery glacial-silt mud.

"This looks like a good spot," Davis said. He pulled in, and we unloaded the boat and pitched our camp on an elevated mound of dry land surrounded by a sea of waving grasses and reeds.

"Listen to all those birds," I said, taking in our surroundings.

As soon as we had turned off the outboard in the channel, the calls of ducks and geese could be heard from afar, and birds flew overhead every so often. We were in the marshland proper, and the thousands of waterfowl that inhabited the small pools dotting the wetlands in the distance made their presence known.

"You need to be careful walking across the marsh," Jake advised us. "It's not as easy as it looks."

As we explored the nearby marshland, we discovered what he was talking about. Some of the land was firm and relatively easy to walk on, but it could turn into a bog that necessitated hopping from one grass tussock to the next. We frequently hit deadends at a channel, and after seeing firsthand how fast these filled up with water, we were careful not to walk though any of the glacial mud that had a reputation for quicksand-like properties. The ducks proved particularly wary and took flight if they saw us or heard our approach. We didn't do any hunting that first day, choosing instead to bed down early as the sky darkened and the temperature quickly dropped. I was soon lulled to sleep by the lonely calls of thousands of ducks interspersed with the occasional honking of geese.

The next day dawned cold and clear as we arose early, ate a quick breakfast, split into two hunting parties, and headed off in opposite directions. As Gig and I went off together toward the north, he said, "Most duck hunters sit in blinds and use decoys to lure the ducks to them."

"Well, I don't think we'll find a blind out here and we don't have time to build one. No one said anything about decoys either," I replied.

"Real duck hunters have dogs to retrieve their ducks from the water," he added.

"Well, we'll just have to retrieve our own ducks," I answered. "Let's find a shallow pond where we can hide in the tall grass and wait for the birds to land."

"Good plan," Gig agreed.

We set up in a thicket of reeds and tall, dry grass tussocks, with a clear view of a brackish pond. We had crawled as quietly as possible into position, hoping to surprise some ducks on the water, but the pond was deserted. The cries of ducks and geese were thick on the air, and we assured ourselves that it would only be a matter of time before a squadron of ducks would appear within range.

"Won't be long now," I said.

V-shaped formations of Canada geese circled and flew off high overhead. Four white Tundra swans whistled by, close enough for us to make out the distinctive yellow spot at the base of their otherwise black bills. Hundreds of ducks hurried by, sometimes in pairs, sometimes singly, and sometimes in triangular flocks, but always far out of range and never approaching our pond. As the day wore on, the sun beat down and warmed us to the point of drowsiness. It was a pleasant way to spend a morning, listening to the calls of the birds while lying in a pile of dry, warm grass, surrounded by the wide, open marsh with the majestic Alaska Range sparkling in the distance—and not another person in sight.

"There they are!" Gig whispered, nudging me awake and pointing to a spear-head of Mallard ducks flying low over the grass, heading right for our pond. As they passed from north to south in their landing glide, we both sprang up and began blasting away with our shotguns. The phalanx of ducks aborted their landing, speeding off with a rapid steady beating of their wings, and we were left staring at three dead ducks floating twenty yards away in the cold water.

"Gig, do you think they'll float to shore?" I asked.

"No, I don't think so," he replied. "If you fetch these, I'll get the next batch."

It was a warm enough day, so I stripped down and started wading into the cold, brackish water, hoping that I would be able to wade out all the way to the ducks. After sloshing out ten feet, the water was chest deep and getting deeper. "Shrivel me timber!" I yelled, barking like a retriever and swimming the rest of the distance. Collecting the ducks, I stroked one armed back to shore.

"Good boy," Gig said, patting me on the head as I emerged from the water. I shivered myself to warmth and made a mental note to try to shoot ducks over land next time.

We shot a few more ducks that day and then headed back to the small elevated area that marked our camp. Jake and Davis had more success, returning with five ducks each, as well as two Canada geese. We traded notes on how the hunting had gone that day, and after hearing our story of fetching ducks out of the pond, they stared at us in disbelief.

"You swam after the ducks?" they asked with a laugh.

"Well, yeah. Didn't you?" I asked.

"No. We shot them so they would land in the grass where we could pick them up," Jake said with a superior smirk.

"Oh," I said.

"Well, we shot some over the land too," Gig added defensively.

After cooking up a welcome hot meal on the camp stove, we watched the purple light of the setting sun reflect off high wispy clouds that streamed rapidly in from the southwest.

"Looks like we might have some weather tomorrow," remarked Jake.

The next day greeted us with a steady drizzle falling from low dark clouds that shut out any view of the surrounding shoreline and mountains. "It's a good day for ducks," Gig said.

Splitting up into our respective hunting parties, we sallied into the rain. Lying in the cold, wet grass was just as miserable as it had been pleasurable in the warm, dry grass the day before.

"Don't even look at a duck if it's flying over the water," I said to Gig, as the rain dripped down my neck. "They must call this weather good for ducks because it's good for their survival." Most of the ducks were hunkered down in the ponds, and we could see very few birds flying from place to place.

"The only chance we'll have to shoot any ducks today is if we startle them out of a pond," Gig said, as we mucked our way across the marsh.

"Hey, that's not a bad plan, Gig," I said. "We could split up, and one of us could flush ducks from one end of a pond to where the other is waiting."

"Okay, you be the hunting dog first," he replied, walking off to station himself at the end of a likely looking pond.

"But I was the dog yesterday," I complained to his retreating back.

Our plan was effective, and after hours of damp work, we had a few more ducks to show for our trouble. We headed back to camp soaking wet. This was our last day on the flats, so we broke camp and loaded the gear, along with the bounty of ducks and geese, into the inflatable, heading for the take out area near Eklutna. We had close to the limit of five ducks per day each, and all in all had spent three days in the kind of place that few people experience.

"We should reach Eklutna close to low tide," Davis said. "This outgoing tide will help push us back out the inlet."

We motored out of the marsh and into the bay proper as the temperature dropped and the weather deteriorated. The steady drizzle was replaced by drenching downpours, interspersed with sleet and snow squalls. To make matters worse, the clouds lowered and became a fog bank that intermittently enveloped us, which led to complete directional disorientation.

"Nice weather," I commented, staring into the impenetrable thickness of a fog bank as it closed in on us.

"Where's the compass?" Jake asked.

"I don't have one," Davis said. "You guys?" he inquired.

We looked at each other and shook our heads no. If you have never been in a small boat on the ocean shrouded in a blanket of thick fog, it's hard to imagine just how disorienting it really is. After continuing to motor through the fog for twenty minutes on what we thought was the correct heading, we were surprised when the fog temporarily lifted to find ourselves headed out toward the open sea.

"This will never do," Davis said, shaking his head. "We don't have enough gas to motor blindly around in the fog all day."

"The fog comes and goes," Jake said. "Let's use the engine when it lifts and just drift when we can't see."

While floating quietly down Knik Arm on the ebbing tide, we stared at the blank whiteness of the fog and tried to avoid the sleet and snow that wanted to work their way beneath our foul weather gear.

Jake decided to cheer us up. "I hope we don't drift into the artillery range," he said.

"Artillery range?" I asked.

"Yeah, the army base uses the Eagle River Flats as an artillery range, and it's right next to where we need to land the boat," he replied.

"They won't be shooting on a day like today," Gig said.

"No, but the flats are covered with thousands of unexploded shells," Jake went on. "We wouldn't want to have to walk through there."

The salt marsh estuary at the mouth of the Eagle River had been used for artillery practice by the neighboring military base since the late 1940s. The military has estimated that there are over a hundred thousand unexploded mortar and artillery shells buried in the shallow marsh and mud. Over recent years, scientists have discovered that white phosphorous leaking from the shells has poisoned waterfowl foraging for food in the ponds and marsh bottom sediment. There has been an unusual increase in mortality of ducks, geese, and swans in the Eagle River Flats, and several lawsuits have been filed against the military. So far there is no evidence that the white phosphorus has traveled up the inlet to the Knik Duck Flats. Back in 1978, we were blissfully ignorant of these details, but still we had no desire to become possible targets by floating by or landing in the area.

Fortunately for us, the fog lifted long enough to show us our destination for a few minutes at a time. During these brief interludes, we started the outboard and headed for the takeout point. When the fog descended again, we turned off the engine and continued to drift. In this fashion, we made our way slowly, but safely, back to where we had put in three days before. It had taken us over nine hours to reach Eklutna, and the tide was headed toward full by the time we landed.

"You two run up and get the truck, while we deal with the boat," Jake said.

It felt good to crank up the heater in the truck as we drove back down the dirt road to collect the gear. Dusk was hurrying toward night as we approached the dip in the road where it crossed the marshy section.

"Gig, there wasn't any water on the road when we crossed here a few minutes ago, was there?" I asked.

"No, that was only ten minutes ago, so it can't be that deep," he replied. The dry dirt roadbed could be seen exiting the water no more than three truck lengths away.

"It has to be the tide coming in," I said. "We'd better hurry."

I recalled how quickly the tide could fill a small area, so I eased the truck into the water slowly and carefully. It did not appear to be more than a few inches deep, barely coming up to the bottom of the rims on the wheels. About halfway across the ford, as I was starting to feel comfortable with the crossing, the truck lost all traction, and the tires spun uselessly without any purchase.

"Put it in four-wheel drive," Gig suggested.

"It's in four-wheel drive," I said.

"Try rocking forward and backward," he suggested next. The wheels continued to spin uselessly.

"The water must have made the glacial-silt covering of the road too slippery for the tires," I said.

"The tide is still coming in," Gig said. "And the water is now over the hubs." Of course, by then, it was dark as we weighed our diminishing options.

"We could use the winch on the front of the truck, if we could rig a deadfall on the other side of the gully," I said. It was a mechanical take-off winch, and so as long as the engine was running the winch would work.

"Good idea," Gig said. "I'll run over and get Jake and Davis to help us."

They were no more than a quarter of a mile away, waiting with the gear on elevated ground by the boat landing. Gig put his waders on and jumped out of the cab. I watched him in the headlight beams as he ran through the black water in front of the truck, racing the tide. He took ten strides and then completely disappeared under water. Before I could hop out of the truck or even think about what to do, he popped back up and made his way back to the cab after ditching his full waders that had been dragging him down.

"Are you all right?" I asked, as he returned soaked and shivering.

He must have stepped off the road, because I don't recall a pothole deep enough to swallow him along that stretch. The water was approaching the top of the tires as Gig tried to warm himself in front of the heating vents. The headlights now illuminated an expanse of dark water surrounding the truck. We sat miserably in the middle of it.

"There's no way we can cross now," Gig said, shivering and pointing out the obvious. As the water rose to the level of the bottom of the doors, I realized we were out of options. Shutting off the engine and the lights, Gig and I crawled out the windows to perch on the roof of the cab.

"Just how high is high tide?" I wondered aloud.

While Cook Inlet was reeducating me about the cold hard facts of thirty-foot tides, we heard Jake and Davis shouting for us from the trees on what now looked like the other side of a small lake. We shouted explanations as best we could, but there was nothing to be done except sit and watch the tide roll in. After what seemed like a lifetime of shivering on the roof of the cab, high water stopped at the level of the hood.

"Hey, look," Gig said. "The seawater is covering the seat of the cab."

"Yeah, thanks, Gig. I see that," I muttered. "I can just imagine what all that salt water will do to my truck."

I meditated on the phenomenon of the moon's gravity pulling water back out to sea, and just as fast as the tide came in, it flowed out again. Eventually, we were able to open the doors and let the water drain from the cab. After another age slowly ticked by, all four of us were standing on damp ground staring at the truck's engine in the beam of a flashlight.

"It's a Jeep," Jake said. "Just dry off the distributor cap and start it up."

Hoping beyond hope, I dried off the battery connections and the distributor cap with my shirt, and in a testament to Jeep pickup trucks everywhere, the engine started on the first try. I kissed the truck, and we piled into the still wet, muddy cab. Now that the water had receded, the tires dug into the dirt road like we were on dry pavement. After throwing our gear into the bed of the truck, we drove back over the dirt road without incident, finally making it home to Wasilla in the early morning hours.

The next day, I faced the reality of a truck that had been partially submerged in silty seawater. With Bill Justin's help, I drained the gear housings, relubricated all the joints, and took apart most of the engine to soak the parts in kerosene. After putting it all back together, I heeded everyone's advice, sold the old Jeep pickup, and used the proceeds to buy a new used truck.

"Well, that was an expensive hunting trip," Gig pointed out.

"Yeah, we should have just gone down to the store and bought some chicken," I replied. However, I relearned some important lessons, everyone survived unscathed, and Gig and I now had yet another cold, wet, miserable, sleepless night to reminisce and laugh about.

Ice Fishing

There is a long list of things that I don't understand—golf, rap music, NASCAR racing, our litigious society, the expanding culture of victimhood—but close to the top, I have to put ice fishing. I just don't see the draw of sitting around a hole in the ice, waiting for a fish to bite. I always preferred to go skiing or ice climbing in the winter, so I usually declined all invitations for ice fishing. Now, I understand that many people will take issue with this, and they will point out that there is a whole industry and culture that supports ice fishing. They say that it is all about the camaraderie of sitting in a shack, communing with one's friends, but I still think ice fishing is just an excuse to escape from the house and go drinking. John kept pestering me to go ice fishing with him, and one winter I finally relented and agreed to go.

The area around Wasilla was dotted with lakes, and judging by the number of fishing shacks scattered over the frozen lakes in the winter, ice fishing was a popular pursuit. I had heard people talk about ice fishing before, so I was familiar with the usual procedure. Most fishermen use a gas-powered ice auger to drill a hole in the ice before placing their fishing shack over the hole. These shacks can be anything from an old outhouse, preferably a two-holer, to large, comfortable buildings with furniture and woodstoves. There are some intrepid souls that fish out in the open, hovering over their holes and constantly skimming ice from the surface, while they wait for the elusive lake lunker to bite. Most fishermen use salmon eggs for bait, but some prefer artificial lures. On the Alaskan lakes, they fished for landlocked salmon, rainbow trout, artic char (also known as Dolly Varden), and artic grayling.

On a clear, cold, blustery twenty-below winter day, John and I gathered our fishing gear, which consisted of a sledgehammer, a colander for skimming ice, monofilament line, a couple of lures, salmon eggs, and a bottle of brandy.

"You did borrow someone's fishing shack, right?" I asked hopefully.

"Well, not exactly," John replied.

"What does not exactly mean?" I asked, crunching across the snow to his beat-up old pickup truck.

"You'll see," he said with a grin. We rattled down the road in his truck the few miles to Lake Lucile.

"Oh, great," I whined. "The wind is blowing the snow horizontally across the ice now."

"That should drop the chill factor a few more degrees," John said gleefully.

There were a couple of trucks parked on the ice along side some fishing shacks in the distance, and a lot more trucks were parked at the bar overlooking the lake, but there was no one that I could see huddled over a hole in the ice, exposed to the elements.

"Are you sure we have to do this?" I asked, as he drove out onto the ice and proceeded to spin a few 360s. "We could just go to the bar like everyone else."

He didn't reply. Every so often, John stopped at a hole that had been previously augured to see if he could smash through the new-formed ice with the sledgehammer. After a few failed attempts, he finally found a fairly fresh hole and cleared it of ice.

The wind was still whipping across the lake as he climbed back in the cab muttering, "Yow, that wind's cold."

I opened my door and started to get out, saying in a dejected voice, "Let's get it over with so we can go back home and get warm."

"Where are you going?" John inquired with a smile. "That's not how we ice fish in Alaska."

I jumped back into the truck, and he drove over the cleared hole, positioning the truck so the hole was under the steering column by the driver's side of the cab. He swept back a small rug that had been covering a rusted out hole in the floor by the accelerator pedal, baited a hook with some salmon eggs, lowered the line through the hole in his floor, and tied the line off to the blinker lever on the steering column. He put his feet up on the dash, took a swig from the brandy bottle, and said in a satisfied voice, "Now this is ice fishing."

We kept the engine running with the heat on. Every so often the blinker flashed, and we pulled up a Dolly Varden or an artic grayling into the cab. As the level in the brandy bottle receded, I had to agree that ice fishing was not so bad after all. In fact, I had such a good time on this ice-fishing trip that I figured I would never be able to improve on it, so I've never bothered to go ice fishing again.

Montague Island

One November, while we were still hanging sheetrock for Richard, he offered us the chance to go deer hunting on Montague Island as an early Christmas bonus. "I have a friend who is willing to fly us to the island in his Cessna and pick us up a few days later," Richard said. Soon Gig, John, and I were winging our way out of Anchorage, over the Kenai Peninsula, and out across Prince William Sound to the western shore of Montague Island.

Montague Island separates the Gulf of Alaska from the western entrance of Prince William Sound and is about sixty miles southeast of Seward. The island, approximately fifty miles long and between five to twelve miles wide, is the twenty-fourth largest island in the United States.

"There's the beach," the pilot yelled over the noise of the engine.

On the southwestern shore, lay a narrow beach suitable for landing a bush plane with oversized, underinflated tundra tires. The beach had been created courtesy of the March 28, 1964 Good Friday Earthquake, also known as the Great Alaska Earthquake. The tectonic Pacific Plate had slid under the edge of the North American Plate to create the quake. It initially had registered 8.6 on the Richter scale, but recently some scientists have reassessed the magnitude scale for very large quakes and reassigned a force of 9.2 to this particular earthquake. That would make it the strongest earthquake to strike North America in recorded history and one of the strongest ever known worldwide. (The Richter scale is used to express the total amount of energy released by an earthquake and is not a linear scale, but rather a logarithmic scale, so each increase of one unit on the scale represents a thirty-two-fold increase in released energy.) The epicenter of the quake had been near the west coast of Montague Island in the Gulf of Alaska, and parts of the western shore of the island had been lifted more than forty feet, exposing the underlying seabed and creating a shelf-like beach where there had been only a steep, rocky shoreline before. The quake triggered a destructive Pacific-wide tsunami as well as many local tsunamis in the Prince William Sound area. The quake and associated tsunamis all but destroyed most of Alaska's largest shoreline communities, seaport facilities, fishing industry, and killed 115 people in Alaska.

As our plane touched down on Montague Island, bouncing on the beach a few times and taxiing to a stop, huge Pacific swells broke along the shore.

"I'll be back in three days, weather permitting," the pilot said.

After we dumped our gear in the sand, the pilot revved his engine and took off down the beach, becoming airborne in a surprisingly short amount of time. As the plane faded to a dot on the horizon, silence was broken only by the sound of waves crashing along the shore.

"There's a small camp right up there by the tree line," Richard said. "Let's carry the gear up there."

A previous group of hunters had put together a lean-to shelter, covered with visqueen, and had dragged driftwood and wooden crates from the beach to use as makeshift benches and tables around a campfire pit. It was November, and there was a foot or two of new snow in the forest, but most of the snow had melted from the immediate vicinity of the shoreline.

"It will be dark soon," I said. "I'll gather some wood for a fire."

"It's still light enough to do a little hunting," Richard replied. "The fire can wait."

The Sitka black tail deer we intended to hunt was native to the coastal rainforests of southeast Alaska and northern British Columbia. It was a relatively small deer: not much bigger than a large dog. An average doe weighed around eighty pounds and a buck about 120 pounds. They had small antlers, with a typical adult displaying three points on each side. The deer were reported to be colorblind and unable to distinguish stationary objects, but they made up for these shortcomings with acute wariness. The slightest movement drew their attention, and they prepared to flee. These deer were not native to the region. They were introduced onto the area by the Cordova Chamber of Commerce between 1916 and 1927. The deer population exploded in the luxurious habitat, and they spread into the surrounding area, including Montague Island. The deer particularly thrived on Montague and other closeby islands because of several favorable environmental factors: a relatively mild climate, protection from deep snow provided by the canopies of the old growth forests, access to forage, and minimal predation from wolves and coyotes that were not as plentiful on the islands as on the mainland. Excessively deep snow made it hard for these small deer to find food, and following a significant snow fall, the deer congregated toward the shore area where the snow tended to be less deep.

That November, hunting regulations allowed us to take five deer each, and they could be either bucks or does. "Look over there," John whispered, pointing toward a small cluster of deer wandering about the shore close to the conifer forest. Without any organized hunting plan, we started shooting deer left and right, as darkness rapidly enveloped the island. Muzzle flashes punctuated the evening, as we shouted at each other to watch where we were shooting.

"Stop shooting!" Gig yelled a minute later. "It's getting too dark." Assessing our marksmanship by flashlight, we were pleased to find no human casualties.

"There must be at least twelve deer here," I said surprised, counting the motionless forms strewn about the beach.

Now came the daunting task of gutting twelve deer in the dark and carrying them back to camp, where they were hung from a log suspended off the ground between two spruce trees. After that bloody bit of work we took a cold dip in the dark ocean and warmed up around a blazing campfire as the chilly Alaskan night set in. Early the next morning, we finished our deer quota by shooting another eight deer. This was one of the few hunting trips that did not include a miles-long slog, carrying a hundred pounds or more of dead animal on my back, since most of this deer slaughter took place within a few hundred yards of our camp-site. We now had two days to explore the island, without having to think about hunting, before the plane was scheduled to return, weather permitting.

The western shore of Montague Island faced the wide open Pacific Ocean, and if you could drift southwest in a straight line, you would eventually hit Asia. The island was a great spot for beachcombing, which I have always enjoyed—sifting through the treasures that washed up upon the shore and wondering about where they came from. I had already noticed that our camp table and chairs were mostly made from wooden Japanese beer crates that had washed ashore. I spent a couple of days exploring miles of the western shore and found a considerable amount of interesting flotsam that had been deposited above the tide line. Most of this trash seemed to be of Japanese origin and included many empty wooden beer crates stenciled with Japanese characters, as well as plastic bottles and containers covered with Japanese writing.

The shore was littered with weathered shoes and boots, old bits of nets, polypropylene line, and other pieces of fishing debris, but the best discovery was a number of torn nets with colored glass balls still attached that had been used to float the nets in some far off country, presumably Japan. All the net floats I had ever seen in Alaska and the rest of the United States were made out of Styrofoam or plastic, and I could only speculate how long these glass balls had been traveling across the wide Pacific. The thick glass balls were mostly a dark green or deep blue color and were the size of grapefruits, although one was the size of a soccer ball. These were the treasures that I collected and took home as souvenirs of the Montague expedition. Over the years, I gave some away as gifts and must have misplaced the rest, because today I only have the memory of discovering those beautiful glass balls.

It was not too far fetched to imagine this bounty from the sea navigating the currents of the Pacific, traveling from Asia to the shores of Alaska. There was a warm ocean current, flowing northeast from the Philippine Sea past southeast Japan, known as the Japan Current. In Japan, it was called the *Kuroshiro* or "Black Stream" because of the dark blue color of its water. This current was analogous to the Gulf Stream in the Atlantic Ocean: transporting warm, tropical water northward. Once past Japan, the current merged with the North Pacific Current that flowed east as part of the general clockwise circulation of water in the northern hemisphere.

As the North Pacific Current approached North America, most of the water was deflected south to continue the clockwise circulation between the west coast of North America and Hawaii, now called the California Current. There was, however, a northern branch of the North Pacific Current that curved counter-clockwise to form the Alaska Current that flowed along the coasts of western Canada and Alaska. Once it turned southwest near Kodiak Island and the Alaska Peninsula, it was known as the Alaska Stream. This current was responsible for the relatively mild climate experienced in southeast Alaska and as far north as the Anchorage area.

I imagined my colorful glass balls breaking off a Japanese fisherman's net in the midst of a storm somewhere along the coast of Japan and bobbing across the surface of the ocean, traveling thousands of miles. Against all odds, they washed up on the shore of Montague Island unbroken, and waited half-buried in the sand for a beachcomber to wander by.

The weather held out for us, and three days later, a telltale buzzing echoed out of the clear blue sky and materialized into a small plane. The plane circled the beach one time, and with a wave of its wings, landed in the hard-packed sand just below the high-tide line. I think the pilot was a little surprised to see the pile of twenty deer carcasses wrapped in visqueen with legs sticking out here and there. Being a typical bush pilot, his only comment was, "Looks like you had a good hunt. Start stuffing them in the plane." We managed to cram most of the deer, which after being field dressed were not very big, and some of our gear into the Cessna.

"We'll have to make two trips," Richard said. "I'll stay here with John, and you two go on the first run."

I sat uncomfortably on board on a pile of dead deer, looking out at the Pacific Ocean breaking upon the shore, as the plane started off down the beach, gather-ing more and more speed. It took longer than usual for liftoff due to the excess weight, but we were airborne with plenty of beach to spare and headed back to the small-plane airport in Anchorage.

After the other hunters and the rest of the deer carcasses had been retrieved from the island, we loaded our share of the deer—fifteen of them—into the back of the pickup and headed for the trailer in Wasilla. It was cold and the deer were half frozen by the time we arrived home. Fifteen deer was quite a haul, even these small Sitka black tails, and we still needed to butcher and process them for the freezer.

"It's too cold to do this outside," I said, looking at the half-frozen pile of deer that was stuffed in the back of the truck.

"We can line the kitchen with visqueen and do it there," Gig suggested.

We brought the deer in and stacked them on the floor like cordwood. We organized our assembly line and began the task of butchering, separating the different cuts of meat, and wrapping them in preparation for freezing.

After a few hours of work, I said, "We're getting there. There's only a couple more left."

"Yeah, but look at the bloody mess we made of the kitchen," John said.

There was a knock at the door, and Bill Sr. walked in and gazed at the horror scene in front of him. He took in the two dead deer, still splayed out on the floor, the blood splattered, plastic-lined kitchen, and the three of us standing there covered with blood, holding our dripping knives and meat saws.

"I see you had a successful hunt," he began.

"Don't worry, Bill, we'll get it all cleaned up," I said.

"Oh, I'm not worried about this mess," he said. "Sally will tell you I've certainly done worse myself. No, I came by to ask y'all to leave. I know those dogs have been living inside the trailer, and you promised me they would stay outside."

"Well, you're right, Bill," I said sheepishly. "I'm sorry."

When the cold weather had set in, I hadn't been able to bear to keep my aging dog, Nancy, outside. She was a short-haired dog and not made for the Alaskan winters, but we had grown up together, and I loved her as part of my family and wanted to keep her comfortable in her old age. The other dogs were doing just fine outdoors and had taken to the cold like the huskies that they were.

"I'll give you a week to pack up and leave," Bill finished.

We gave him a big pile of deer meat to thank him for all he had done for us, and a week later, we left on good terms, but facing the prospect of surviving an Alaskan winter without a place to live.

Chapter Seven:
Mount Saint Elias

Gig and I lived mostly out of the back of the truck for the rest of the winter. John continued to work for ARCO, and we saw less and less of him that winter since he lived with different friends, here and there. Gig and I had split from Jake at that point, and we spent the majority of the winter hanging sheetrock on our own, mostly in the Anchorage area.

"I'm tired of moving from house to bus to trailer to truck," I said to Gig. "This year I'm going to save enough money to buy a piece of land and start building a house of my own so we won't be continually faced with these housing problems."

"Living in the truck isn't that bad," Gig said, "especially when all we do is work."

We usually worked until eleven or twelve o'clock at night, so it wasn't that much of a problem to lay out a sleeping bag on a pile of sheetrock or climb into the back of the truck and curl up with the dogs for warmth. For a couple of hundred dollars each, we joined a health club in Anchorage and used it for taking showers, and on extra cold days, we used the Jacuzzi and steam room to defrost and warm up. Our diet consisted mainly of bread and Adam's chunky peanut butter, which we bought in gallon jars. We supplemented the peanut butter sandwiches with an occasional meal at the local Fat Boy restaurant, where we got to know some of the regular customers.

"There she is again," Gig whispered, watching an elderly couple who were pushing through the door. As usual, they were dressed in their Sunday best, and you could tell the old man was particularly proud to parade in with such a ravishing beauty.

"She really put it on thick this time," I whispered back, as everyone at the salad bar stared at the woman. I think she needed a new prescription for glasses because her bright red lipstick was not only caked on, but she had drawn a red oval at least an inch in diameter away from her lips, and sometimes she dotted her nose as well.

One of our best sheetrocking jobs that winter was at a mini-cache self-storage facility. The long rows of garage-like storage rooms were designed so that almost no sheets needed to be cut: we just picked up the sheets and nailed them to the studs.

"For someone getting paid by the square foot of sheetrock hung, this is almost like free money," I told Gig.

"Yeah, no complicated angles to measure and cut, no tiny closets to try to nail in, and no thirty-foot ceilings to deal with; just pristine sheet after sheet to lift and nail, and then move on to the next storage room," Gig said.

The only drawback was the cold weather, since we were essentially working outside. During the month we spent working on the mini-cache, the temperature rarely got as high as zero degrees and was twenty below or colder most days. The storage rooms were not heated, because the doors couldn't be installed until after we hung the sheetrock. We dressed for the weather, of course, but on many days we stopped and spent an hour or two thawing out in the Jacuzzi of the health club before returning to work through half the night. All in all, I counted it a successful winter, as I was able to save enough money to purchase two acres of land in the Wasilla area and had some leftover to make a start on the house I had designed during my spare time shivering in the back of the truck.

Sadness did visit me late that winter as my old dog, Nancy, slipped away from me one bleak day, just as winter was getting ready to give way to mud season.

"She's really slowing down," Gig said, while we were visiting friends in Wasilla for a few days.

"The arthritis is so bad she doesn't want to walk anymore," I replied. "She hasn't eaten in two days. This is probably the end for her."

We had been inseparable for the past twelve years of her life, and I was despondent when she wandered away from the house we were visiting and disappeared into the Alaskan bush. I'm not sure how she mustered the energy to travel, as she had been barely walking for the past two weeks. My other dog, Denali, and I spent the next two days searching the area, tramping through the woods calling Nancy's name, but we found no trace of the big black dog. My heart hopes she found a quiet, peaceful spot to curl up and die, but not being able to find her left me with an uneasy, incomplete sense of loss. I found myself frequently visiting those woods over the next few months, wandering the game trails until I could finally put her to rest in my mind.

In the spring of 1979, with Gig's help, I cleared a spot on my land for my house and driveway and rented a backhoe to dig the hole for the foundation, a series of trenches for a septic system, and a twelve-foot-deep trench from the foundation to the site of my future water well. I buried a flexible copper water line in the trench deep enough to prevent it from freezing in the cold winter temperatures and left one end sticking out of the ground.

"Drilling the well will have to wait," I told Gig. "It's too expensive now."

"Maybe next year," he said.

Since I was building the house without any financing, I would just have to wait until I could afford the well. The first priorities were building the foundation and framing in the structure. Fortunately for us, a friend lent us a camper off the back of his pickup truck that we parked on my land to live in.

"Hey, we're really moving up in the world now," I remarked to Gig, as we moved out of the truck and into the camper.

"Yes, very luxurious. We can really impress the girls now," he agreed.

We worked on the septic system and foundation at night after sheetrocking all day, and soon called in a cement truck to pour the footings. I subcontracted out the cement block foundation work and, before summer arrived, had the floor of the house in place, covering the combination crawl space and basement. I framed in the house, wall by wall, as I found the money, and by fall, I had a roof over the house with visqueen covering the windows and doors. While Gig was gone working on a firefighting crew in northern Alaska, I spent a month on my first serious mountaineering expedition.

"Want to climb St. Elias?" Harry (my Hatcher Pass climbing partner) asked me early that summer. "I'm organizing what will be only the second ascent of the mountain via a ridge from Mount Newton."

"I've never been on an expedition like that," I told Harry.

"You'll do great," he said.

The route he proposed climbed Mount Newton and then across a knife-edge ridge that connected with St. Elias through Russell col. St. Elias was on the Alaska-Yukon border and at 18,009 feet, was the second-highest mountain in both Alaska and Canada. Overlooking the Gulf of Alaska, the mountain was a target for storms off the ocean, and on average, received a hundred feet of snowfall per year. Because of the terrible weather, it was infrequently climbed.

Vitus Bering, the Danish explorer in Russian employ, had sighted the almost perfectly pyramidal-shaped mountain from the deck of his ship, the *St. Peter*, on July 16, 1741. He also noted in the ship's log, the vast glacier that emanated from the coastal mountains and spread out like a fan toward the shores of the Gulf of Alaska. This ice field, the Malaspina Glacier, was a classic example of a piedmont glacier. Several valley glaciers exited the St. Elias Range onto the broad coastal plain, and when these glaciers were no longer constrained by their valleys, they merged and spread out into a single, fan-like piedmont glacier. The resulting Malaspina Glacier was the largest glacier in Alaska at 1,120 square miles and was frequently noted to be larger than the state of Rhode Island. Using seismic sensors, the glacier has been found to be over eighteen hundred feet thick, and the weight of the ice pushes down its basin as much as nine hundred feet below sea level. Over the most recent twenty years, by comparing satellite radar images and laser height measurements, scientists have discovered that the average thickness of the glacier has been reduced by sixty feet, giving some support to the global warming theory. Until Mount McKinley/Denali was spotted by Europeans, St. Elias was thought to be the highest peak in Alaska. Four unsuccessful attempts were made to scale the mountain between 1886 and 1891.

The mountain had first been climbed in 1897 by the young Italian adventurer and mountaineer, Luigi Giuseppe Maria Ferdinando Francesco, better known as Luigi of Savoy, the Duke of Abruzzi. The Savoy family held sovereignty over most of Italy in the nineteenth century, and therefore the Duke was a royal prince. He was twenty-four years old at the time of his St. Elias expedition and had previously climbed in the Alps, scaling the Matterhorn with the famous English climber, Albert F. Mummery. The Duke's St. Elias expedition was sponsored by his uncle, the king of Italy, and included four Italian mountain guides, as well as a photographer, a physician, a lawyer, and a fellow naval officer.

The Italians hired eleven American porters in Seattle, who sailed to Sitka on a chartered schooner, the *Aggie*. The Italians took a steamship from Seattle to Sitka and then towed the *Aggie,* with the porters on board, to Yakutat, a small village close by the Malaspina Glacier.

At Yakutat, the Duke hired a group of native Tlingit men to help carry the thousands of pounds of expedition gear to the start of the route on the Malaspina Glacier. The gear included five fold-up iron bedsteads that weighed fourteen pounds apiece, on which the Duke and the other four high-ranking Italians intended to sleep comfortably above the glacial ice and snow, leaving the guides and the porters to sleep on cold spruce boughs. Once on the glacier proper, the team struggled to drag the loaded wooden sledges around and over crevasses, through ice falls, and around seracs. In classic siege expedition style, it took the Duke and his team approximately one month to ferry everything across the glaciers to the base of the Newton icefall, which they proposed to scale in order to reach Russell col, and then on to the summit of St. Elias.

The Duke's Italian guides cut steps up and through the Newton icefall, and all ten Italians, with the Duke's iron bed in tow, climbed easily up the steps, avoiding several avalanches on the way. Thirty-seven days after starting across the

Malaspina glacier, they pitched their high camp at Russell col, six thousand feet below the summit of St. Elias. The next day dawned perfectly clear and windless, and the Duke and the other nine Italians all reached the summit.

After his St. Elias success, the Duke continued his adventurous career: traveling to the source of the Nile, making an attempt at the North Pole, and also attempting a climb of K2, the second highest mountain in the world. It would be another fifty years before another human would stand on the summit of St. Elias.

In 1979, our climbing team consisted of four members, including me. My friend Harry was the organizer and leader of the expedition. A lifelong Alaskan, he lived in Wasilla with his wife and two young daughters and owned a title insurance company. He was an active climber in the area, and after being introduced by a mutual friend, we began climbing together in the Hatcher Pass area. Harry was somewhat smaller than me—strong, compact, and cheerful. As often as not, he had the telltale raccoon-like facial suntan of a climber who often wore glacier goggles. I had never met the other two members of the team: Bob and Einar. Bob was a tall, lanky lawyer from Anchorage with a wispy beard and much more mountaineering experience under his belt than I had. Einar was also from the Anchorage area. Tall and powerful, with a full Alaskan beard, he was a quiet veteran of many Alaska climbing seasons who lived for climbing. I was the inexperienced member who had never been on a full-fledged expedition before, but with Harry vouching for me, I was warmly included in the group.

"We should plan for a month-long expedition," Harry said. "We'll drive from here to Kluane Lake in the Yukon, and a bush pilot will fly us into the St. Elias Range."

"I've been to Kluane Lake a few times before," I said.

Just organizing an expedition of this duration was quite a feat. Each of us had his own personal climbing equipment: packs, ice axes, crampons, climbing harnesses, carabineers, ascending devices, ice screws, snow flukes, snow pickets, cold-weather gear, and down sleeping bags rated for twenty below. In addition, the communal team gear included three high-altitude tents, climbing ropes, two white-gas stoves with cooking pots, a month's supply of fuel for the stoves, snow shovels, snow saws for building igloos, hundreds of bamboo wands capped with florescent tape for marking the route, a large, bulky radio for contacting the bush pilot for a ride out, sleds, and a mountain of food.

"Separate the food for each camp and put it into these labeled stuff sacks," Harry instructed me.

There was heavy, bulky fresh food for base camp, including cheese, bread, watermelon, eggs, and beer. For the higher camps, much lighter, freeze-dried dinners, powdered soups, ramen noodles, instant hot chocolate, Tang, instant oatmeal, candy bars, dried fruit, tea, and instant coffee.

"We've planned on five successive camps," Einar said. "Four of them on Newton, and one at Russell col at the end of the ridge. From there we should be able to make the summit attempt, just as the Duke and his team did."

The different stuff sacks full of food were marked with the camp numbers to easily identify which bags went where. As we packed this immense pile of gear and food into Harry's truck, I had a hard time imagining how we were going to cram it all into a small plane along with the four of us, never mind carry most of it up a mountain.

A day's drive brought us to the Destruction Bay area on Kluane Lake in the Yukon Territory, and we met our bush pilot on a perfectly clear, sunny, summer day.

"I just flew two climbers into the Seward Glacier last week, so you won't be alone on the mountain," he informed us. "They're only planning to climb Newton and not traversing over to St. Elias like you."

Somehow, we loaded ourselves and all the gear into the ski-mounted, single engine Cessna 185 and were soon flying over Kluane National Park. The plane arced out over the turquoise-blue waters of the lake and circled back toward the St. Elias Mountains, following a series of glaciers cutting their way through the foothills. Flying over these glaciers from eight thousand feet gave me a bird's eye view of glacial topography.

There are essentially two main types of glaciers: valley glaciers, such as we were flying over, and continental glaciers, such as the huge ice sheet that covers Greenland. A glacier forms when the climate is cold enough to allow snow to accumulate over time. The snow eventually turns to ice and begins to flow outward and downward under the pressure of its own weight and the pull of gravity. As this glacial ice builds on itself and is compressed, the ice crystals grow larger, and the air spaces between them decrease. This process makes glacial ice extremely dense and is responsible for its other-worldly, deep blue color. Glacial ice is so dense that only the blue-light wavelength has the energy to escape the ice crystals, making the ice appear blue.

"You can really see the different glacial features and how they affect the landscape from up here," I said over the noise of the engine. The plane had flown over a scrub forest that gave way to the terminal moraines of glaciers.

"I've never seen all the different types of moraines at the same time before," Harry yelled, pointing down at the glacier.

The terminal moraine forms at the snout or terminal end of a glacier and marks the furthest extent of the ice. Lateral and medial moraines are long, dark strips of rock and earth that mark a glacier's surface longitudinally, following every curve and twist of the ice. Lateral moraines form along the edges of a glacier as material from the valley walls falls onto the surface of the ice and is carried along as if on a conveyor belt. A medial moraine forms when two lateral moraines merge as two glaciers come together, and the resulting medial moraine marks the centerline of the combined larger glacier. The presence of a medial moraine is evidence that a glacier has more than one source, and we flew over glaciers with three and four medial moraines striping their surfaces.

Thirty minutes after taking off from the shores of Kluane Lake, the plane turned a corner of the fifty-mile-wide Seward Glacier and Mount Logan, and then St. Elias came into view. The mountains seemed to erupt from a sea of glaciers, and in the reflected sunlight, they were startling white against the deep blue backdrop of the sky, with a few dark rock faces peaking through here and there.

"There's not a speck of green down there," I said, more to myself than anyone else, "only snow, ice, and rock."

The plane angled down toward the deceptively smooth-looking surface of the Seward Glacier and landed in two feet of virgin snow, close to a small snow-covered hill that formed the beginning of a long, sinuous ridge that led up to the summit of Mount Newton. After crawling out of the plane and helping to unload our mountain of gear, I stood on the glacier and gazed around, trying to fathom the immensity of the scale of my surroundings. Mount Logan, at 19,250 feet the highest peak in Canada, stood fifty miles away on the other side of the glacier. The vast bulk of St. Elias was hidden behind the thousand-foot hill that marked the beginning of our route.

"See you in a month or so," the pilot said in parting. The plane made a short takeoff run, and we were blasted with icy snow crystals by the prop wash as it roared by. Very quickly the roar receded to a barely perceptible buzz as the plane became a dark smudge on the blue horizon and then, silence. All the planning, packing, and rushing around was now behind us.

"Let's move all the gear closer to the base of the hill and set up base camp over there," Harry said, breaking the silence and pointing toward the hill that marked the base of the north ridge of Newton. Distances are deceptive on the surface of a glacier. From the air, it looked to be only a short jaunt to the base of the ridge, but in reality, it was a two-mile slog through heavy and sometimes even slushy two-foot deep snow.

"This fresh snow must have covered the other climbing party's tracks," Einar said.

Once the sleds were loaded, we shouldered our packs, roped together in teams of two for crevasse protection, and slowly slogged toward the ridge and the spot that would become our base camp.

"Man, I never thought it would be this hot on a glacier," I muttered to myself, as the sun reflected off the snow and baked the overlying air. It was not long before I was drenched in sweat and stripped down to long underwear. I draped a bandanna under my baseball cap, desert-style, for sunburn protection.

It took a couple of hours to cross to the base of the ridge, and periodically, a low, thunderous boom rolled across the glacier from the vicinity of St. Elias. I looked for storm clouds in the clear blue sky, until Harry shouted down the rope, "Avalanche." The base of the north ridge blocked our view of St. Elias, so we could not see any of the distant avalanches, but the frequency of the thunder certainly made me wonder what would be visible from the ridge itself.

"Keep me on belay while I probe around for any hidden crevasses," Harry instructed me, once we finally reached the hill. After he checked the perimeter, we unloaded the sleds and set up our three tents. We staked out black plastic garbage bags and covered them with snow to take advantage of solar heat to melt the snow and collect water.

"All right, let's head back to the landing site and pick up the rest of the gear," Einar said.

Trudging slowly back and forth in the same tracks was a preview of the coming climb. Our plan was to climb the mountain in the time-tested, classic siege manner. That is, we would ferry loads up the mountain, establishing successively higher camps as we went. After caching a load of supplies, we would retreat to the previous camp to sleep before moving more supplies up to the higher camp. This meant we would essentially climb the mountain twice, but it was the only way to move a month's worth of food and fuel up the peak.

"The real advantage to the siege approach is that it allows you to slowly acclimatize to the altitude," Harry said.

It is a common misconception that the percent of oxygen decreases with increasing altitude. The percent of oxygen in the air remains essentially the same (approximately 21 percent) up to 50,000 feet, but what does change is the barometric pressure and thus the partial pressure of oxygen. With increasing altitude, barometric pressure decreases and gases, like air, expand so that at altitude there are fewer oxygen molecules in a given volume of air (40 percent fewer at 12,000 feet), even though the concentration or percent remains constant. (The partial pressure of a gas refers to the contribution that each gas makes to the total pressure of the atmosphere.) At sea level, the barometric pressure, as measured in millimeters of mercury (abbreviated as mmHg), is 760 mmHg, and the partial pressure of oxygen (PO_2) is 159 mmHg. At 20,000 feet, the barometric pressure falls to 349 mmHg and the PO_2 to 73 mmHg.

Our bodies, of course, need a constant supply of oxygen to support cellular respiration. The lower partial pressure of oxygen at high altitude translates to lower oxygen saturation in the blood and less oxygen available for use by the cells of our bodies, which is called hypoxic hypoxia. This lower oxygen saturation can lead to altitude-related illnesses, such as acute mountain sickness (AMS), high-altitude pulmonary edema (HAPE), and high-altitude cerebral edema (HACE). The likelihood of sustaining an altitude-related illness depends on the elevation, the rate of ascent, and individual susceptibility. AMS embraces a constellation of symptoms that include headache, dizziness, fatigue, shortness of breath, decreased appetite, nausea, sleep disturbances, and general malaise. HAPE occurs when fluid builds up in the lung tissues from capillary leakage, thereby preventing effective oxygen exchange. HACE occurs when fluid leaks into the brain, resulting in altered mental status, confusion, ataxia (unsteady walking), coma, and if not treated, death. Fortunately, our bodies can adapt somewhat to higher altitudes through the complex, but not yet completely understood, process of acclimatization.

This process requires complex interactions between several of the body's systems, including the respiratory system, the cardiovascular system, and the endocrine system. Some of the changes are immediate, and others take days and even months to occur. All the changes help the body to more efficiently deliver oxygen to the tissues, despite the decrease of oxygen in arterial blood, and help the body to cope with the lower partial pressure of oxygen at altitude. Once over twenty thousand feet or so, the body no longer really adapts to the altitude, but instead it begins a slow spiraling process of deterioration. Once over twenty-six thousand feet, a climber enters the "death zone," where the deterioration process from lack of oxygen puts them at extreme risk even with supplemental oxygen.

"We don't need to worry about the altitudinal death zone on St. Elias," Einar said, "only the usual mountain dangers that can leave you just as dead."

"Avalanches have been the major killer of climbers on this mountain," Harry added. The relatively warm temperature, combined with exceptional snowfall, created unstable snow formations that were the prerequisites for avalanches.

"Don't forget about the crevasses," Bob said. "On glaciers and mountains like this you need to be constantly vigilant." When different sections of a glacier moved at different rates, internal stresses built up in the ice, causing it to split apart and form crevasses. These crevasses sometimes were obvious and easily avoided, but more often than not, they were covered by snow bridges and invisible to anyone on the surface of a glacier. Staying roped together and being aware of the dangers were the only ways to stay safe while traveling over these glaciers.

Once base camp was organized, we made our first supply carry up to camp one, just below a small knoll overlooking a fairly gentle slope that would lead us up and onto the north ridge of Newton. Harry and I became a team on one rope, while Einar and Bob made up the other rope team. Taking turns breaking trail through the deep snow throughout the hot day, we finally dumped the few hundred pounds of supplies, and stashed it all in one of the tents to protect it from marauding ravens before heading back down to base camp to spend the night.

"I'm glad we brought all this fresh food with us," I said, "especially the beer."

The weather continued hot and sunny the next day, and we loaded the rest of the supplies into packs and sleds, leaving one tent, a few days worth of food and fuel, and the bulky radio at base camp.

"Collapse the tent and wand the area so we can find it when we return," Harry said. "We may not see base camp again for a month."

Continuing in this slow and plodding fashion, we established camps two and three over the course of the next five days. At camp three, we were finally on the north ridge of Mount Newton, after crossing a small bergschrund and ascending a steep headwall. A bergschrund is a crevasse that separates the flowing ice from stagnant ice at the head of a glacier and can be a tiny crack or a wide, gaping hole.

"Stop staring into the hole and get a move on," Harry yelled down to me, as I gazed into what seemed like the deep blue depths of eternity. A cold icy breeze wafted up from out of the gash in the glacier, sending a chill down my spine. In response to Harry's urging, I gingerly stepped over the crevasse and followed him up the headwall.

"There she is," Harry said, after we had finally gained the ridge. The imposing bulk of St. Elias dwarfed our position on Mount Newton.

We could then see, as well as hear, the many avalanches that roared down the slopes of St. Elias and spilled out onto the distant Seward Glacier. As temperatures climbed during the day and warmed up the snow, we could see distant white plumes silently roll down the faces and steep headwalls of all the surrounding mountains, and seconds later, we could hear the sound of their passing, much the way the sound of thunder hesitantly follows the flash of distant lightning. We were well out of the way of any avalanche danger, and the sound and sight of the white clouds of snow pouring down the distant mountains became so common-place that soon we no longer looked up at the sound.

The ridge broadened out onto a small plateau, before continuing up along a true knife-edge that was no more than a foot wide and sloped steeply down a thousand feet on each side. On the plateau, just before the knife-edge began, we dug a large, comfortable snow cave that would serve as camp three.

"Let's spend a day or two here to rest and acclimatize," Harry suggested.

"I can't believe we've had nothing but sunshine," Bob said.

"That's bound to change sooner or later," Einar said, pointing at the sky. "Look at those mare's tails."

High over the white face of St. Elias, high-flying, feathery cirrus clouds, known as "mare's tails," streamed in from the ocean, heading in our direction. They were formed when an approaching cold front began to lift an area of warmer air, so they frequently signaled the approach of bad weather. They were shaped by strong winds in the upper atmosphere and were made out of ice crystals that were blown into wispy curls, resembling the tails of horses.

The next planned camp, camp four, lay just below the summit of Mount Newton.

"Let's carry as much food and fuel as we can to camp four and then return here for the night," Harry said the next day. This would mean our longest day of climbing yet, encompassing a good bit of the ridge and then back down again.

"We'll need to keep an eye on that sky," Einar added, pointing to an ugly, grayish cloud billowing up from the ocean side of St. Elias.

The first obstacle on the ridge was the knife-edge that stretched a few hundred yards. It was only a foot wide and was exposed on both sides. Before traversing over this part of the ridge, Harry shortened the climbing rope to seventy-five feet and tied the excess onto my pack.

"You're going to lead this section, right?" I asked.

"No problem," he replied, edging out onto the thin ribbon of snow. "If I fall, jump off the other side of the ridge."

I stared uncomprehendingly at him and said, "Are you crazy?"

"No, there's no way to belay safely on this part of the ridge, and if I pull you off the same side, we'll both end up dead at the bottom. If you jump off the other side, we'll balance each other out and only fall forty feet or so. Then we can jumar back up the rope," he explained.

I couldn't argue with the logic and slapped him on the shoulder, saying, "Okay man, but please don't fall."

Harry eased out onto the foot-wide ramp of snow, using his ice ax for a balancing point, as I gave him an ice-ax belay from the safety of the plateau. He moved along smoothly and confidently, and after seventy-five feet he was off belay and I was following along behind him. After a few minutes, I became used to the rhythm of step, plant the ice ax, step, plant the ice ax, over and over, while balancing my eighty-pound pack. I tried not to look down the slope too much and concentrated on following carefully in Harry's boot prints.

"See, piece of cake," Harry said, as I joined him on the other side.

Before long, Bob and Einar were beside us, and we were once again plowing upward through the deep snow. The ridge widened and wound its way toward the summit of Newton. Alternating the lead between the four of us, we plodded on, hour after hour.

"Make sure you wand the trail every hundred feet or so," Harry advised.

As the ridge started to narrow once more, we found the first evidence of the other climbing party in the form of a shallow snow cave carved into the west side of the ridge. "They must have camped here before moving higher up the mountain," Harry observed.

"Pretty small snow cave," Einar added. "Let's stop here and have lunch."

"I don't like this snow," Harry said, gazing skyward as a few white flakes began to sift down out of the gray sky. "Still, the clouds aren't that thick, and there's no wind yet." The horizon line to the east was still clear, but the summit of St. Elias was now obscured by an ugly lenticular cloud, and the sky to the west looked a lot darker than it had before.

"Let's hustle to camp four," Einar suggested. Lunch was cut short, and we continued to trade leads up the ridge, keeping an eye on the weather.

A couple of hours later, we came on a construction that was part snow cave, part igloo. It sported dozens of bamboo wands sticking out of its roof like porcupine quills. It was no more than a few hundred yards below what appeared to be the summit of Mount Newton. Two climbers met us at the entrance of this ice palace and invited us in for a cup of tea. The cave really wasn't large enough to fit all of us, and the snow was now falling much more heavily and beginning to accumulate.

"Thanks for the offer," Harry said, "but we need to hightail it back down to our camp with this weather descending. Can we dump our loads here in your cave?"

"Sure, no problem," one of the climbers replied. "This is the first real snow we've had since we arrived."

As we left their camp, the wind picked up, roaring over the summit of Newton, and before long, we were in whiteout conditions, blindly groping our way downhill as we searched for the next wand. I reached the shallow snow cave that served as our lunch stop and belayed Harry to me.

"We can't continue in this storm," Harry yelled at me over the roar of the wind. "We'll have to bivouac in this cave."

"You're right," I agreed. "It would be way too easy to wander off the ridge in this storm."

We took turns for an hour enlarging the snow cave until all four of us could just fit in and spread out our sleeping bags. The entrance was rearranged so that there was a small tunnel leading out at a level below the sleeping platform. This allowed the cold air to collect in the tunnel area and kept the main body of the cave slightly warmer. As the wind howled and the snow blew outside the tunnel entrance, we took stock of our situation in the dim light of the snow cave.

"Well, I wouldn't call this cave spacious," Bob said.

"Yeah, but at least it's cozy," Harry replied. Our body heat warmed up the cave, and we could peel off storm gear.

"I'd much rather be in here than out there in a tent," I added, listening to the wind moan outside.

"All right, how much food do we have?" Harry asked, as we unloaded our packs and tallied up the communal supplies. Each rope team carried a stove and spare fuel, so there were two stoves and plenty of fuel to melt snow for water. We all carried our own Styrofoam sleeping pads and sleeping bags as well as a few extra personal items of clothing.

"Well, I've got one candy bar," I said.

"Yeah, I've got one too," Einar added.

"I've got nothing," Harry and Bob answered in unison, after double-checking their packs and coat pockets. We had just unloaded more than a week's worth of food and fuel below the summit of Newton and had almost two more weeks of food back at camp three.

"I wish I had carried an emergency stash of food," I said.

"You can only carry so much," Harry replied. "Besides, the speed of the storm took us all by surprise."

"We'll be all right," Einar added confidently.

"Well, let's eat then," I said, splitting the two candy bars in half and passing them around.

We were all tired from the long day of trudging up the ridge with heavy packs and fighting our way down through the blowing snow, but even if we went to sleep a little hungry that night, at least we were snug and cozy in our snow cave. Besides, how long could it possibly continue to snow this hard anyway?

When I awoke the next day, I found the entrance to the snow cave completely blocked with snow. Light filtered dimly through where the tunnel entrance had been situated, and I could faintly discern the muffled roar of the wind through the wall of the cave.

"I'm going to shovel out the tunnel and have a look around outside," I said, bundling up and grabbing a snow shovel.

"You'll have to shovel the snow back into the cave first," Harry said. "Once you break through to the outside, I'll shovel it out to you again."

The tunnel was five feet longer than it had been the day before, due to accumulated new snow, but I finally broke through to the outside world. It was snowing harder, and the wind was blowing stronger than when we took shelter for the night, if that was possible. Visibility was no more than a few feet, and it would have been dangerous to wander off away from the tunnel entrance. Harry shoveled the excavated snow to me, and I transferred it outside. From then on, we took turns clearing the tunnel every few hours and emptying any full pee bottles outside. Otherwise, there was nothing to do but lie in our sleeping bags and talk about food. Every once in a while, one of us would fire up the stove and melt some snow for water.

"You know, one of the conveniences of living in a snow cave is that you can just reach out and put some of your wall into the pot to melt, without having to get out of your bag," Einar said, plopping a chunk of the wall into the pot.

"Hey, what do we have here?" Harry said, triumphantly uncovering a spot in a corner of the wall where it looked like the previous occupants had dumped one of their leftover dinners. There were a few identifiable noodles with what looked like specks of carrots and maybe a piece of celery frozen in some dirty snow. "We could brew up some garbage soup," he said.

"Ah, no thanks," the rest of us chorused. "We're not that hungry yet."

The storm kept up, and the tunnel kept getting longer and longer. No one had any reading material, and all conversations eventually ended up returning to the subject of food. We took turns torturing each other with the memories of some of our favorite meals.

"All right, your turn to torture us now, John," Harry said.

"Okay, a few years ago my father took me out to dinner at a small restaurant in New Hampshire run by a Swiss chef," I began. "I started the meal with a hot, flaky, golden, baked-brie pastry appetizer, smothered under a ragoût of wild mushrooms in a red-wine pan sauce. It was of course, washed down with a cold, crisp, refreshing lager."

"Oh, that would be good," Bob said. "Don't stop."

"A savory spinach and herb salad, encrusted with goat cheese and sprinkled with warm bacon vinaigrette, followed," I continued, "accompanied, of course, by a 1968 Gervey-Chambertin. The wine was a deep purple-burgundy color and had a smoky nose, with hints of plum and raspberry aromas. On the palate, it had a full, lush fruit taste, with cherry, blackberry, musk, and licorice predominating, and boasted a long and satisfying finish."

"Keep going," Harry said.

"No, don't," Einar said.

"A small crystal glass of watermelon sorbet to clear the palate preceded the main course of chateaubriand," I went on, "accompanied by roasted, red new potatoes and sautéed baby carrots with zucchini blossoms. The chateaubriand was carved at the table and seared to perfection on the outside with a pinkish center. The meat was melt-in-your mouth tender, oozing delicious warm, red juice."

"Stop," Bob pleaded.

"Dessert consisted of freshly baked, warm shortcake, topped with just-picked, ripe wild strawberries with homemade vanilla ice cream and smothered with whipped cream. Coffee enhanced with a shot of Bailey's rounded out the meal," I finished.

"Oh, that hurts," Einar complained.

By the third storm-bound day, we were desperate enough to scrape up the leavings of the prior party's leftovers and make the garbage soup. There really wasn't much to be found, only some tinted snow with a few frozen noodles and unidentifiable orange and green bits. It did more to boost our morale and relieve boredom than it provided nutrition. After thoroughly boiling the "soup" for a few minutes, we distributed it equally and quaffed it down. In reality, it was barely tinted water with a few colored specks floating in it.

"Tastes like chicken," Harry said.

"A subtle nose of freeze-dried turkey tetrazzini," I added. "Light on the palate but thoroughly satisfying."

By the fourth day, all talk of food had subsided, and we tried to doze as much as possible to keep our minds off our shrunken bellies and the incessant, muted roaring of the wind outside the snow cave.

On the fifth day, we awoke to a new sensation: silence. I crawled out of my sleeping bag, suited up, and wormed my way down what was by then a fifteen-foot-long tunnel into the outside world. Blinding sunlight, reflecting off the freshly fallen snow, greeted me, and there was not a breath of wind to disturb the ridgeline. The heavy snowfall had already jump-started the avalanche concert on the northeast face of St. Elias, and every few minutes a new one rumbled down and ran out onto the Seward Glacier. The ridge connecting Mount Newton to St. Elias looked immense in the clear morning light, with a huge overhung cornice towering over the almost sheer face that fell thousands of feet to the glacier below. I made a mental note to stay well back off the cornice rim if I ended up traversing that ridge. Gazing down the north ridge of Newton, I saw nothing but pristine snow.

"Not a track or a wand in sight," I said.

"That's okay, there's only one possible route down to camp three," Harry replied. "We won't need wands to find our way today. I can't believe how much snow has accumulated."

"It will be a lot easier moving downhill to camp three than trying to break trail through this snow up to the food stash below the summit of Newton," Bob said.

It did not take much to motivate us to break camp, rope up, and head down to the food awaiting us at camp three. "Even going downhill isn't very easy," Einar called back to us, after thrashing his way down the first twenty feet.

Most of the day had worn away in a fog of hunger and deep snow before we found ourselves staring at the knife-edge portion of the ridge separating us from camp three.

"I can almost taste the food now," Harry said dreamily. Without hesitation and with a growing sense of excitement and relief at almost being there, we all trudged carefully across the narrow ribbon of snow leading to the plateau.

"Where are the wands marking the roof of the cave?" I asked, incredulously looking around at the expanse of smooth, unblemished snow that covered the plateau.

"We marked that cave with at least a dozen wands," Harry added in a voice of bewilderment and crushing disappointment.

"Oh well, no rest for the wicked," Einar said. "Give me that shovel, and I'll start digging. There are only so many places you can hide a snow cave." Wading through the snow to where we thought the cave and our precious food should be, we began to dig.

"Hey, look at this!" I yelled triumphantly an hour later, when I crunched into a bamboo wand with the shovel and saw the attached florescent-orange surveyor's tape pop up.

"All right!" Bob shouted. It was another hour before we located and cleared the entrance to the cave and liberated a bag of freeze-dried dinners and candy bars.

"There was at least twelve feet of new snow covering that entrance," Einar said in a very tired voice.

"Here, eat these," Harry said, handing us a bag of candy bars and dried fruit. "I'll melt some snow and whip us up some real freeze-dried turkey tetrazzini."

We spent two days eating and recovering our strength, and on the morning of the third day after regaining our supplies, we saddled up into our familiar rope teams to begin the slow ascent back to the summit of Mount Newton.

"I was hoping that we could just follow the tracks we made coming down," Harry said. "But the wind has blown the snow around so much that it's like we had never been here before."

"Yeah, this isn't climbing," I agreed, taking over the lead. "It's more like swimming through snow."

When you were breaking the trail, you had to lean into the pile of snow that usually was over your head and breaststroke with your arms to pull yourself forward. With each step, your leg sank through the snow up to your crotch, and you then repeated the procedure in what seemed like an endless procession. It wasn't much better for the second person, but the forth person in line had a relatively easy time of it. We took turns leading until we physically couldn't do it anymore and then traded off. It was an excruciatingly slow, exhausting, step-by-step process.

"Hey, what's that?" Einar said sometime in the late afternoon, as the unfamiliar sounds of people talking drifted down from above. Soon, two climbers appeared and headed in slow motion toward our hard-won trail.

"Let's just sit here and let them break trail downhill to us," I said.

This happy meeting of the two trails soon turned awkward. After a short whispered conversation with the other party, Harry announced, "I'm going to abandon the climb and head down the mountain with these guys. I just don't feel good about the climb anymore." This came as a complete surprise to me, as we hadn't discussed abandoning the climb. Harry obviously had been thinking about it and was missing his wife and children. He didn't want to ruin the expedition for the rest of us and had been willing to continue on our accounts, but his heart wasn't in it anymore. Meeting the other two climbers presented an unexpected opportunity to descend safely with them and at the same time not compromise our expedition. Einar, Bob, and I all looked at each other, weighing the possibilities in our minds.

"Well, I would still like to go on," said Einar in his usual quiet voice.

"Me too," seconded Bob. "Although I think we really need a team of three to have any chance of success."

Turning to me, Einar said, "There's no pressure on you to continue. If you want to go down now, that's fine. There'll be no hard feelings."

I know the five days without food had weakened everyone somewhat, but I still felt fairly strong and was not quite ready to give up on the mountain. "All right, I'm with you," I said and received a hearty slap on the back from Bob.

"I know you guys will summit," Harry said, giving us the second stove, his snow flukes and pickets, extra wands, and most of the food and fuel from his pack. As he tied into the other team's rope, he said in parting, "I'll leave my truck for you at Destruction Bay and hitchhike back to Alaska. See you all back in Wasilla. Good luck."

I tied into Bob and Einar's rope and watched Harry slowly disappear downhill. Then with mixed feelings, I turned uphill to face the task at hand.

"At least we can follow their trail from now on," Einar said. "That should be better."

We were sadly disappointed to find that the going wasn't all that much easier. The other climbers had tried to float over the surface of the snow and take the widest possible steps while going downhill. Trudging uphill, we were forced to take two or three steps to every one of theirs, so the hard work of trail breaking through that deep snow continued. Hours passed, and we switched off the lead frequently. Our progress was depressingly slow, and to make maters worse, the wind picked up and the temperature started to drop.

"Man, I can't break trail anymore," Bob sighed. "I'm exhausted."

Einar and I switched off as best we could. A lingering twilight that passed for darkness that time of year descended on us, and we measured our slow, steady progress in hours instead of distance. Finally, we were able to spy our goal, the camp-four snow cave, marked with wands glittering in the moonlight only a couple of hundred yards further up a gentler slope. Unfortunately, we knew that it would take us the better part of two hours to cover the distance.

"I can't go any further," Bob said. "I need to stop here and rest for a while."

"Bob, you need to keep going," Einar insisted. "We have to make it to the camp. You can't fall asleep here in the snow."

"No, I can't do it," he said. "You'll just have to go on without me."

"Go ahead and break trail, Einar," I said and untied Bob from the rope. "I'll stay here with him for a while and then catch up to you." Einar continued the difficult work of pushing the trail uphill, and I helped Bob get his pack off.

"I have some Dexedrine in here somewhere for just this situation," he mumbled through his exhaustion, looking through his pack. After he washed a tablet down with some water, I left him lying on his pack in the snow and trudged upward to help with the trail breaking.

"I'm sure I've been this exhausted before," I said to Einar after overtaking him, "but I just can't remember when that might have been." It was with a great sense of relief that we finally stumbled into the entrance of the snow cave.

"We made it," Einar said happily.

"Great job, Einar," I replied. "Without you we never would have made it." Einar's beard was encrusted with snow and ice, and all that could be seen of his face were two tired-looking eyes peaking out of the white ruff. "Why don't you melt some snow and I'll go back down for Bob," I suggested. I dumped my pack in the snow cave and headed back out the entrance. I thought for sure I would find him sleeping where I had left him, but he had mustered up a tenth wind, or the Dexedrine had kicked in, for I found him struggling up the trail not far from the snow cave.

"Here, give me your pack," I offered, and we stumbled together toward the softly glowing snow cave that was now illuminated from within by Einar's headlamp. More than twenty hours after starting out that morning, the three of us huddled safely in camp four, drinking hot soup in our sleeping bags before slipping into an exhausted slumber.

I'm not sure how long I slept, but when I awoke, sunlight was reflecting off the snow at the entrance to the cave, and our sleeping bags were coated with a fine mist of frost.

"Hey, let's go check out the summit of Newton and have a look at the ridge over to St. Elias," Einar said.

Every muscle fiber in my body protested from the previous day's struggle, but after a cup of instant oatmeal, I was ready to explore. Without heavy packs on, it was an easy scramble up over the ridge to the summit. Once we crested the ridge, a completely different environment greeted us. On the north side of the mountain everything had been soft, deep snow, but on the summit and southern exposures everything was covered solidly with rime ice in fantastic, feathery formations. Crampons were essential on this terrain, and what a pleasure it was to step onto something solid and not have your boot disappear three feet into soft snow. In a few minutes, we had crossed the icy surface and were standing on the 13,811-foot summit of Mount Newton, gazing down at the Newton Glacier and toward the Pacific Ocean.

"The wind scoured the summit and the connecting ridge to St. Elias and deposited the snow on the north side of Newton," Einar said.

"That's why it was so deep," Bob added.

The rime ice was incredibly thick on the dome of the summit. Rime ice is a white ice that forms when water droplets in fog, mist, or in this case clouds, freeze to the outer surfaces of objects. The only objects on the summit of Newton were a few rocks sticking out of the ice with long feathery fingers of rime ice pointing northward.

"Let's climb down to the ridge and get a better look at it," Einar suggested.

A short distance from the summit, the next obstacle presented itself. To gain the ridge proper, we had to negotiate a small, rocky corner that was coated with transparent glaze ice with thousands of feet of vertical exposure down to the Newton Glacier.

"I'll lead this section," Einar said, gathering all our ice screws. Gingerly stepping onto the near vertical glaze with the front points of his crampons, he placed ice screws where he could, and wherever possible, tied off slings for protection around rocks jutting out from the ice. Soon, we were all past the exposed corner and contemplated the expanse of ridgeline leading to Russell Col over on St. Elias.

"That's an impressive ridge," Bob said with a whistle, as the full extent of the challenge came into view.

"It's pretty steep," Einar agreed. "The southern exposure is thousands of feet, and look at the size of that cornice overhanging the north side of the ridge."

"I remember looking at that from the hunger bivouac," I said. "We need to stay well back from the edge of the cornice."

The scale of the vista was huge, and it was hard to judge the distance across the ridge to Russell Col, but from our vantage point it looked to be a long way off. Over the undulating course of three miles, the ridge loses almost two thousand feet of altitude from the summit of Mount Newton to the saddle-like Russell Col.

"There's where the Duke gained the ridge," Bob said, pointing toward the 2,500-foot slope where the Duke of Abruzzi climbed from the Newton Glacier up to the col. It appeared to be much less steep than the ridge we intended to traverse, but we could see that the Duke's route would be constantly bombarded by avalanches sweeping down from the northeast face of St. Elias. A few years before our climb, a party of five had tried to follow in the Duke's footsteps up the headwall to the col, but four of them had died in an avalanche on the treacherous slope.

"From Russell Col it looks to be a straightforward climb to the summit of St. Elias," Einar observed, gazing at the relatively easy six-thousand-foot snow slope on the other side of the col. "This ridge is the crux of the climb," he said. "Our last camp will be at the col, and we'll summit from there, just like the Duke. I'll leave a rope fixed at the rocky corner to make our return passage easier tomorrow."

"Let's eat, prepare our gear, and get a good night's sleep before beginning the final push to camp five," Bob added.

I thought about how different this expedition-type climbing was from my usual rock and ice climbing. Climbing frozen waterfalls and cliffs seemed so much more straight forward than the slow and exhausting plodding up a big mountain. The rewards of rock climbing were intense and immediate. That kind of technical climbing enabled you to focus on the here and now, and your mind didn't wander through the mundane minutia of daily life if you were leading the climb of a difficult section of rock or ice. Your only focus was on the next handhold or toehold. Rock climbing does wonders for your concentration. On these expedition climbs, on the other hand, there really was not that much technical climbing involved, and I found the rewards were subtly different. Although dangers on big mountains were ever present, it was vastly different than technical rock climbing. There were invariably long periods of utter boredom, when stormbound in a tent or snow cave, and plenty of time for your mind to wander, while slowly breaking trail through deep snow or trudging along a ridge. You did develop a situational awareness, a presence of mind made necessary by living day after day surrounded by the constant dangers of a big mountain, be they crevasses, avalanches, overhanging cornices, the cold, or the altitude. A sense of isolation and the grandeur of the scenery surrounding you intensified the higher and longer the climb became. After a while, this fostered a greater sense of self-awareness and produced a liberating experience not found during the usual experiences of daily living. I have hardly ever been able to access that feeling during "normal living," and I wonder if that is what Buddhist priests, Zen masters, and other spiritual people are able to do. Or is it, as writer Frances Fukuyama would say, that we merely try to find an outlet for our desire to be recognized by recreating the conditions of historical struggle where danger, disease, hard work, and the risk of violent death are ever present.

"The weather looks like it will hold for us," Bob said the next morning, as we traversed the summit of Newton once again and negotiated the fixed rope at the exposed rocky corner.

"At least we're only carrying one load across," I said, staring at the exposed ridge. We had loaded a week's worth of food and fuel, as well as one tent to be used on the col for camp five, and that made our packs relatively heavy for traversing this steep ridge.

Einar was by far the strongest member of the party and had become the de facto leader. "John, I think you should lead off across the ridge. I'll go second, and Bob will follow last," Einar said. "We won't be able to set up belays everywhere along the ridge, and we'll just have to follow each other strung out on the rope most of the time. Being in the middle will give me the best chance of catching you if you fall," he added.

"Okay, I can do that," I said, staring at the intimidating stretch of ridgeline. "Give me all the ice screws and pickets."

The ridge was not vertical ice, but it was steep enough that I needed to frontpoint with my crampons across long stretches, while sinking the point of my ice ax in for further balance. Sometimes I was able to sidestep, or use French technique (stepping sideways with the crampons for purchase) on the less steep sections, and place the occasional ice screw or snow picket for protection. All the while, I was staring between my cramponed boots down thousands of feet to the Newton Glacier and concentrating on not picking a route too high up on the overhanging cornice. Occasionally, I came to a small shelf or large rock that made a decent belay station and belayed the other two to me. After a short rest, I collected the ice screws that Bob had retrieved on his way across and led off again. For hour after nerve wracking hour, we went on and on, and Russell Col slowly approached closer and closer.

We were not far above Russell Col when, lying back on a small rock ledge at a rest stop, I noticed huge mare's tails streaming out above St. Elias and blowing to the northeast. I had been concentrating on leading across the ridge so much that I had not taken any notice of the sky. "Einar, look at those clouds," I said, pointing at the ugly cloud formation. "They look exactly like the ones that preceded the last storm."

"Yeah, I've been watching them gather for the past two hours," he answered. "They seem to be getting a lot thicker."

We all knew what those clouds meant on St. Elias from our prior experience. We actually had been fairly lucky during the last storm, as some storms here have been known to rage on and on for two weeks or longer. Staring up at the approaching weather pattern shook my commitment to reaching the summit of St. Elias. The hard climbing was just about all behind us, and I had been leading across that ridge for six hours. Russell Col was not more than a half hour in front of us.

"I don't know, you guys," I said. "I have no desire to end up stormbound in a tent on Russell Col for a week or more." We had already been on the mountain for almost four weeks, and reaching the summit just didn't seem that important to me anymore.

"Well, we don't really know what the weather is going to do," Bob said. "I think we should continue on to the col and see what tomorrow brings. We're almost there."

"We have a week's worth of food and fuel with us," added Einar, "and we could always ration that if we needed to."

"The col isn't protected," I went on. "Look at it. It's completely windswept, just like this ridge is. There's not going to be any digging into that for a snow cave, and if we get caught there, we'll have to survive in the tent."

"Well, that's true," Einar agreed. "And if the storm descends as quickly as the last one, we'll be stuck there for sure. Still, I'm up for going on, but we need a unanimous decision."

"It's up to you, John, to decide if we should head back or go on," Bob said to me.

"If you vote to go back that's fine with us too," Einar continued. "We've done a lot on this climb, and I'll be perfectly satisfied with our attempt if we head back now," he added, lessening the pressure of my decision.

I stared at St. Elias, at the closeness of the col, at the long path of the trek back across the ridge, at the gathering clouds, and then at Einar and Bob. "I want to head back," I said simply.

"Then back it is," Einar said. A feeling of relief flooded through me as they pronounced themselves satisfied with the climb. Einar later confided to me that it was never all about reaching the summit for him, but that he came to the mountains for the freedom and the solitude that eluded him at lower elevations.

I led the six-hour return trip back across the ridge, following the crampon trail we had just made along the face of the ridge. We made it back to the summit of Mount Newton without incident and down to camp four for a much-needed hot meal and a couple of hours of rest as the clouds continued to thicken over the summit of St. Elias.

"I think we can make it all the way to base camp tonight when it gets cold enough to firm up the snow lower down," Einar said.

A full moon rose in the east, casting a silvery light to guide our descent down the north ridge of Newton. We made great time, glissading down in a few minutes some sections that had taken us half a day to climb. Before the sun rose to turn the snow on the Seward Glacier to slush, we arrived at base camp exhausted, but happy to be off the mountain.

The radio crackled into life, and Einar contacted the pilot. "The weather is closing in," his static-filled voice said, "but I think I can still make it in to pick you up. Make sure you pack down a landing strip for me."

With wary eyes on the mass of clouds that now obscured the summit of St. Elias, we packed up base camp, stomped out a landing area in the snow, and then fell asleep on our packs to await the arrival of the plane.

The roar of a small plane flying low directly overhead startled us awake. The pilot circled the landing strip and then landed skis down into the wind. He gunned the engine to turn the plane around, and we hauled our gear over and piled in. I had one final glimpse of an ugly lenticular cloud devouring most of St. Elias, and then we were off the Seward Glacier heading toward Destruction Bay.

I had spent almost a month seeing nothing but snow, ice, and rock. Green leaves, grass, and a warm summer day greeted us on the shores of Kluane Lake. "What I want more than anything is a green salad, some fresh fruit, and a bath," I said.

Chapter Eight:
Gold Mining

In 1979, on a cold and clear October day, Gig and I left the truck next to a small roadhouse off the Glenn Highway, a few miles east of Gunsight Mountain, strapped on skis and heavy packs, and along with our two dogs, headed north into the Talkeetna Mountains. We had been seduced by the lure of gold, just as countless thousands before us had been.

"Gig, the price of gold is going wild," I had told him in the early fall of that year. "Let's drop everything and go gold mining." We dreamed of finding wealth lying at the bottom of some forgotten Alaskan stream.

"You know that prospectors have been over the state with a fine-toothed comb since the late 1800s," he said.

"Yeah, but we also know that there are still successful, ongoing gold mining operations scattered throughout the state," I replied. "Besides, think of what a great adventure it would be."

As we had researched the geology of the gold-bearing regions and the process of staking a mining claim, we had reasoned that there would be areas that had been overlooked by the prospectors of old or that sites found to be unproductive back then could be economically viable now with the current price of gold. In truth, we didn't need much of an excuse to adventure into the Alaskan bush to live out a prospector's fantasy.

Gold has been highly valued and sought after from prehistoric times onward, not only for its rarity and beauty, but also for its utility. Gold is an element, one of the noble metals that resist corrosion and oxidation, and this resistance to deterioration and the relative softness and malleability of the metal have made gold a favored material for jewelry and kingly baubles since civilization first began. There are Egyptian hieroglyphs dating from 2,600 BC, as well as earlier Mesopotamian writings, that documented the value of gold to ancient peoples. Gold was first used as coinage around 700 BC in the kingdom of Lydia. The ancient ruler of this Asia Minor kingdom was Croesus, whose name has symbolized gold as a source of wealth.

When gold was unmoored from its fixed rate of $35 per ounce in the United States in 1967, its value had climbed steadily. In the fall of 1979, fueled by an energy crisis, brought on when OPEC tightened the oil supply, and fears of a world wide depression, the price of gold began to skyrocket, doubling in value in less than six months. By January 1980, the price of gold stood at $850 per ounce.

We were interested in placer gold. That is, gold that had been concentrated by natural erosive and weathering forces and had accumulated in the sand and gravel of streambeds. There were bands of gold-bearing quartz mineralization through-out the state, and one such band ran unevenly through the Talkeetna Mountains.

Tens of millions of years ago, sometime in the Cretaceous period, hot, molten, igneous rock shot through fractures in the bedrock of the Talkeetna Mountain area and distributed uneven veins of gold-bearing quartz. Over ensuing millennia, the exposed veins weathered and eroded, and the gold settled in streambeds in the form of placer gold—nuggets, small flakes, and gold dust.

Unlike the Yukon area directly north of the Alaska Range that was the source of most of the gold discovered during the Klondike Gold Rush, most of the Talkeetna Mountain area had been glaciated during the last ice age. In general, glaciers tended to erode and disperse any accumulated placer deposits, while scouring the overburden and exposing bedrock. That was good news for lode prospectors, who hoped to find buried rich veins of gold ore, but it was bad news for placer miners. The glaciation of the Talkeetna Mountains, however, had been spotty during the last ice age, and some of the glacial depositions had subsequently been redeposited as new placer deposits. Our plan was to search for gold in valleys that demonstrated a lack of recent glaciation, hoping that would improve our chance of discovering placer gold.

"There are the areas of mineralization," I said, pointing at a geologic map of the Talkeetna Mountains. "Now, we only need to determine which areas are open for staking a mining claim."

About 60 percent of the land in Alaska (222 million acres) is owned by the federal government. This includes national parks, wildlife refuges, national forests, military reserves, and the North Slope Petroleum Reserve. When Alaska became a state in 1959, it had been given the right to choose approximately 100 million acres of federal land to become state land, including parts of the Talkeetna Mountains. In 1971, the Alaska Native Claims Settlement Act had given Native Alaskans control of 44 million acres. Less than 1 percent of Alaskan lands were privately owned. The majority of the land in the Talkeetna Mountains belonged to the federal government and as such was open to mining. The state lands in the area in general were also open to prospecting and mining. At the land recording district office for the Talkeetna Mountain area in Palmer, we found a map of existing, valid, mining claims and lapsed claims that we could compare to our map of mineralization of the area.

"That's the spot," Gig said, pointing to a small river valley in the eastern Talkeetna Mountains, "Sheep Creek."

"That's where we can stake our claims," I agreed.

The requirements were essentially the same for staking a placer mining claim on either federal or state lands. First, there had to be a discovery of a valuable mineral, although there was no standard that clearly stated what amount or concentration of a mineral was considered valuable. Second, the four corners of the claim had to be physically marked on the ground and a location notice posted on one of the corner posts. Lastly, a certificate of location had to be filed at the appropriate recording office within ninety days of posting the claim. Placer claims were limited to twenty acres each, and one person was allowed to stake two claims per month in any one recording district. Once the claim had been properly posted and recorded, the claim holder essentially had all the surface rights, as well as the mineral rights, which an owner of the property would have. In order to maintain his rights, the claim holder had to do $100 of assessment work each year and file an affidavit of annual labor. Usually, the government continued to hold the fee simple title to the land, but a claim holder could apply to patent federal lands after $500 worth of work had been done and recorded.

Armed with this knowledge, Gig and I were ready to venture into to the Sheep Creek drainage area, which we hoped held our golden fortune. Winter had already descended on the Talkeetna Range, and we could speed into the area by using cross-country skis.

"I reckon it's about twenty-five miles to Sheep Creek from the road," Gig said, looking at the map before starting out.

"That's if we follow this valley," I said, pointing at the map. "If we do that, we'll have to cross Alfred Creek at its mouth. I doubt it's frozen at this time of year, and we don't know how deep it might be."

"You're right," Gig replied. "We should probably cross over the eastern edge of Syncline Mountain and hit Alfred Creek near its source."

"That looks good," I agreed. "There are still a number of smaller streams to cross, but I'm sure we can manage them."

"A week or so should give us enough time to explore the area, pan for gold along the way, find the mother load, and stake our claims," Gig said.

"Yeah, right, Gig," I said. "I'm sure we'll be able to do all that in a week."

From the roadhouse parking lot, a tractor trail climbed a thousand feet to Belanger Pass on Syncline Mountain. After skiing over the pass, we headed down the snow-covered trail, following Pass Creek into the Alfred Creek drainage basin. The dogs ran ahead of us, flushing perfectly camouflaged white puffballs of ptarmigans into the air. At the head of the valley, we gained the north side of Alfred Creek and followed it about nine miles downstream to where it joined the much larger Caribou Creek. From our study of the map in the Palmer Recording District office, we knew that all the land around the Alfred Creek drainage area already had valid placer claims in place. Halfway down Alfred Creek, we came upon a relatively large placer mining operation that had been shut down for the winter.

"This looks like a big operation," I said, examining the mining shacks that were built on a gravel bench overlooking the river. Mining equipment was stored under plastic sheets, and heavy metal sluice boxes were stacked neatly on top of each other.

"They would need a bulldozer to move one of these sluice boxes," Gig said. "I bet they drive bulldozers over that tractor trail in the summer, and from the looks of this valley, they bulldoze the whole riverbed into these sluice boxes."

"They must move a lot of material," I said. "I wonder how much gold they find?"

"Enough to keep them coming back," Gig said. Seeing the amount of effort and expense someone was willing to invest in this area gave us confidence that there was still gold in "them thar hills."

"Let's try panning for gold in these little tributaries flowing out of the Horn Mountains on our way down to Caribou Creek," I suggested.

Panning for gold was somewhat of an art form, and we had practiced it in our front yard prior to leaving for the Talkeetna Mountains. We each carried a flat-bottomed metal pan about fourteen inches in diameter, similar to an oversized pie plate. Sand and gravel from a likely source were shoveled into the pan and mixed with water. The pan was tipped to forty-five degrees, and the water and material were swirled in a circular fashion to settle the heavy gold. The worthless, larger-volume, low-density material would spill over the lip of the pan, and the smaller, heavier materials, such as black sand, gold, and gemstones, would be left behind—or so we hoped.

The smaller tributaries that we were crossing had mostly frozen over, and we had to break through the ice to get at the sand and gravel in the streambeds. We spent a few cold, wet days, kneeling in the snow and slowly swirling sand around and out of the pans. We were occasionally rewarded with "color."

"Look at this!" Gig yelled, proudly holding out his pan with a few minute flecks of shiny yellow mixed in with the black sand.

"Gold!" I cried, gazing lustfully at the tiny specks and forgetting all about my frozen fingers and wet clothes. The excitement of actually finding some minute particles of gold drove us forward in our quest for Sheep Creek, where we knew there was a section open for staking placer claims.

We skied down to the mouth of Alfred Creek and then upstream, along the north bank of Caribou Creek, which originated high up in the Talkeetna Mountains from a nameless glacier and was fed by many other creeks. By the time Alfred Creek contributed its waters to the river, Caribou Creek was a swift-moving glacial river, twenty to seventy-five yards wide.

"Man, that looks cold and deep," I said, standing on the bank overlooking the rushing silt-laden water. "I'm glad we don't have to cross that."

As the crow flies, it was only about six miles from the mouth of Alfred Creek to where Sheep Creek emptied into Caribou Creek, but as we skied, we traversed a lot more ground.

"Hey, look at that cabin over across the river," Gig said, when we were halfway between Alfred and Sheep Creek.

"It looks well maintained, but no one's there now," I said. "It could be another mining camp."

Continuing along the north bank of the river, we followed a game trail that led up a steep ridge, and then, we descended into the Sheep Creek drainage.

"Finally, the promised land!" Gig said, as we started up the valley.

Sheep Creek was a fast-running, clear stream that coursed through the lower reaches of a wooded valley. At its widest point, it might have been twenty yards wide and three or four feet deep. About three miles upstream from its mouth, it plunged over a fifty-foot waterfall and rushed through a short, narrow gorge before flowing onto the broader valley floor.

"This is where we should stake the claims," Gig said, staring at the area where the water lost speed and power after issuing from the gorge—a likely spot for the river to give up its golden burden.

Over the next two days, we paced out and posted the four twenty-acre claims that we could legally hold. We also did some panning and were rewarded with a small amount of color that constituted our "discovery." I was so caught up in the rush of gold fever that I have no recollection of having appreciated the beauty of the country that we had just spent a week traveling through. After posting the required location notices at the corners of each claim, we retraced our tracks out of the mountains, back to the truck. The very next day, we recorded our claims at the Palmer Recording office and officially became Alaskan gold miners.

We spent that winter at my partially finished house in Wasilla, and in our spare time, we prepared for the coming mining season that would begin when cold weather released its grip on the icy rivers. Our pile of equipment slowly grew and took over the living room.

"We're going to need a sluice box," I said. The miners of old had built large wooden sluice boxes and constructed elaborate stream diversions. They then laboriously shoveled the streambed overburden into the sluices. The modern sluice boxes we had examined at Alfred Creek had been welded together out of thick steel and could only be moved around with heavy equipment, so they were out of the question for us.

"I've been going through this catalog of mining equipment, and I think this gas-powered dredge is the answer," Gig said, pointing to a picture of a miner smiling out from the page with a sluice full of gold.

"Ah, the Gold King," I said, looking over his shoulder. "That looks like it should work."

After Gig's catalog discovery, we planned to use a small gasoline-powered dredge to suction sand and gravel from the streambed and then run the material down a sluice to separate the gold. The gas engine mounted on a large, inflated inner tube, with a lightweight metal sluice attached. The entire unit floated on top of the water. A long, heavy-duty, plastic suction hose, with a curved, wide-mouthed, metal nozzle, was used to vacuum the streambed. The overburden material was flushed down the sluice box by water that was suctioned out of the streambed along with the gravel. The sluice was fitted with riffles every few inches to create eddies in the current so that the heavier gold would settle out.

"I wonder how much gas that thing will use," I said. "This will commit us to transporting gasoline into the claims all season to keep the dredge operating."

We had hoped that we could feed ourselves and the dogs by hunting and fishing, and that intermittent trips out of the mine area would be necessary only to resupply our gasoline stores and any other mining-related equipment needs. The closest we could get a vehicle was about twenty-five miles, so we would have to carry everything on our backs that went into the mines. A five-gallon jerry can of gas weighed over forty pounds, and we had no idea how long five gallons would last us.

"Well, we can't afford to have a helicopter drop a season's worth of gas at the site," Gig replied. "So why don't we borrow an idea from the old-time miners and buy a couple of pack horses to help us?"

"Horses again, hmm," I said. "We didn't do so well with the last ones."

That was a busy winter for the both of us. We were living in my house and had managed to close it in with windows and doors prior to winter's arrival. In between sheetrocking jobs, we continued to work on the interior of the house. It was a vast improvement over our previous living arrangements. A wood stove kept us warm, and there was a kitchen with an antique refrigerator, as well as electricity and separate bedrooms for each of us. The only drawback was the lack of running water—drilling a well was still in the future.

We bought two wooden pack saddles, along with all the horse paraphernalia we thought would be needed. "I think you've mastered the diamond hitch packing knot," I congratulated Gig, as he read directions from a book and practiced tying yet another load onto a pack saddle in the comfort of the living room. As spring approached, we started looking around for two horses that would meet our needs.

"Steve probably has a horse for sale," I said, thinking of a friend in Palmer who owned a horse farm. "Let's stop by there and take a look."

"You need a couple of pack horses to go gold mining?" Steve asked at his farm the next day, letting doubt color his tone of voice. "Well, Kodie here has some packing experience, and I suppose I could sell him." Before I knew it, I was the proud owner of a handsome quarter-horse gelding.

"I hope he's not like the last gelding," Gig said, staring up under the horse.

"There's a herd of horses coming in from the Yukon to a farm up the road next week," Steve advised us. "You can probably pick up another horse there."

The next week, we found ourselves leaning on a corral fence, dickering over horses with a weathered old cowboy. Gig had sold his truck for $1,200 and had brought the cash with him for his horse purchase.

"I could let that big bay over there go for $2,500," the cowboy said.

"Too expensive," Gig replied. "How about that one?" he asked, pointing to a dappled gray.

"$2,400," the cowboy said.

"Too much," Gig responded. "What about that chestnut over there?"

"$2,000."

"No, too much," Gig answered. "And that one?"

"$1,900," the cowboy replied.

"I can't afford that," Gig said.

"Well. How much money can you spend?" the grizzled cowboy asked, tilting back his hat.

"$1,200," Gig said quickly. "What about that palomino?"

"What a coincidence," the cowboy said with a smile. "She costs $1,200."

"Okay, I'll take her," Gig said.

"Gig, I don't think telling someone the maximum amount you can spend is the proper way to dicker for horses," I whispered.

"Oh, like you know how to be a horse trader," he replied. "As I recall, you traded your last horse for a shotgun."

The young palomino mare had a good disposition and seemed healthy enough, but we had no idea if she had any packing experience. Gig named her Suzie, after a former Alaskan girlfriend.

By the end of April, we had collected a mountain of equipment, including a large army surplus canvas tent, the gasoline-powered dredge, a metal sluice box, a wet suit, pack saddles and canvas pack bags, packs for the dogs, jerry cans for the gas, gold pans and cloth bags for our treasure, a Colman stove with fuel, a few weeks' supply of bulky dry food, and assorted camping gear. We also had an arsenal of guns that included a .300 magnum rifle, the .30–30, the .22, and two .44-caliber pistols that we strapped to our hips, stupidly thinking they could be used for bear protection. All dressed up, standing beside the fully packed horses with guns dangling at our sides, we pictured ourselves looking like a couple of prospectors from the 1800s.

The snows melted in Wasilla, break up came and went on the Susitna, and May arrived. We could stop dreaming about it and finally start living our gold mining adventure. After borrowing a horse trailer and loading the truck with all the equipment, we drove ourselves, the two horses, and the two dogs, Denali and Rask, to the roadhouse on the Glenn Highway that would be our staging base for the trip into the goldfields.

"I can't believe that horses can only carry 25 percent of their body weight," I said with a disappointed sigh, driving by Gunsight Mountain. "Steve said not to pack more than 250 pounds on them."

"If we load each horse with four jerry cans of gas, that only leaves another ninety pounds we can put in their packs," Gig said.

"Our packs are going to weigh well over a hundred pounds, as usual," I pointed out.

"At least the dogs will be carrying packs too," Gig said.

"What an auspicious day for starting out," I added, driving through the cold drizzle into the roadhouse parking lot. "What do you think the temperature is, forty degrees?"

"No, closer to thirty, I'd say," Gig answered, as we stepped out of the truck and watched our breath rise in white puffs. "Let's at least get a hot breakfast here before we start." As we lingered over coffee, we could see the horses shivering in the cold drizzle where they were tied up to a railing out in the dirt parking lot.

"Time to go," I said, and as we left the warmth of the roadhouse behind, the drizzle turned to sleet, and then to snow.

The winter snow drifts had all but melted from the trail as our sorry-looking contingent started trudging, with backs bowed, down the muddy path. The tractor trail, similar to a narrow, washed-out dirt road, led us over the headwaters of Squaw Creek, and instead of continuing northward over Belanger Pass as we had done the previous winter, we turned southwest and followed the creek bank as it wound its way down the valley that separated Gunsight Mountain from Syncline Mountain. After a few miles of traveling, men and animals warmed up enough to ignore the mixed snow and sleet that was drenching us. Along the north bank of Squaw Creek there was a decent trail, a remnant of a long-deserted road that most likely fed an old mining claim years in the past.

"Gig, look at that," I said a few hours out from the roadhouse. "I think somebody lives there."

Close to the river and partially hidden by a cluster of spruce trees was a rough shelter made from spruce poles covered over with clear visqueen. Out of the top of this unlikely looking house poked a small, rusted metal chimney from which issued a thin stream of blue smoke. The dogs started barking, and to be friendly, we hailed the cabin. Out of the makeshift cabin door emerged a painfully thin, bearded, middle-aged man accompanied by two teenage boys, somewhere between the ages of fifteen and eighteen. All three had pistols and large knives conspicuously strapped to their belts.

"We're on our way to our gold claims up on Sheep Creek," we explained, as they looked over the two horses, the dogs, and our mountainous packs.

"Well, come on in for a cup of coffee and get out of the rain," the thin man offered.

After tying the horses to a tree and relieving the dogs of their packs, we followed our new neighbors through the door. It was surprisingly warm inside the twenty-by-twenty-foot plastic-enclosed structure. A small wood stove made out of an old fifty-gallon metal drum gave off welcome heat, and a dented and blackened tin kettle steamed on top of the stove. Inside the shack, we met the man's quiet wife, from whom we thankfully received two cups of hot, bitter instant coffee. Two rough-planked bunk beds were stacked against one wall, and a slightly larger bed lay beside another. A sparse scattering of kitchen utensils, dented pots, and a few boxes of food lined a shelf behind the stove. A makeshift table crowded the center of the room with four upright stumps for chairs, over which an old Colman gas lantern hung from a supporting spruce pole.

Naked Playboy centerfolds graced the wall by the bunk bed, where presumably the two boys slept. The older boy had the beginnings of a scraggly beard, and long, black, greasy hair hung limply from underneath his battered cowboy hat. He sat on the lower bunk staring at us while he fingered the handle of his knife and caressed the butt of his pistol, never uttering a word.

"We're gold miners too," the younger boy blurted out.

"Be quiet," his father hissed at him.

"How long have you been here?" I asked, hoping to ease the tension.

"Well, let's see. We've been livin' here for four years now," the father said. "We stay here all year round and only go into town a few times a year for supplies."

"You've been mining here the whole time?" Gig asked.

"Yup," he replied.

"Well, how have you been doing?" I asked, trying to encourage him to reveal more information.

"We get by," he said simply.

"You should see what we found yesterday!" the younger boy began excitedly, rummaging under the bed and producing a small wooden box.

"Shut up!" his father snapped at him.

"Yeah, we found it right there in Squaw Creek," the younger son said, pointing out the door and ignoring the lethal gazes of his father and brother.

Before his brother could snatch the box away, the boy opened it and produced a huge, flat, gold nugget that barely fit in the palm of his hand. His father swore at him as he handed it to us to examine, and his brother stared at us all the harder. Our eyes grew large, as the luster and the weight of the nugget rekindled the gold fever in us and reassured us that we were in the right area.

After only a few minutes in the cabin, we felt distinctly uncomfortable, and I was glad that we were armed with pistols at our hips and had rifles slung over our shoulders, giving us the illusion of superior firepower in those cramped quarters.

"More coffee?" the wife asked.

"Ah, no thanks," I said quickly.

"We need to get the horses moving before they freeze," Gig added, handing the heavy nugget back to the father. Once out of earshot of the family, he whispered, "Did you see the size of that nugget!"

"It was huge, and I couldn't believe how heavy it was," I whispered back.

"That family was a little spooky," I added, "especially the older boy."

"Did you see how he stared at us the whole time and never said a word?" Gig went on. "I think we should call them the Deliverance Family."

"If they're successful gold miners, why do they live in such squalor?" I wondered aloud.

Over the course of the subsequent mining season, we occasionally crossed paths with the family and stayed on friendly terms, but never again did we venture into their cabin.

We continued down the trail that paralleled Squaw Creek, and we eventually came to the fast flowing, glacial-silt-heavy Caribou Creek and found that the trail led up onto an elevated bench that shadowed the northeastern bank of the river. A few miles further along, Gig said, "Look at that old truck," as we unexpectedly came across an ancient flatbed truck parked in a grove of trees. Its rusted-out cab had at one time been painted yellow, and most of the windshield had been shot out. The cab was missing its doors, and all four oversized tires were long flat. The rear axle was broken, and saplings were growing up through the rotted wooden truck bed.

"This thing's been parked here for years," I said. "There must have been a road here at one point."

"I think this is about halfway between the roadhouse and Sheep Creek," Gig said. "Looks like a good place to break for lunch."

After relieving the horses of their burdens, we tied them to the truck bed before climbing into the cab to temporarily escape the freezing rain. Our breath rose in white clouds as we watched the rain trickle down the inside of the shattered windshield. Soon enough, both men and horses were shivering, and we had to leave this cozy spot and repack the horses. An hour later, the trail opened out of the conifer forest into a field that eventually led down to the mouth of Alfred Creek.

"That's a little wider than I remember from last winter," I said, staring at the thirty-yard-wide river of swiftly moving water while the horses drank greedily.

"I wonder how deep it is," Gig said.

"Only one way to find out," I replied. "We'll have to keep our boots on for the crossing."

"Unbuckle the waist belt of your pack," Gig suggested. "That way, if you fall, it will be easier to get out of it."

The river proved to be only mid-thigh deep, but with heavy packs on, it was hard to keep our footing against the swift current. The horses were much better at crossing the river than we were, and we soon learned to hang on to their pack saddles for support.

"That wasn't so bad," I said, sitting down and raising my legs to let the ice cold water drain from my boots.

"The dogs had no trouble swimming the river without their packs on, but I don't know if I could have done it without hanging onto the horses," Gig said.

With numb feet squishing in our boots, we continued along the northern bank of Caribou Creek. After another hour of tramping, I said, "Hey, there's that log cabin."

"And somebody lives there," Gig added, pointing at the thin stream of smoke rising from the chimney.

Four people emerged from the cabin and ran down to the river to shout across to us. A big, burly, bear of a man with a huge white beard and long white hair led the procession. He was dressed like some Hollywood producer's idea of a mountain man with a red plaid wool shirt, buckskin-fringed pants with matching vest, and a leather cowboy hat. Close behind followed a teenage boy and two teenage girls.

"Come on over for supper," the mountain man shouted at us over the noise of the rushing water, and the teenagers waved excitedly.

"They don't look like the Deliverance Family," I said to Gig.

"No, but this river is at least twice the size of Alfred Creek," he said.

"We should be able to make it, if we just hang onto the horses," I suggested, and once again, we stumbled into the ice cold water.

"You're just in time," the mountain man boomed, shaking our hands after we made it across. "The wife's just putting supper on the table."

It was indeed a family that greeted us on the other side of the river. We dubbed them the Mountain Man Family, consisting of Al, the mountain-man father, his wife, Vicky, their fifteen- and sixteen-year-old daughters, Becky and Kathy, and their slightly older, gangly son, Carlo. Unlike the Deliverance Family, these people were friendly and not the least bit scary.

"Can we lead the horses?" the older girl asked, as she and her sister stroked the necks and foreheads of the two horses and patted the wet dogs.

"Girls love horses," Al said, leading the contingent of people and animals up to the cabin, where we unburdened the horses and staked them out in a field of new grass. Then, Vicky beckoned us all into the warmth of the cabin to shelter from the still falling rain.

"We're from the Tucson, Arizona, area," Al began. "Some friends from Anchorage are letting us stay at this cabin and work their gold claim this summer."

"Had any luck?" I asked.

"Well, we really haven't started mining yet," he said. "We've only been here for a week. I wanted to get the family away from Arizona to escape all those urban distractions that were ruining the kids," he continued, while the three kids rolled their eyes. "Yep, we're gonna live off the land here."

"So you've had some experience in the Alaskan bush before?" Gig asked.

"Well, no, but back in Arizona I've had plenty of experience. I worked in Old Tucson," he explained.

After only a week of wilderness living, their son and daughters were overjoyed at the distraction of visitors and the chance to talk to someone besides their parents. It turned out that Al really wasn't a mountain man after all, but back in Tucson he had played the part of one at a tourist trap, called "Old Tucson," outside the city. He was one of the actors who had recreated "wild west" drama scenes, such as bank robberies and shootouts on the streets of Old Tucson. In addition, he had driven tourists around town in a horse-drawn stagecoach. Unfortunately for him and his family, this mountain man illusion had not given him the skill he needed to flourish in the Alaskan wilderness.

"Have you been hunting?" I asked.

"Every day," Carlo spoke up. "But so far we've only managed to shoot a couple of squirrels."

"Haven't seen much else around," Al said.

"I wish we had brought more supplies from town," his wife added, serving up the food.

"Oh good, biscuits and gravy again tonight," Kathy said with sarcasm.

"Pa said we'd feast on moose and salmon all summer long," Becky added with a giggle.

"And so we will, Becky," her father said, smiling. "Don't you worry."

A week into their Alaskan adventure and they were already running low on supplies, and dinner that evening consisted of Bisquick biscuits, smothered in greasy gravy made out of Crisco.

"Ma'am, this is delicious," Gig complimented her. "We have some extra supplies out in the pack saddles we could share," he continued.

"I'll fetch a few of those freeze-dried dinners," I volunteered.

At least they had a nice cabin to live in, warmed by a wood cooking stove and furnished with rustic chairs, tables, and beds. There was even a wood-fired sauna close by the river.

"The day's wearing thin, boys," Al said. "If you want, you can spread your bed rolls out here on the floor and spend the night."

"Thanks Al, but we're a little anxious to get to our claims over on Sheep Creek," Gig said.

"This is just our first supply trip," I added. "We need to go back out for another load in a day or two."

"Well, stop in whenever you're passing by," he offered.

As we forded Caribou Creek once again, I made a mental note to drop off some food for Arizona Al and his delightful family on our next trip through. Safely across the river, we continued upstream, following a narrow game trail as it wound its way up a steep ridge.

"Come on, Kodie!" I cursed, pulling hard on his halter to try to force him up the last few yards of the steep grade. He pulled back equally as hard, lost his balance, and falling backward, knocked Suzie over as well.

"Watch out!" Gig yelled, as both horses tumbled down the steep hill, scattering the carefully packed gear from the packsaddles. Racing downhill after them, we expected to find two injured horses, but they proved resilient. Once freed of the packsaddles, they were able to roll to their feet, and we found them grazing happily along the side of the trail.

"I think we had a little too much weight on there for that steep section," I said sheepishly.

"Yeah, we still have a lot to learn about packing horses," Gig replied.

"Let's carry all this gear over the ridge ourselves," I suggested.

Once safely over the ridge, the trail zigzagged down to Sheep Creek and continued northwest along Caribou Creek. We left the trail and followed Sheep Creek upstream to the spot we had staked out the previous winter, and in the gathering dusk of the early May night, we gladly shed our heavy packs, unloaded two tired horses, and pitched a small tent before preparing to fall into an exhausted sleep next to the dogs.

"Well, here we are, Gig," I said. "We did pretty well today."

"Yeah, except for the horses falling down the hill. It only took us about fourteen hours, including stopping to visit our neighbors," Gig agreed. Over the course of the season, we cut the time it took us to cover the twenty-five miles from the roadhouse to the gold claims down to eight hours.

The next day, we set up camp and explored up and over the bench that separated the Sheep Creek drainage from the Billy Creek drainage area. The Sheep Creek Valley was wooded only along the edge of the creek in the lower portion of the valley. The tree line started at an altitude of around thirty-two hundred feet at this latitude, which was approximately the elevation of our camp. We climbed a gently sloping, alpine meadow landscape that was just starting to blossom with small, delicate wild flowers. This tundra-like bench formed the approach to Sheep Mountain, rising in the distance steeply to a jagged peak at fifty-five hundred feet.

As we crested a rise, Gig dropped to the ground, grabbed at the dogs to restrain them, and whispered, "Over there, caribou." Three caribou were grazing slowly away from us toward the mountain in the distance. "If we can crawl to within range, we could bag ourselves a couple weeks' worth of meat."

"We could drop some off for the Arizona Family too," I added.

After a crawled stalk, Gig shot the closest caribou from about a hundred yards away. After gutting and quartering the animal, we carried it back to camp in two trips. This was the first of many caribou that fed us that season.

"We can make a refrigerator by digging down into the permafrost," Gig said. "I read about it in one of the old mining books."

We dug down into the moss-covered tundra and hit permafrost at a depth of two feet. After hollowing a space out of the frozen dirt and lining it with moss, we had a functional refrigerator-freezer that kept meat from spoiling for two weeks. The next day, we retraced our trail back out to the highway to pick up a second load of supplies and on the way dropped off a haunch of much-appreciated caribou at Al's cabin. After trekking back to Sheep Creek for the second time in four days, we were finally ready to begin gold mining.

Because of its weight and size, the dredge had to be carried into the claims in pieces, but once reassembled and floated onto the river, it was ready to go. The water was initially two feet deep in the pool where the river emerged from its small gorge and started to spread out. The dredge operated just as advertised, suctioning sand, gravel, and rocks up to three inches in diameter.

"I hope bedrock isn't too far down," I said. "The book said the pockets of placer gold will be in the nooks and crannies of the bedrock."

"Let's get to work," Gig said.

We developed a daily routine. One of us donned the wetsuit and grabbed the working end of the suction hose while the other manned the sluice box, throwing out any large rocks that emerged from the hose in order to keep the excess gravel flowing down the sluice and to prevent it from backing up into the suction hose. After an hour or so, we washed all the accumulated material from behind the riffles of the sluice into a bucket and used the gold-panning technique on that sand to remove any gold. At first, there was a small amount of gold dust and sometimes a few tiny flakes of gold to show for a long day's labor. We worked steadily every day for two weeks and occasionally found small nuggets behind the riffles that could be picked out before washing the sand into the bucket. Small red and purple garnets also sometimes graced the gold pan, half buried in the leftover black magnetic sand in the bottom of the pan.

As our river hole became wider and deeper, the work became a lot colder, and we found that we could last only about an hour in the cold water with the wetsuit on. Most of the time the suction work was preformed kneeling down, and before long there were holes worn in both knees of the wetsuit that no amount of neoprene cement and patches could repair.

"No bedrock yet," I shivered, finishing an hour-long stint at the end of the suction hose. "Just more sand and gravel."

"We'll get there," Gig said. "We just have to keep at it."

The small flakes and bits of gold we had collected continued to give us the incentive to get back into the icy water day after day.

Forty gallons of gasoline lasted us close to two weeks, so every two weeks we needed to make the pilgrimage out to the highway, where there was a gas pump at the roadhouse. If we needed any other supplies, one of us had to drive the truck into Wasilla, while the other waited at the roadhouse with the horses. One caribou also lasted about two weeks, so every couple of weeks we took a day off for hunting. There were always caribou and moose wandering through the valleys, and we spotted small herds of Dall sheep grazing on the slopes of the surrounding mountains.

"I'm getting pretty tired of eating caribou all the time," I said. "Why don't we try for a sheep?"

Hunting sheep was much more involved than hunting caribou. The sheep were wary and disappeared the moment they smelled us or glimpsed our approach. When trying to get close to the sheep, we traveled up valley to circle behind the mountain the sheep were on and then climbed the back side to drop down on them from above. This process took hours, and by the time we climbed the back side of the mountain and came down over the top, they were usually long gone. Most of the time we ended up just shooting a caribou, since that was so much easier.

To break the monotony of eating caribou every day, we fished for trout and artic grayling in the river. When we ran low on food, we were not above fishing with our pistols. The concussion from a .44 round placed close to a fish temporarily dazed it, and the fish floated to the surface where it could be scooped up.

"I think Bill Jr. would like this kind of fishing," I said when returning to camp with a string of trout. "Look, three with one shot."

Throughout this time, we continued to share our bounty with the Arizona Family in the cabin downstream. They rewarded us by cooking a meal in the cabin, and the girls frequently heated up the sauna for us, when they saw us passing by on the way into or out of the claims.

The dogs were in dog heaven, running wild and eating meat every day. The horses were also faring well, having lush pasturage along the river bank. They didn't seem to mind the walk out or packing loads back into the claims, for they soon appeared to learn that at the end of a long day's carry, there would be an extra ration of grain.

"We've been at it a month now," Gig said one night, as the camp fire burned low, "and we really don't have much gold to show for ourselves."

"I know," I said, "but the river hole is getting deeper all the time, and sooner or later we'll hit bedrock and be rich."

"I guess you're right," he replied.

"And besides," I added, "we're having just as much fun out here as the dogs."

"Let's take a day off to explore up to the source of the creek tomorrow," Gig suggested.

"Okay, we're running low on meat anyway," I said.

On our way to the source of Sheep Creek the next morning, we discovered a half-decomposed caribou in the middle of the river, not far upstream from our camp. "We have to get that out of there," I pointed out.

"You're right," Gig agreed. "That's the source of our drinking water."

The caribou appeared to have met its fate by falling off an overhanging cliff into the river, probably while having been chased by a bear or a pack of wolves. Gig and I preformed the unenviable task of removing the rotting carcass from the river, and we dragged it up a bank away from the creek, where nature could continue its work.

Almost all the four-thousand- to five-thousand-foot mountains on our map of the area were unnamed, so we felt free to name them ourselves. Upstream, past the waterfall at the head of the gorge, the creek issued from between two steep, rounded mountains, one of which was more perfectly shaped and slightly taller than the other. To two sex-deprived gold miners they looked like the breasts of a reclining woman.

"Look, it's the Big Tit," Gig said, bestowing the name on the largest of the peaks.

This had more than sexual connotations for us, since we normally also referred to the generous Alaskan state welfare system as the Big Tit also. We avoided it ourselves, but we had many acquaintances whose only mission in life seemed to be to work as little as possible in order to become eligible for unemployment benefits, food stamps, state-sponsored housing assistance, and any other handouts a state overflowing with oil dollars was willing to supply.

"We need to climb up there, Gig, to see for ourselves the source from which all that state milk flows," I said.

"You're right," he agreed. "Then we can suck on the Big Tit like everyone else."

As a cold rain began to fall, we made the pilgrimage and were rewarded with a few eagle feathers from the summit, not to mention another caribou for the larder on the way back home.

Gig and I weren't the only ones whose imaginations had been piqued by the thought of gold mining in Alaska. My brother and two of my uncles came to Alaska that summer to try out our gold-mining adventure firsthand. The first uncle, Paul, arrived for ten days in the middle of June, with his two young sons, age nine and ten, and his father-in-law, who had to be approaching seventy. They hadn't done much camping before and had never done any hunting, but they had the adventure of a lifetime that summer and still talk about it today. With our visitors in tow, it took us two days to make the trip into Sheep Creek, instead of the usual eight hours. They panned for gold, helped with the dredge, fished in the river, ate caribou, and enjoyed an experience that could not be reproduced today.

By the middle of June, our dredge work had converted the original two-foot-deep pool of water into a six-foot-deep pool that was approaching the limits that could be handled with a mask and snorkel. There was still no bedrock in sight at the bottom of our working hole, and the wetsuit was shredded beyond repair—putting it on before descending into the hole was becoming a cruel joke.

"I'm going to buy you guys a drysuit when we get back to Anchorage," Paul promised us.

At the end of his trip, he not only kept this promise, but he also purchased us a hookah system that could be connected to the dredge engine. The hookah system was a device that supplied a diver with air from a compressor that ran off the gas powered engine of the dredge. A long plastic hose with a scuba-type breathing regulator on one end was connected to the compressor and allowed the diver to breathe underwater without the traditional bulky scuba gear. The hookah enabled us to stay submerged at the bottom of the hole and vastly improved our efficiency. The drysuit was an unheard of luxury for the first few weeks, but eventually the constant wear and tear turned it into another wetsuit.

Toward the end of July, our second set of visitors arrived—my uncle, Dick, and my younger brother, Kevin. Dick, who was fourteen years my senior, had introduced me to the joys of hiking and camping in the White Mountains of New Hampshire years earlier in my life, and I was happy to return the favor by introducing him to Alaska. My younger brother wasn't much of an outdoors person, but he was always a good sport and a lot of fun to have around.

"You guys are doing great," Gig encouraged them, as we plodded toward Sheep Creek loaded down with supplies.

"Yes, the last group took two days to walk in," I said. "We're going to make it in one."

The walk into the gold claims was never easy. Your boots were almost always wet from river crossings, and a significant part of the trail led through bog-like areas that required jumping from tussock to tussock while trying to balance a heavy pack. This proved to be a bit much for my brother, and by the time we neared the cabin, we had long since relieved him of his pack, splitting the extra burden between ourselves and the horses.

"I don't think your brother is doing too well," Dick said to me, while we waited for him to catch up.

"You're right," I said, watching Kevin sway into view. "He's staggering like a drunken sailor, and what is that noise?" A shrill off-key shrieking intermingled with humming became louder as Kevin approached.

"He's singing to himself in his delirium of exhaustion," Gig said. "You're not a very good brother."

"We can rest at the Arizona cabin," I said. "It's just around the bend."

The girls had heated up the sauna for us, so we stopped for a couple of hours, giving Kevin a chance to rest up for the final push to Sheep Creek. My brother still views this part of his trip as a nightmarish hallucination, and he remains unconvinced that the sauna was real. He was too tired to participate anyway, and washing off in the icy, glacial river afterward was not an idea he would have entertained. By the time we arrived at our camp on Sheep Creek, Kevin had long since gone beyond his usual endurance limits, and that night he slept the sleep of the dead.

"Gig, the tundra refrigerator is running low again," I said the next morning. "Hey, Dick, do you want to go exploring up around the source of the creek and see if we can find any game?"

"Sure, that sounds great," he said.

"How about you, Kevin?" Gig asked.

"Are you crazy?" Kevin groaned. "I don't think I can stand, never mind walk."

"You can rest here in the tent," I said. "We should be back in six hours or so. Here, I'll leave you my .44 just in case."

"Just in case of what?" he asked nervously.

"Just in case you need it," I replied. "You know: wilderness, bears, alien abduction, that sort of thing."

Kevin was not a gun person, and I don't think he had ever handled a pistol before. I gave him the short course on how to shoot the gun and pointed out the obvious danger of shooting himself or someone else by accident. We left him lying in the canvas tent that doubled as a field kitchen and storage area with the .44 close by one hand and a pile of food by the other.

"We're leaving the horses here with you," Gig told him. "They're okay just wandering around camp."

"And remember," I said in parting, "don't shoot us when we return."

The three of us spent an enjoyable day exploring, but did not come across any caribou or other approachable game. Far off in the distance, high on a mountain side, we caught a glimpse of a herd of mountain goats and watched them disappear once they spotted us. In the late afternoon, we returned to camp to find Kevin still lying in the tent staring at a cocked .44 that he had gingerly put down on a stump and pointed business end toward the door of the tent.

"I heard some rustling around and snapping of twigs and thought it had to be a bear," Kevin began, obviously relieved to have us home. "I grabbed the pistol and cocked it just like you showed me. After an hour or so, I peeked out the tent and realized it was only the horses moving around, but I forgot how to uncock the gun. I've been staring at it sitting on that stump all day hoping it wouldn't go off."

"Are you sure aliens didn't come and experiment on your brain," I laughed, lowering the hammer on the pistol and returning it to its holster. "Don't worry; I'll never leave you alone with a gun again."

It was time to get back to work in our underwater hole. The pool was at least eight feet deep by this time, and frequently we thought we had finally reached bedrock, only to discover it was yet another large boulder buried in the sand and gravel. We had to dig out around the boulder and roll it out of the submerged hole to continue to suction the bottom.

Kevin volunteered to help us dredge, but he was a lot larger than either Gig or me, and I had my doubts if we could stuff him into the drysuit.

"Suck in your gut a little more and I think we'll have it," I told him, zipping the suit up from behind. "There you go," I said. "Now you look just like the Michelin Tire Man."

"What about the weight belt?" Gig asked, trying to see how much it could be adjusted.

"That will never fit," I said.

"I don't need the weight belt," Kevin said. "I'll be able to work without it." He belly flopped into the river and bobbed helplessly at the surface like a bloated walrus.

"That won't work," Gig said, shaking his head.

"I know what we can do," I said. "Let's put the weight belt into this backpack and put that on him." I fitted him out with the pack, but the weights weren't enough to overcome his buoyancy. "Well, I'll just add some rocks," I said, stuffing a couple of large stones into the pack.

"Yeah, that should keep him on the bottom," Gig replied.

"Are you sure about this?" Kevin asked me nervously.

"Oh, sure. No problem," I assured him, slapping him on the shoulder. "You're good to go."

He waded into the hole with the dredge nozzle in hand and disappeared in a cloud of bubbles. When the bubbles cleared, we could see him lying face up at the bottom of the river waving his arms and legs helplessly in a futile attempt to roll off his back.

"You know, you're really not a very good brother," Gig said, as I dove into the river to rescue Kevin.

After freeing him from the backpack and pushing him to shore, I said, "Good try, man. Don't worry; you're relieved from any further underwater duties."

Toward the end of Kevin and Dick's two-week stay, we spotted the herd of Dall sheep on one of the closer mountains overlooking Sheep Creek. We had chased those sheep many times without success that summer, but hope sprang eternal.

"Maybe today's our day, Gig," I said, staring up at the white dots slowly moving up the green slope of the mountain.

"Maybe," he replied, "we're almost out of caribou, so we might as well try."

"Dick, you and Kevin stay here with the dogs," I said. "We'll be back in a few hours. Maybe with dinner."

Working our way upstream, we were careful to stay close to the bank at the bottom of the gorge and out of the line of sight of the herd. Once past the front slope of the mountain, we continued around and up the backside, and following a faint game trail, we eventually came over one of the two summit peaks. We inched up the next summit hill on our bellies and we poked our heads over the top.

"There they are!" Gig whispered excitedly, catching sight of five Dall sheep grazing about a hundred yards away down a steep slope.

The sheep came instantly alert the moment our heads broke the skyline, and as they turned to flee, Gig and I both shot simultaneously. One sheep started tumbling downhill as the other four disappeared in a flash of white. For a split second, we looked at each other incredulously and then sprinted downhill after the tumbling sheep, as it gained momentum and headed toward the edge of a cliff.

"Don't let it roll off!" Gig shouted.

I dove for the sheep as it sailed off the edge, missing it by a few inches with Gig tumbling to the ground next to me. "So close and yet so far," I panted, as we both lay there staring over the edge of the cliff at the sheep as it bounced once off a ledge and then hit a grassy slope a hundred feet below and rolled to a stop.

"There's no way to make it down this cliff," Gig said.

"We'll have to take the long way around," I agreed. It took us an hour to make our way back up to the summit and find another way down to the base of the cliff.

"There it is, Gig," I said, approaching the grassy run out at the base of the cliff. "One perfectly tenderized mountain sheep."

We weren't interested in trophies, so we left the head and horns with the entrails as so much extra weight. Dressed out, the sheep weighed somewhere around 120 pounds, light enough for just one of us to carry. "I'll do it," I volunteered, stripping down to my underwear to keep my clothes from becoming covered in blood. Gig hoisted the sheep up onto my shoulders and with blood dripping down all over me, we headed back to camp, as the dark shadows of dusk started to creep up from the valley.

I don't think my brother was impressed as I approached the camp in my boxers, covered in blood, carrying the headless sheep carcass.

"I'm not really related to you, am I?" he wanted to know.

"You'll be singing a different tune after we barbecue this baby," I replied, dropping the sheep at his feet.

After an invigorating swim in the icy river to wash off the blood, I helped Gig make a bonfire on the rocky river bank and improvised a spit to roast the sheep. As an added treat, we constructed a temporary sauna from a few spruce poles covered with visqueen and heated river rocks in the fire to warm up the sauna. By pouring water over the hot rocks, we filled the sauna with steam, and soon we were drenched in sweat and hot enough to swim in the river one more time. The smell of roasting meat filled the cool air, as we stood around the fire pit slowly turning the sheep on the spit. In the approaching Alaskan dusk, we cut off succulent chunks of steaming meat with our knives and stuffed ourselves in an orgy of roasted sheep.

"Well, that was another overly full day," I commented.

"This will go down as one of my more memorable feasts," Dick said.

After this last set of visitors departed for home, we were left to carry on with our mining operation as before. The cold underwater work continued as the hole was enlarged and became ever deeper. Most days we were rewarded with small amounts of gold, but we definitely were not getting wealthy yet.

"Hey, look," Gig said one morning after another cold, unproductive shift underwater. "We wore a hole in the metal nozzle. It's not working right anymore."

"I don't want to walk out and then drive to Anchorage to buy a new one," I whined.

"Hey, I bet that mining operation over on Alfred Creek would be able to fix it," Gig replied.

"Yeah, they must have some welding equipment with all that heavy machinery," I agreed.

With the dogs trailing along, we mounted the horses and rode bareback the fifteen miles over to Alfred Creek. The mining operation was much larger and more involved than I had imagined from our winter visit. They had two D-9 Cats that they used to scrape the whole river valley overburden into the long metal sluice boxes they had fabricated.

"Look at that," Gig said. "They can process the same amount of sand and gravel through their sluice in five minutes as we did in three months."

"That's depressing," I agreed. "It's probably the only way to viably mine placer gold in this day and age."

The miners were friendly enough, and one of them gladly repaired our nozzle by welding on a patch while we waited. Like miners everywhere, they were exceedingly closed mouthed about the details of their operation and how much gold they had discovered.

"The nozzle is stronger now than when it was new," I said, when the miner handed our equipment back. "Can we pay you for the repair?"

"No thanks," he replied, "glad to help out a neighboring miner. Good luck." And with a wave, we mounted the horses and headed back to Sheep Creek.

As before, every two weeks, one or both of us had to walk out for resupply with gasoline, and along the way we would usually drop off a haunch of caribou or moose for the Arizona family. Returning to Sheep Creek after one of these solo excursions with the two horses and the two dogs, I had my first encounter with a wolf pack. Soon after leaving the rusted-out truck that marked the halfway point, the trail crossed a wide-open field before turning back into the conifer forest. Halfway across the field I noticed the horses were becoming skittish, and the dogs were not running ahead as they usually did. Over the summer, the horses had proved to be very good at detecting any nearby wild animals, so I stopped the caravan and scanned the border of the forest for what was spooking them. At first I didn't see anything unusual, but when both the two dogs and the two horses decided they wanted to be between my legs, I was sure that we were not alone.

A gray shadow stepped out of the woods fifty yards away, on the far side of the clearing, and stared at us.

"Wolf," I whispered to my four-legged companions. Of course, they already knew what it was: a wolf, with long, lanky legs and gray, matted fur. The first wolf was soon joined by three others that emerged from different corners of the field to stand silently as sentinels. I glimpsed other figures trotting through the shadows of the trees, keeping more or less out of sight. Gig's extra-large dog, Rask, whimpered pitifully as he vied for a position between my legs with the other three. The horses had their ears laid back and snorted softly through their nostrils. I knew that generally wolves were not known to attack humans and that the pack was probably just curious about us, but all the same I tightened my grip on the two halter ropes and chambered a round into the breech of the .30–30. The wolf that first appeared let out a spine-tingling howl that was answered from the surrounding forest. As the eerie echoes of their cries faded, they all melted into the woods, apparently satisfied with their inspection. The whole encounter lasted no more than a few minutes, and I never caught another glimpse of the pack or heard another soulful howl that mining season, but the memory of the sight and sound of those wolves can still send a chill running down my spine.

Toward the end of summer, as Gig and I were approaching Caribou Creek on one of our supply trips, we were sidetracked by shouting coming from the vicinity of the Arizona cabin.

"There," Gig said, pointing toward the river, "it looks like Al is stuck in the middle of the river."

The water in Caribou Creek was unusually high, following a few days of heavy rain, and there, perched in the middle, clinging to a half submerged rock, was the mountain man himself. His family was yelling to him from the opposite bank and trying unsuccessfully to throw him a rope. When they spotted us, they waved and shouted frantically.

"Hang on Al!" I called. "We'll use the horses."

Clinging to the horses while fighting against the powerful current, we rescued him, and got him back into the cabin next to the hot cook stove.

"He was in that water for twenty minutes," Vicky said, wrapping him in a blanket as Carlo stoked the fire.

He was able to speak after the uncontrollable shivering had subsided somewhat, "I-I-I saw a m-moose across the river and decided to try for it. The r-r-river has never been that high before."

"Lucky we happened by when we did," Gig said.

"Sure is boys," Vicky agreed. "We thank y'all once again."

"Yes, th-thanks again," Al shivered.

"You're staying for supper," Vicky added. "Girls, go fire up the sauna for them."

"John," Gig whispered, "too bad we don't have our usual caribou haunch to give them."

"Well, we could see if we could track that moose," I said hopefully. "Let's cross the river, and if we don't find it in half an hour we'll just come back."

Moose tracks led from the sandy river bank toward a patch of brush, and about a half mile from the cabin we spied a lone moose making its way toward the steep bench that led up into the Horn Mountains. We dispatched the moose easily and, using the horses, soon had four quarters of moose hanging in the family's cache. It was at this moment that Becky presented Gig with a gift to express her undying love.

"You have the most beautiful blue eyes I ever did see," she whispered, holding a homemade necklace out in front of her. "Gig, I really love you."

"Oh, Gig, you lucky dog," I said, watching while she placed it around his neck and he stared at the squirrels' foot necklace that was still oozing blood from the amputated feet and staining his shirt red.

"Ah, thank you, Becky," he choked out, his face almost matching the color of the stains on his shirt. "I better put this away somewhere safe." Packing his new fashion accessory into the saddlebag, he glared at me and whispered, "Not another word about this."

As the end of August closed in, we woke up one morning to find Gig's horse, Suzie, lying on her side with the other horse grazing beside her.

"John, do you think Suzie is okay?" Gig asked, when she was still lying on her side after breakfast.

"Sure, they sometimes rest for a while lying down," I answered, but a few hours later, after we spent the morning working in the river, she was still in the same position.

"That's not right," Gig said, as he pulled off the drysuit and hurried over to the horse. "Something's wrong with her."

"Come on Suzie, get up," I encouraged her, but her only response was to move her head back and forth, trying to reach some grass with her mouth. She had eaten all the grass within reach of her head. "Gig, she can only move her head and neck," I said, "but not the rest of her body."

"There's no sign of any trauma," he replied, looking her over carefully. "And she doesn't appear to be in any pain."

"She's breathing normally," I noted. "And her digestive system seems to be working," I added, pointing to the pile of fresh manure lying behind her.

"I don't understand it," Gig said. "She was perfectly healthy yesterday, and Kodie seems fine." The other horse continued to graze in circles around his fallen friend.

"Maybe it's just a temporary thing," I offered. "Something she ate perhaps. If we bring her grass and water, she might get over it." She ate and drank eagerly, but was no better by the next day.

"Al should know something about horses," Gig said, feeding Suzie yet another handful of grass.

"Yeah, that's right," I replied. "He drove a stagecoach in Arizona. I'll take Kodie down and bring Al back to have a look. You stay here with her."

A few hours later, I returned with Al and Carlo, and all four of us stared helplessly at the stranded horse. "Well, I don't know," Al said slowly. "I don't take care of the horses in Arizona; I just drive the stagecoach. Maybe if we can get her up on her feet she'd be okay."

"How are we going to get a twelve-hundred-pound horse up on her feet?" I asked.

"We could build an A-frame out of logs," Gig suggested, "but we don't have a winch or a block and tackle to pull her up with."

There were no veterinarians out in the Talkeetna Mountain wilderness, and we had no delusions of being able to bring one to camp. Over the next three days, we fed and watered her, but her condition deteriorated to the point she had trouble lifting her head, and her face was bloodied from continuously banging it on the ground.

"We can't watch her suffer like this anymore, Gig," I said. "She isn't going to get any better, and the right thing to do is to shoot her."

"I know," he replied sadly.

"I'll do it," I offered.

"No, she's my horse. I'll do it," he said. The loud crack from his .300 magnum rifle echoed back and forth across the valley, and we then had a twelve-hundred-pound dead horse in the middle of our camp.

"We can't leave her here," I said.

There were bears living in the area, and we had seen a few over the course of the season. The leavings from our hunting excursions always disappeared within a day or two, and we assumed it was mostly due to scavenging bears. Digging a hole in the rocky, frozen ground was impossible, and it would not be long before a bear, following the scent of death, might visit camp.

"We'll have to cut her up and carry her over the bench a few miles," Gig said.

"I don't want to load her on her friend, Kodie," I said.

"No, you're right," he replied. "We can just carry her ourselves."

"You know, Gig," I said, "they eat horses in Europe. Do you think we should save some of the meat?"

"We could save a little, but there's not much room in the icebox," he replied.

We put a small amount of horse meat into the tundra refrigerator (after all, it was a delicacy in some parts of the world), and we divided the rest of the carcass into sections small enough to carry. In retrospect, of course, it was not a smart idea to eat meat from an animal that could possibly have had an infectious disease that caused those neurological symptoms, but we were living life close to the bone then.

A tarp served as a makeshift sled for the entrails, and we dragged them away from camp two miles up onto the bench separating Sheep Creek from the next drainage area to the west. Returning for the rest of the carcass, I volunteered to carry the severed head and neck while Gig struggled with part of a hind quarter.

"This is the most awkward thing I've every tried to carry," I muttered, stumbling across the alpine meadow weighted down by that heavy head slung over my shoulder. Blood dripped down my back into my pants from the severed neck and Suzie's dead eye starred at me the whole way. Six hours later, all remnants of the horse had been deposited two miles from camp, and we were now down to a single pack horse. We later visited the spot where we had deposited Suzie's remains, and other than a red stain on the trampled grass, there was nothing left of her.

As the end of September approached, ice started to form in the calm pools of the river at night. Our mining season had come to an end. After five months of work, the underwater hole was now twelve feet deep, and still there was no sign of bedrock. Our yield of gold was sparse. The Arizona clan had already departed, and soon we were packing up for the last walk out.

"Well, we didn't get rich, Gig," I said. "And we never did reach bedrock."

"No, but I wouldn't trade this year for anything," he answered.

"I hope I never have to eat caribou again," I laughed.

"Can you believe John is going to carry all this stuff out with his helicopter?" Gig said.

Instead of packing out all our equipment on one horse and our own backs, we wrapped the canvas army tent around as much of the gear as possible, tied it into a bundle, and left it on the alpine bench. John had spent the year managing an exploration camp for ARCO and offered to pick up our equipment free of charge by taking a small detour on one of his frequent flights over the state. We pinpointed the location of the camp on a map, and when he found it, he attached a cable to the bundle and slung it out under the belly of the helicopter, delivering it to us courtesy of ARCO. I doubt a favor like that would be possible now in this day of corporate oversight and liability concerns.

I saved a small glass vial of shiny, yellow placer gold and another of reddish-purple, multifaceted garnets that I gathered from the Sheep Creek gold claims. Gig and I did not become wealthy with gold that year, but we did end up far richer in experiences, memories, and with a priceless lifelong friendship. Sometimes late at night after everyone else has gone to bed, I find myself sitting before the fireplace, staring into that small vial as the firelight glitters off pieces of golden dreams, and I try to rekindle the feeling of freedom, excitement, and adventure of those youthful years.

Peter with the truck, Whaler, and kayaks on the Alcan Highway somewhere in the Yukon Territory.

The Copper River Delta near Cordova, Alaska.

The farmstead in Sutton, Alaska.

An avalanche on Mount St. Elias.

The knife-edge on the north ridge of Mount Newton.

Twelve feet of fresh snow covering the entrance to the snow cave at camp three on Mount Newton.

Mount St. Elias from close to the summit of Mount Newton.

Inside a snow cave on Mount Newton.

The author on the summit of Mount Newton.

The three-mile-long ridge connecting Mount Newton to Mount St. Elias.

The author's home under construction in Wasilla, Alaska.

Gig and Suzie taking a break in the old truck marking the halfway-point into the gold claims.

The dredge in action at the Sheep Creek gold claims.

The author's dog, Denali, overlooking the Sheep Creek gold claims.

Gig with Kodie and Suzie at the gold claims.

Gig tending to the sheep barbecue and the visqueen sauna at the gold claims.

The author waiting at the Talkeetna Airstrip for a bush pilot to fly him into the Alaska Range.

The Ruth Amphitheater in the Alaska Range.

Mount Foraker from the Kahiltna Glacier.

Alpenglow on the Alaska Range.

Moonrise at 14,200 feet of the West Buttress Route on Mount McKinley.

The view from the tent camp at sixteen thousand feet on the West Buttress Ridge of Mount McKinley.

The author skiing in the 1983 Iditaski.

Chapter Nine: Mountaineering Adventures

"Let's build a few speculation houses together," Harry suggested, as we were climbing in Hatcher Pass one day.

"How would that work out?" I asked.

"You build them, and I'll take care of the financing and all the other details," he said. Since he owned a land title company, Harry was familiar with the legalities and process of building houses.

"Well, that should be a lot better than hanging sheetrock all the time," I said.

And so, I became a general contractor, building houses in the Wasilla area. Gig helped me most of the time, when he wasn't off working as a smoke jumper, fighting wildfires in northern Alaska. I designed most of the houses, although over the years, I built a few custom architect-designed houses also. Harry arranged the construction financing, purchased the land, and took care of all the legal paperwork involved in selling the houses. Some years, we built only one house if it was large and complicated, and other years, we built three or four starter houses in one of Wasilla's growing subdivisions. The real estate market was booming in Wasilla, and we never had any trouble selling the houses. After all the expenses and wages were taken care of, Harry and I split the profit fifty-fifty.

Harry had also started a wilderness adventure school for young people, and he eventually purchased Genet Expeditions, one of the climbing concessions leased from the federal government on Mount McKinley. He asked me to help him, and I discovered that I enjoyed teaching young people. I helped him with groups in the Hatcher Pass area and joined him on many expeditions to the Alaska Range and other mountains throughout Alaska. During the climbing season, I often abandoned the building projects to join these expeditions for three or four weeks at a time.

Mount Drum

"Want to help me guide a trip to Mount Drum?" Harry asked, early one summer.

"Sure, who's going?" I replied.

"I'm taking a group of teenagers as part of the wilderness school," he said. "Come on. It'll be fun."

Like a silent sentinel guarding the western fringes of the Wrangell-St. Elias Range, the snowcapped stratovolcano, Mount Drum, rises 12,010 feet out of the boggy tundra. Stratovolcanoes are composite volcanoes, composed of layers of both lava flows and pyroclastic material vomited up by the volcano. Mount Drum has been dormant for somewhere around half a million years, but in its prehistoric past, a Mount St. Helens-like eruption had destroyed the southern half of the volcano, spewing rock, ash, and lava over a wide area. Although not considered a difficult climb, the approach to the mountain was somewhat unusual.

A chartered bush plane waited to take us to the beginning of the climb from the small town of Gulkana. It was a short flight of a few miles from the Gulkana airstrip, across the silty, braided Copper River to a dry creek bed that wound through a gully that the pilot optimistically called a landing strip. From here, a two days' march across wet, spongy, mosquito-infested taiga and tundra terrain brought us to the base of a glacier where the real climb began.

Even though this was not a siege-like expedition with a month's worth of food and supplies to pack in, there was still a substantial amount of baggage to move to the base of the mountain. Shouldering heavy packs, the half dozen teenagers, along with Harry and I, began the slog westward toward Drum, which glittered in the sunlight like a jewel in the distance. We frequently lost sight of Drum following the slowly rising, but undulating, landscape, and as we drew closer and closer to the mountain, it came to dominate the skyline. Two days later and thirty-two hundred feet higher in elevation, we stood at the terminus of a glacier, looking up at the snow-covered ridge, which wound its way to the volcanic cone that constituted the summit of the mountain. Weather permitting, it would be a relatively short, non-technical, two-day climb to the top.

On a warm day with clouds streaming in from the southwest, we began the climb from the end of the glacier in three separate rope teams, up onto the ridgeline. Snow cover began somewhere around five thousand feet of elevation.

"Hey, Harry. Those clouds look similar to the ones that preceded that storm on St. Elias," I said, casting a wary eye at the sky.

"We'll watch the weather closely," he replied. "Einar told me about a natural ice cavern somewhere around eight thousand feet on this ridge that's big enough to camp in. Maybe we can use it tonight if we can find it."

The weather deteriorated as the day wore on, and by early evening, the clouds had descended, cloaking the summit. The wind picked up, howling banshee-like, and then it started snowing, hard.

"Where's that cave?" I shouted at Harry over the wind.

"Einar said it can be entered through a narrow, downsloping crevasse at a spot where the ridge flattens out at eight thousand feet," he hollered back. "Should be right around here somewhere."

With visibility dwindling, we searched the area for the entrance hole. There were several unpromising crevasses scattered around and between a few large pinnacles of ice (seracs), and we were just about to give up hope when one of the teenagers found a wand stuck a couple of feet into a small slit in a snow wall between two of the seracs.

"Over here," Gordie, one of the younger teens, shouted, pointing at the wand.

Working with my snow shovel, I enlarged the slit and transformed it into a tunnel barely wide enough to crawl through without a pack. The possibility of finding a natural shelter instead of building a snow cave or setting up tents in the storm was intriguing enough to lead me onward, down through the hole. Harry belayed me, and I wormed my way through the tunnel as it twisted and sloped gently downward for seventy-five feet into the mountain. Just as I was beginning to worry about how I would be able to turn around in the close confinement of the walls and retreat to the surface, the tunnel opened onto a huge cavern. A soft, diffused light filtering in from the outside world brought the features of the cavern into dim relief. The room was at least seventy-five yards long and fifty yards wide with a flat floor sloping down to the edge of a crevasse along the far side of the chamber. The ceiling soared a hundred feet overhead and was dotted with gigantic icicles hanging down like stalactites. Scattered about the floor were the shattered remains of a few of these crystal giants. As I took it all in, I was vaguely aware of distant, muffled shouts intruding from outside. I probed the floor in the immediate vicinity of the tunnel with my ice ax for hidden crevasses and then retreated back to the group that was huddled around the entrance hole.

The contrast between the two worlds was startling. The cathedral-like cavern was quiet and peaceful, while outside on the ridge a storm raged, and the snow blew horizontally.

"What did you find?" Harry shouted at me.

"It's definitely the ice cavern," I shouted back. "It's huge. Let's get out of this blizzard." Pushing our packs in front of us, we soon had the entire climbing party gathered in the cavern at the tunnel outlet.

"Belay me, and I'll probe the floor for crevasses," Harry said, and a short time later he reported that the floor appeared to be safe.

"Let's pitch the tents over there, away from those hanging death icicles," I suggested, pointing toward the giant ice fingers hanging precariously from the ceiling.

In that huge, ice-chandeliered cathedral, the dome tents looked small and out of place. A ten-yard-wide crevasse along the far wall reflected a ghostly bluish glow at its lip that melted into an impenetrable blackness of unknown depths. Taking turns throwing chunks of ice into this black pit, we listened to the echoes as they bounced off the frigid walls and traveled down into the icy blackness.

"Don't want to fall down there," I pointed out rather needlessly.

We melted ice for water and spent a comfortable night sheltered from the weather. In the darkness, the soft glow of headlamps shining through the fabric of the tents cast multicolored highlights against the ice walls of the cavern that reminded me of the light of stained glass windows in a great cathedral or of a futuristic scene on some far off distant ice world in another galaxy. In my mind, this remains the most unique and otherworldly camping site I have yet encountered in the mountains.

The next morning, we emerged from the tents and crawled back through the tunnel to the ridge outside. The storm had abated, leaving low, gray, fog-like clouds surrounding the mountain.

"Great day for climbing," I commented.

"Well, let's start off and see what the day brings," Harry said. "At least it's not snowing anymore, and the wind has died. Make sure to wand the trail adequately."

Plodding upward toward the summit, I placed wands like a trail of bread crumbs as the rope teams climbed higher. After hours of foggy climbing interspersed with tantalizing, brief glimpses of the mountain when the clouds momentarily parted, the altimeter read twelve thousand feet, and there was no more upward sloping snow to climb.

"This is it," I said, belaying the group to the top.

We had reached the summit and stood gazing into the thick whiteness of the clouds. It was not the crystal clear summit day with vast vistas that mountaineers dream of, but I thanked the mountain for the memorable gift of the ice cavern, and we made our way uneventfully back down the ridge, retrieving wands as we went.

The Ruth Amphitheater

"The Ruth is one of the best spots in Alaska for climbing," Harry told me. "You can set up base camp on the glacier and pretty much find something close by to climb in any direction. I'm taking a group in for the wilderness school soon. Why don't you join me?"

Thereafter, Harry and I took many trips into the Ruth Amphitheater with groups of teenagers and even children as young as ten years old. We taught them the basic skills needed for glacier travel, crevasse rescue, ice climbing, and mountaineering. From our base camp, we skied throughout the Ruth and climbed some of the surrounding peaks. One year, we took a group of paraplegics in for a couple of weeks of ski touring, harnessing ourselves like sled dogs, and explored the far reaches of this vast glacial wonderland.

The Ruth Amphitheater was just southeast of Mount McKinley in Denali National Park, where huge masses of glacial ice flowed off the East Buttress and Southeast Spur of McKinley and filled the enormous bowl-like amphitheater. The three forks of the Ruth Glacier—the West Fork, Northwest Fork, and North Fork—merged in the amphitheater and flowed through the Gateway, surging past the towering granite walls of Mount Barrille and the Gargoyle, then into and through the Great Gorge of the Ruth. In the Great Gorge, the ice has been discovered to be thirty-eight hundred feet thick, and sheer two-thousand- to five-thousand-foot granite cliffs erupted from the ice to define the narrow gorge between Mount Barrille, Mount Dickey, and the Mooses Tooth. Many of Alaska's most famous and difficult climbs were in the immediate vicinity of the Ruth, including the Rooster Comb, Mount Huntington, Mooses Tooth, and the impressive Yosemite-like granite walls of Barrille and Dickey. You could spend a lifetime climbing here and still not be able to see it all.

The famous bush pilot, Don Sheldon, had first pioneered the high-altitude glacial landings necessary for flying into the area. He carried spruce boughs with him and threw them out the window of his plane onto the surface of the glacier, using the depth perception generated by the color contrast between the green of the spruce and the white of the snow to gage his landings. In 1966, after carrying all the materials he needed strapped onto the struts of his bush plane, he had built a small, hexagonal cabin on a rock outcrop that cleaved the Ruth Glacier between Mt. Barrille and the Rooster Comb. The cabin still stands there today. We often used this cabin, known as the Mountain House, as base camp for our Ruth forays. Standing at the Mountain House, you could look west at the steep, undulating ridge of the Rooster Comb, east across the Glacier to the snow covered peaks of Barrille and Dickey, and North out across the vastness of the confluence of the forks of the Ruth Glacier to Mount Dan Beard.

We flew out of the town of Talkeetna, the base of operations for several flying services that flew climbers and sightseers into Mount McKinley and the Alaska Range. In those days, we flew with Talkeetna Air Taxi, a company founded by Don Sheldon and subsequently bought by Lowell Thomas Jr., the son of Lowell Thomas, the famous American writer, broadcaster, and adventurer who made Lawrence of Arabia famous. Lowell Thomas Jr. had been a pilot in the U.S. Air Corps during World War II, lieutenant governor of Alaska from 1974 to1978, and produced an adventure TV show for CBS. He was an exceptional bush pilot and flew a ski-mounted, turbo-charged Helio Courier. At that time, he had Doug Geeting working with him, and we frequently had the pleasure of flying with Doug as well.

The flight into the Ruth left the small Talkeetna runway and headed out over the confluence of the milk-silty Susitna and Chulitna Rivers, across wet, spongy, alpine terrain, dotted with small lakes, and then onward into the Alaska Range. Usually, the plane followed the lower reaches of the Ruth Glacier up into the mountains, flying through the Great Gorge and turning northwestward at the corner of the Gateway to land on the glacier just northwest of Mount Barrille at an elevation of approximately five thousand feet.

It helps to understand the geologic forces, and plate tectonics in particular, that shaped this part of Alaska in order to truly appreciate the spectacular topography of the area.

The Earth is made up of several layers, and at its core is presumed to be a solid ball of iron, surrounded by an outer liquid core of molten iron. Surrounding the dual core is the mantle, composed of different layers of rock. The heat and pressure within the mantle has caused this rock to slowly flow, and over time, perhaps a billion years, there has been continuous exchange of rocky material between the layers of the mantle. The rigid outer layer of the Earth, the lithosphere, makes up the relatively thin, cold, hard crust. The lithosphere is broken into roughly twenty fragments, or plates, that ride upon the hot, not-quite-solid rock of the upper mantle, the asthenosphere. Heat from radioactive decay and the Earth's core, as well as the crushing pressure of the overlying rock, causes the rocky material of this part of the mantle to set up convection cells, and the rock slowly flows like warm caramel or squeezed silly putty. The convection currents cause the plates of the lithosphere to move, and the continents embedded in the plates move passively with them. This movement is slow, on the order of a couple of inches per year, but the heat engine of the mantle inexorably drives plate tectonics—the force responsible for the wandering of the continents, the eruption of volcanoes, the building of mountain ranges, and the destructive power of earthquakes.

When two plates collide, one plate subducts under the other, and the material of the plate is eventually recycled in the mantle. This usually happens along continental margins and deep ocean trenches. While one plate subducts, the edge of the other plate is forced up, resulting in mountain building. Oceanic crust is denser than continental crust, and therefore, prefers to subduct into the mantle when it meets continental crust. While one edge of a plate subducts, new oceanic crust is formed at the opposite edge of the plate in mid-ocean ridges. In this fashion, over hundreds of millions of years, oceans open and close, and continents come together and break apart like giant, slow-motion jigsaw puzzles.

Geoscientists call this process of continental coalescence, breakup, drifting, and re-accumulation Wilson cycles. It is thought that there have been at least six cycles of supercontinent formation, where all the continents came together to form one super landmass, and then subsequently broke up. Somewhere between two hundred and three hundred million years ago, all the continents coalesced to form the supercontinent of Pangaea (meaning all lands) surrounded by a super-ocean, Panthalessa (meaning all oceans).

Sometimes small blocks or fragments of continental crust break off from a continent as two plates collide or scrape by one another. These blocks, called terranes, are swept along with the rest of the plate as it slowly moves. In this fashion, terranes can collide into and merge with continents, yet the terrane can retain its distinctive geologic history, which is different from the new surrounding area. The rocks north of the Alaska Range are geologically much older than those that form the mountains of the range itself. Perhaps a billion years ago, there were one or more mountain ranges north of the present-day Alaska Range that over hundreds of millions of years were eroded away. The eroded material deposited on the floor of a shallow sea and under mounting pressure, this sediment transformed into mudstone and sandstone.

A few hundred million years ago, the Pacific plate began acting like a giant conveyor belt, delivering a number of terranes to Alaska that had broken off the continental edges of Central and North America, and in geologic slow motion, these terranes crashed into the Alaska coastline. Pressure from subduction of oceanic crust and the newly arrived land masses began to cause uplifting of the area that now forms the Alaska Range. The basalt of the oceanic crust and some of the attached continental crust of the terranes subducted down under Alaska, heading for the mantle to be melted and reincorporated. The sedimentary rock that had been the eroded leftovers of those billion-year-old mountain ranges was compressed, heated, folded, and tortured into a new form of metamorphic rock, a black, slate-like flysch.

As dense oceanic basalt subducted, parts of the relatively light, less dense continental rock of the terranes was dragged along with it. Melted by the internal heat of the Earth, this lighter, less dense molten rock began to make its way back toward the surface. Somewhere around sixty million years ago, this magma (molten rock) spewed from volcanic vents north of present-day Mount McKinley and covered hundreds of square miles of land with lava. In the area of the Alaska Range, the overlying flysch was too thick for the magma to penetrate, and instead it formed huge underground magma chambers where the overlying flysch was further baked and changed in a process known as contact metamorphosis. Fifty-six million years ago, these magma chambers slowly cooled into masses of granite called plutons, named after Pluto, lord of the underworld. These plutons were raised up with the rest of the area to form part of the Alaska Range. Mount McKinley is mostly made up of one of these huge plutons as are Mount Hunter, Mount Foraker, the mountains of the Ruth Gorge, and the Little Switzerland area. Sometimes blocks of the dark flysch fell or floated into the cooling plutons, forming inclusion blocks, otherwise known as xenoliths, which can be seen throughout the area. Both the granite plutons and the folded, wavy, black flysch are visible from the Mountain House on the Ruth Glacier.

When these many terranes accreted to the landmass of Alaska, they left a series of discontinuities or geologic faults in the crust. Over the last one hundred million years, many of the faults in the Alaska Range have fractured causing differential movement in sections of the range. Ever since the area was first uplifted, the relentless forces of weathering and erosion have sculpted the mountains. Over the last few million years there have been multiple periods of glaciation and these glaciers have cut, chiseled, and bulldozed the Alaska Range into its present-day appearance.

Among these mountains there are countless outstanding examples of all the various types of glacial erosional landforms. U-shaped valleys carved by glaciers, with the glaciers still occupying the floors of the valleys, curve and twist as the glaciers force their way downhill. Cirques and hanging valleys abound. Arêtes—sharp-edged, knife-like ridges formed by two glaciers eroding opposite sides of a ridge—slice the sky, while horns—pyramid-shaped peaks formed by several glaciers eroding away different sides of the same mountain—pierce the glaciers as they extend skyward.

Within Denali National Park, glaciers currently cover over a million acres of the park, including the Kahiltna Glacier, which at forty-four miles is the longest glacier in the Alaska Range. The Great Gorge of the Ruth is the deepest gorge in North America. Its U-shaped base is thirty-eight hundred feet under the ice of the glacier, which is hemmed in by five-thousand-foot sheer granite walls, making it deeper than the Grand Canyon. Just like the rest of the state, everything about the Alaska Range is huge, and only superlatives can be used to describe it.

Mount Foraker

"I've been thinking of trying an alpine-style ascent of Foraker," Harry said to me early in May 1981. "We could probably make it up and down in less than a week."

"Just the two of us?" I asked.

"Sure. It will be easier that way," he replied.

Mount Foraker, the sixth highest peak in North America, stood 17,400 feet high about ten miles southwest of Mount McKinley. According to Hudson Stuck, the leader of the first successful climb of the south summit of Mount McKinley in 1913, the Athabascan Indians had two names for the mountain. The natives called the mountain *Sultana*, "the woman," and *Menlele*, "Denali's wife." Whatever you called the mountain, it was a beautiful, cross-ridged, ice-crusted granite peak, rising from a surrounding nest of glaciers separated from Mount Hunter and Mount McKinley by the Kahiltna Glacier.

As usual, we flew in from Talkeetna with Lowell Thomas Jr. in his Helio Courier. "Lowell, do you think you could land us as close to the southeast ridge as possible, instead of the regular spot on the Kahiltna?" Harry requested above the noise of the engine.

"Sure. No problem," Lowell replied.

"Hey, Lowell, this seems much bumpier than usual," Harry yelled.

"Really? I didn't notice," Lowell answered.

Flying into the Alaska Range was often a bumpy, gut-wrenching experience, and that day the flight was more like a roller coaster than usual. After shooting through One Shot Pass into the interior of the range, we were in and out of clouds, and strong gusts of wind batted at the small plane like an invisible, gigantic hand. As we approached the proposed landing area, the contrast between the snow of the glacier and the white of the sky became indiscernible, at least to my eyes. Lowell circled the area a few times and then came in for his landing, relying on his altimeter and his instincts to determine where the sky ended and the glacier began. I wouldn't exactly call it a crash landing, at least not by Alaskan standards, but we hit the snow hard and bounced along the glacier several times before coming to a stop at sixty-five hundred feet of elevation.

"I need to adjust that altimeter," Lowell muttered. "Everyone okay?"

As we unloaded our gear, Lowell walked around his plane and inspected it for damage. Beyond a slightly bent strut supporting one of the skis, everything seemed to be in working order. He nonchalantly retrieved a hammer from the plane and straightened the strut by banging on it before waving goodbye and winging off back to Talkeetna.

"Nice landing," Harry commented, once Lowell was gone.

"You know what they say, any landing you walk away from is a good one," I said. "Look how close we are to the ridge."

From our landing position, we could see that the normal approach to the ridge was now a few miles away, back down a small bowl-like indentation the glacier flowing off the ridge of Foraker made before joining the Kahiltna on its journey southward. To the north, not far from our current position, a twisting rib of rock led upward, ending close to the ridgeline.

"That rock rib looks a lot more enticing than the long slog down the glacier to the start of the ridge," Harry said.

"From here it doesn't look like the rock extends all the way to the ridgeline," I said. "And, that's a pretty big cornice overhanging the last snow slope."

"I'm sure we'll find a way over it when we get there," Harry answered.

After skiing up and over to where the rib thrust its beginning slabs of granite out of the glacier, we pitched base camp. The next day, we stashed the skis and the rest of the gear at the base of the rib and hefted our packs filled with a week's worth of supplies. It took most of the day to work our way up the rib of granite, which ended about a hundred feet short of the overhanging cornice. The ridge cast late evening shadows over the bergschrund that separated the cornice from the steep headwall.

"That cornice looks a lot bigger from here than it did from down below," I said. "The rest of this slope is a perfect setup for an avalanche."

"The evening shadow should have firmed things up by now," Harry said. "Belay me over, and I'll see what I can do about climbing the cornice."

I belayed Harry from the end of the rock rib, where I was safe from avalanche danger, and he worked his way slowly up to the overhang. "There's no way to climb over this from here," he called back from the end of the rope.

"Great," I yelled. "Come back and let me try."

"No, you can't get over it, it's too overhung," he answered. "But maybe I can dig through it."

He started chipping away at the base of the cornice with his snow shovel and ice ax. An hour later, he wormed his way through the hole he had made and belayed me up and through the keyhole. We were now standing on the back of the cornice, below the overhang, on a narrow ridge that curved seductively toward the summit far off in the distance.

"Nice work," I complimented him. "I don't see how we can dig a tent platform on this part of the ridge though."

"You're right," Harry said. "We'll have to keep heading up until we find a better bivouac spot."

A couple of hours later, as the sun was approaching its midnight setting, I reached a moderately level spot around eleven thousand feet, just wide enough for a tent. After belaying Harry to me, I said, "This is as flat as it's going to get. We can shovel a platform and camp here."

"Looks pretty exposed, but I guess you're right," he agreed.

We were exhausted from the long day, and I gladly took off my pack and pinned it to the snow with a picket to prevent it from sliding off the other side of the ridge into the void. As I stared at the coil of rope at my feet, I thought, *that's odd, the rope is unraveling fast.* In the blink of an eye, understanding and adrenaline flowed through me past the exhaustion. *Harry must have fallen!* Two thoughts entered my mind. Jump off the other side of the ridge and hope for the best, or fall on my ice ax and hope that I can hold him. Falling on the ice ax and driving the blade deep into the hard snow, I braced as best I could with my crampons. Closing my eyes, I waited for the inevitable wrenching jerk when the rope ran out of slack, but it never came. Opening my eyes, I found a few feet of coiled-up rope still at my feet, and no Harry in sight.

"Harry!" I screamed. There was no answer.

The rope led down the slope on the eastern side of the ridge and disappeared into a hole in what had been a snow bridge hiding a crevasse. I fashioned a fixed belay from a snow fluke and two pickets and rappelled down our only rope to the edge of the hole. Harry had fallen about twenty feet into the crevasse, landing on a shelf of ice beyond which the huge crevasse gaped open into unplumbed depths.

"Harry!" I yelled into the crevasse.

"I'm all right," he called up. "Except for my shoulder."

My spirits lifted when he answered my call from the edge, and I continued the rappel down to the shelf and found him with an injured left shoulder, but otherwise unscathed.

"Can you move your shoulder?" I asked.

"A little," he replied, "but it's pretty painful."

"Let me have a look at it," I said, helping him to sit up. The shoulder didn't seem to be broken or dislocated, but he had only limited use of that arm, and it was clear that the climb to the summit was over.

"What were you doing? I had you off belay," I said.

"I thought I saw a more level spot a little further along," was his lame answer. "Help me off with this pack."

Such is the nature of accidents in the mountains: one moment of carelessness can lead to deadly consequences. Tying his pack off to the rope, we both peered over the edge of the narrow shelf into the black depths of the crevasse. Once again we had been extremely lucky—it was doubtful that I would have been able to hold his fall had he not hit that well-placed shelf.

"Good thing this shelf was here," I said, "or we both would have ended up in an icy grave, wedged in the bottom of the crevasse."

The shelf sloped upward toward the surface of the ridge, and I was able to dig a way out of the crevasse rather than having to jumar back up the rope. "Should we bivouac on the ledge here in the crevasse, or do you want me to set up the tent on the ridge?" I asked.

"I don't want to spend any more time in this crevasse," he replied, staring into the black depths. "Set up the tent."

In the gathering dusk, I pitched the tent on the edge of the ridge, exposed to the wind blowing in from the west, and melted snow for dinner. "How's the shoulder," I asked.

"I'll live, but I can't do much with this arm," he said.

The wind picked up, threatening to blow us off the ridge, and we spent a sleepless, uncomfortable night sitting up with our backs to the tent wall, trying to keep it from imploding.

In the morning light, I collapsed the tent and packed as much gear as I could carry into my pack for the retreat down the ridge. Harry managed to carry his pack using just his right shoulder and waist belt for support. Inching our way back down the ridge, we were thankful to escape the numbing, cold, west wind as we crawled through the keyhole in the cornice. I lowered Harry down the headwall on the rope and glissaded down after him. Then we carefully picked our way down the granite rib back to base camp.

"Lowell's not expecting to hear from us for seven to ten days," Harry reminded me. We had planned to ski to the glacial landing strip used by McKinley climbers on the southeast fork of the Kahiltna Glacier and contact Lowell from there with the base camp radio.

"We should be able to hitch a ride out with somebody else if Lowell isn't around," I said.

The next day, we began the long ski up and across the Kahiltna, with me carrying or trailing most of our gear on my sled, while Harry struggled to ski without using his shoulder. It was a slow journey, but we made it without incident to Kahiltna International two days later and caught a ride out to Talkeetna with Doug Geeting, after he flew in some other climbers. We didn't climb to the summit of Foraker, but the mountain was generous enough to allow us to live to climb another day.

Denali Winter Rescue

On December 15, 1981, a Cessna 185 on a routine sightseeing flight crashed at the top of Mount McKinley's Kahiltna Pass. The small plane, flying out of Talkeetna with a pilot and three passengers, was caught in a mass of sinking air over the Kahiltna Glacier and slammed belly up on the Kahiltna side of the pass, bounced over the top, and came to rest a few hundred yards down the Peters Glacier side, somewhere around 10,500 feet in elevation. When the plane did not return as scheduled, Doug Geeting flew over the area and spotted the crash site just as darkness was descending.

The next day, the National Park Service Rangers from Denali National Park, in conjunction with the Army, staged a rescue attempt using a C-130 as a communications platform and two military CH-47 Chinook helicopters. The weather turned bad, and the helicopters were unable to land at the crash site or even drop supplies, but they did observe at least two survivors at the scene before retreating to Talkeetna.

In the morning, six local, experienced Talkeetna mountaineers, unhappy with the way the rescue of their pilot friend was progressing, convinced the park ranger in command to let them fly on the helicopters as support climbers. The helicopters went airborne with the Talkeetna climbers on board, but they were again turned back by the weather before they could even reach the Kahiltna Glacier.

On the third day after the crash, the helicopters again attempted to reach the site and once again had to turn back. The anxious and frustrated Talkeetna climbers convinced the ranger to drop them off on the lower reaches of the

Kahiltna Glacier and they would try to climb from there to the crash site on foot. The ranger acquiesced to their demands, and they were dropped off in what was essentially a blizzard at the 6,700-foot level of the glacier, seven miles and four thousand vertical feet below the crash site with one week's worth of supplies. Over the next two days, the climbers struggled up the glacier toward the pass through the brutal winter storm. By then, the local news media was second guessing the rescue effort, and the story was receiving national media attention. In order to leave no avenue unexplored under the media pressure, the Park Service asked for the help of any other local rescue groups that could supply support climbers.

"Want to go rescue some people from a plane crash on Mount McKinley?" Harry asked, waking me from sleep late one night.

Harry and I belonged to the loosely organized Alaska Mountain Rescue Group that operated out of Hatcher Pass and the Anchorage area, and we both happily volunteered to help in the effort. Joined by Bob and Einar, who had been with us on St. Elias, we drove to Talkeetna, where we found the two Chinooks waiting at the airstrip.

"The C-130 just reported continuing marginal weather for flying into the pass," a ranger informed us, "but let's take off in the Chinooks anyway and hope for a break in the weather."

The first thing I noticed about the Chinook was its huge size. The CH-47 was a twin-engine, twin-rotor, heavy-lift helicopter with contra-rotating rotors that dispensed with the need for a vertical tail rotor. This design allowed all the power to go to vertical lift and enabled the craft to have a maximum takeoff weight of around fifty thousand pounds. From rotor tip to rotor tip, the overall length was close to a hundred feet. Inside the cavernous cabin there was room for forty-four troops or a tank or two. The back end of the main cabin had a hydraulically controlled ramp that lowered to the ground, and as we carried our gear up the ramp into the vastness of the interior, our footsteps echoed hollowly. Thirteen soldiers of the Northern Warfare Training Center and two park rangers lifted off in one Chinook, and the four of us, along with two local climbers, followed them in the other.

I strapped into one of the fold-down canvas seats that lined the walls of the main cabin, and as the ship prepared for liftoff, I was deafened by the incredibly loud noise of the engines and rotors.

"Do you have any extra ear protection?" I screamed and mimed at the crew chief.

Unfortunately, there were no extra headphones, but he was able to fashion me a pair of earplugs from the filters of two cigarettes, and with my fingers stuffed in my ears over the makeshift plugs, the noise was at least tolerable. The weather did not break, and the two monster helicopters returned to Talkeetna, where we camped beside the airstrip for the night.

"There might finally be a break in the weather," the ranger informed us the next morning.

The C-130 reported a lessening in the cloud cover over the crash site, and in the predawn darkness at 9:00 AM, the Chinooks took off for the Kahiltna Glacier. As we flew up the glacier, the wind remained fierce, and blowing snow obscured visibility. The pilots circled near the top of the pass a couple of times, and the crew chief signaled us to prepare to exit.

"All four of us should rope up together as a team on one rope," Harry screamed over the noise.

"Let's do it here inside the Chinook," Einar said.

When the pilot landed the helicopter somewhere around 9,800 feet, the crew chief lowered the ramp, and out we jumped into a bitterly cold blizzard of snow whipped up by the rotors. The other Chinook landed a short distance away and the soldiers, in their white, air-insulated boots and white winter uniforms, piled out and organized themselves and their gear to climb up the glacier.

"Let's go," Harry said, nodding toward the soldiers. "It looks like they may be awhile."

The four of us strapped on skis and began to travel roped together toward the top of the pass. The pilot had spotted the Talkeetna climbers just below the pass, so we knew they were ahead of us and all accounted for.

"Nothing like landing unacclimatized at ten thousand feet and trying to hurry up the mountain," Harry gasped, as we all struggled to catch our breaths.

Soon enough, we reached the top of the pass and climbed down the Peters Glacier side to the crash site. The Talkeetna climbers had already reached the site, and by the time we arrived ahead of the military, they had fixed polypropylene rope to the top of the pass to make removing the survivors easier.

"We've got two survivors here," one of the Talkeetna climbers informed us as we arrived.

When I reached the plane wreck, I saw it was precariously wedged in the snow on a steep slope with its tail aimed toward the distant Peters Basin. It looked as if a small puff of wind could send the plane skidding thousands of feet to the glacier below. The front of the plane appeared relatively intact, but the pilot-side door had been ripped off and the right wing was broken at the base. Snow had drifted in throughout the interior of the fuselage, and crammed in the back of the plane was a frozen body in a sleeping bag with one gloveless hand frozen onto the wire cables running to the tail section. Another body lay higher up the slope, frozen inside a sleeping bag close to where the two survivors were being tended to. One of the survivors, the pilot, had somehow lost his boots, and he was sitting on a sled with his frozen, stocking-covered feet planted firmly in the snow. He was able to speak and drink some hot liquids, but appeared extremely weak. The other survivor also had badly frozen feet and hands, but he was able to move about on his own steam and was wearing boots.

"How could they possibly have survived those five stormy winter days and nights?" I asked Harry, gazing at the desperate scene.

"I don't know," he replied. "They were essentially out in the open the whole time."

"I doubt they would have survived another night by the looks of them," added Einar.

I learned later that all four people had initially survived the crash, but one passenger was severely injured and died within a few hours. His was the body outside the plane in the sleeping bag. The person I saw dead in the back of the plane had survived until the fourth day of their ordeal, when he died of internal injuries and exposure. Both survivors had significant frostbite injuries; the pilot ended up having both legs amputated below the knees, and the other survivor lost all his toes on both feet along with a couple of fingers.

The pilot was loaded and strapped onto a sled and slowly dragged to the top of the pass, while the other survivor was able to stagger uphill with two climbers supporting him using the fixed ropes.

"It's better to keep their feet frozen until they reach the hospital," an Army medical corpsman advised.

"Yes, unthawing and refreezing is worse than staying frozen," a Talkeetna climber agreed.

The weather continued to improve, and the Chinooks were able to land higher up the glacier, closer to the crash site from where they had dropped us. The two survivors were loaded into one helicopter, which took off for the hospital in Anchorage. In the gathering darkness of the winter afternoon, the four of us, along with the Talkeetna climbers, tumbled into the other Chinook and headed back to Talkeetna. The Northern Warfare Team opted to stay on the mountain and retrieve the two bodies as part of their training mission. They ended up spending the night on the mountain and were taken off by the Chinooks the next day.

When we landed at the Talkeetna airfield in the late afternoon darkness, the back ramp was lowered, revealing the blinding lights of television cameras. The victorious Talkeetna climbers disembarked to cheers from the local Talkeetna crowd and questions shouted at them from the media. Harry and Bob quickly followed them out into the glare of the spotlights.

"Let's get out of here," Einar said to me, nodding his head toward the pilot's door at the front of the helicopter.

"Yeah, I'm with you," I replied. The Talkeetna mountaineers had risked their lives and fought their way up the glacier through the blizzard, neither of us wanted to impinge on their hard-won celebration.

That was the last time I saw Einar alive. The next year, he died in an icefall doing what he loved to do best, climbing in the Wrangell-St. Elias Mountains.

Chapter Ten:
Mount McKinley

I will always associate Alaska's highest mountain with the name bestowed on it by the New York newspaper reporter-turned-gold prospector, William Dickey. In 1896, he named the mountain after William McKinley, who was then a senator and candidate for president of the United States. Dickey called the mountain Mount McKinley in a story about Alaska he sent to the New York *Sun,* along with a sketch of the mountain and his extraordinarily accurate estimate of the elevation, which he placed at twenty thousand feet.

Everyone I knew in Alaska in the 1970s referred to the mountain as McKinley, and so I tend to use that name. Today, the politically correct majority of people prefer to call the mountain Denali, the traditional Native Alaskan name. In 1917, Mount McKinley National Park was established, and in 1980, the Alaska National Interest Lands Conservation Act enlarged the boundary of the park by four million acres, renaming it Denali National Park. The mountain itself is still officially labeled Mount McKinley on the USGS topographic maps.

No matter what name you prefer, Mount McKinley/Denali is the highest peak in North America at 20,320 feet and has a greater vertical rise from base to summit than Mount Everest. McKinley has many difficult routes, but the most frequently climbed route, the West Buttress, which over 80 percent of climbers use, is not technically difficult. However, the mountain's brutal weather, high winds, and polar location make any route extremely dangerous, and many climbers have died on the West Buttress.

The early attempts to scale Mount McKinley resulted in one of the greatest controversies in the history of mountaineering. These first climbs were full of misfortune, deception, and triumph.

The first documented attempt to climb the peak was in 1903 by the Alaskan frontier judge, James Wickersham, from the small mining town of Fairbanks. He and his party left Fairbanks with supplies loaded on mules and bushwhacked their way to the north side of the mountain. After climbing to approximately ten thousand feet, they were turned back by a huge vertical wall of granite, now known as the Wickersham Wall. At the same time that the Wickersham party found the mountain impossible to climb, another party led by Dr. Frederick Cook, a famous polar explorer and a founder of the American Alpine Club, approached the mountain, intending to climb the same route. Cook's party landed from boats on the shores of Cook Inlet and traversed 250 miles of wilderness to reach the base of the mountain. They climbed about a thousand feet higher than Wickersham, but were stopped by the same granite wall. However, Cook continued northward and completed a 750-mile circumnavigation of the McKinley massif before going back to Cook Inlet.

Cook returned in 1906 and again landed at Cook Inlet with a party that included Hershel Parker, Belmore Browne, and a packer named Edward Barrille. Cook tried a different route, but as before, the mountain defeated him. After returning to the shores of Cook Inlet, Cook convinced everyone that the expedition was over. Once Parker and Browne had departed, he wired his sponsors in New York that he was returning to the mountain to make one last attempt. With only Barrille as a companion, Cook traveled back to the Alaska Range, following a glacier that he named after one of his daughters, Ruth, and entered a vast amphitheater, the same one I explored later with a group of teenagers. Cook later claimed that he and Barrille climbed from there to the summit, and Cook exhibited a photograph of Barrille triumphantly holding a flag attached to his ice ax on the purported summit. Although his former colleague Browne and many other Alaskans disbelieved Cook's claim, he was fêted as one of the world's great explorers when he returned to New York. He wrote a book about his successful ascent of the mountain, *To the Top of the Continent.*

In 1909, Thomas Lloyd, one of the Alaskan skeptics of Cook's summit claim, organized a group of seasoned Fairbanks miners known as the "sourdoughs." Led by Lloyd, a miner, and financed by Fairbanks saloon owners, the party of six men left Fairbanks in December 1909 in dogsleds and headed for the Muldrow Glacier area of Mount McKinley. These men had prospected and hunted the area for years, and believed they had discovered a viable route up the mountain. They traveled by dog team to the head of the glacier and set up a camp at approximately eleven thousand feet on the northeast ridge, after which they returned to lower elevations to hunt caribou and moose for food.

After returning to their ridge camp, they set out for the summit. They claimed to have scaled the ridge, planted a fourteen-foot spruce pole on the north summit (which they hoped would be visible from afar with a telescope), crossed over to the south summit, and then returned to the ridge camp all in one day. There were no photographs to document the climb, and many doubted the tale.

Parker and Browne again returned to the northern side of McKinley in 1912 via Cook Inlet. They retraced the sourdough's route up the Muldrow Glacier to the northeast ridge and pushed up the ridge, trying for the summit on June 29. A sudden blizzard turned them back a few hundred feet short of the summit. Their food supplies ran low, and they were forced to retreat off the mountain without trying for the summit again.

In 1913, Hudson Stuck, the Episcopal Archdeacon of the Yukon, led a party from Nenana to attempt to climb the mountain along the same northeast ridge route. Stuck's twenty-one-year-old protégé, Walter Harper, who was half Athabascan and half Irish, was part of the party. Like the sourdoughs, they used dog teams to ferry supplies to the head of the Muldrow Glacier and established a camp on the ridge at approximately 11,500 feet.

The climbing party of four advanced up the ridge and found it drastically changed since the 1910 and 1912 climbs. An earthquake had transformed part of the ridge into huge jumbled blocks of steep ice. Stuck's party had to spend three weeks of hard labor cutting steps in the shattered ridge in order to traverse what had taken the sourdoughs less than a day and the Parker-Browne expedition only a few days. They finally surmounted the ridge and made a succession of camps in the Grand Basin, the highest at eighteen thousand feet. From there, they made their final push to the summit on June 7, a perfectly clear day.

Walter Harper was the first person to set foot on the summit, followed by the other three climbers. They were able to see the spruce pole left by the sourdoughs over on the north summit, thereby confirming the sourdoughs' claim to have reached the lower of the two summits. Stuck and his party also confirmed that the true summit was completely different than the one described in Cook's account, further damaging his reputation. Stuck's successful team returned to Nenana three months and four days after setting out. In 1914, Hudson Stuck published *The Ascent of Denali*, in which he described the expedition and also urged to return to the mountain's traditional native name, Denali. Walter Harper, who perished in a shipwreck in 1918, is remembered by mountaineers who cross the Harper Glacier, the highest glacier on Mount McKinley, encompassing the Great Basin of the summit plateau.

After Stuck's revelations, Frederick Cook was disgraced and expelled from the Explorers Club and the Artic Club of America. He fell on hard times and eventually was jailed for fraud in an oil-property scheme. After spending seven years in Leavenworth prison, he was pardoned by President Franklin Delano Roosevelt, but he lived out the remaining years of his life in poverty. His claim to have reached the summit of Mount McKinley still had a few supporters, however, and the controversy continued until 1956 when, Bradford Washburn used high-resolution aerial photography to locate the exact spot where Cook had taken his faked summit photo.

I became personally involved with the mountain again in the spring of 1982, several months after participating in the rescue of the air crash survivors, when Harry asked me, "Want to help me guide an expedition on McKinley? I have a group of teenagers that have signed up for the West Buttress route."

"Sure, when?" I asked.

"Let's shoot for June," he replied.

We planned for twenty-five days on the mountain and would ferry loads and move camps in siege fashion, as we had on Mount St. Elias. Doug Geeting flew the group, six teenagers, Harry, his wife, Dianne, and me, into the southeast fork of the Kahiltna Glacier and landed at Kahiltna International (the nickname for the glacial landing strip) at 7,200 feet. This was a base-camp staging area, where there were usually many climbing parties milling about, either starting or finishing climbs. The air taxi operators hired a base-camp manager, who spent the climbing season in a canvas tent on the glacier, coordinating flights in and out and assisting with any rescue communications.

"Can you believe Mugs Stump just climbed the Moonflower Buttress?" Harry asked, as we organized our base camp on the glacier.

I looked across in awe at the intimidating vertical ice-and-rock wall of the Moonflower Buttress of Mount Hunter that Mugs Stump and a New Zealand climber had successfully climbed a few days before. Mugs had described the climb to us earlier that day in his usual understated fashion, making it sound like just another day of ice climbing rather than the desperate, cutting-edge climb that it had been.

"At least the West Buttress won't look like that, right?" I said.

The next day, it was down to business. We ferried loads down Heartbreak Hill to the main fork of the Kahiltna and cached supplies around 7,600 feet at what would become camp one. Over the next week or so, we made our slow, plodding way up the glacier. We took a right at Kahiltna Pass and established a camp at 11,500 feet. Climbing McKinley successfully was all about taking advantage of good weather and understanding just how fast the weather could change on the mountain. Up to that stage, the weather had been perfect, and we had enjoyed relatively warm, sunny days. Then, the next few days turned colder, and the wind came up as we ferried loads around the aptly named Windy Corner and up onto the wide, spacious plateau at 14,200 feet.

"We should be out of the wind on the plateau," Harry said.

"That will be nice," I replied, adjusting my goggles against the icy blast.

The 14,200-foot plateau was used as a rest and staging area for the upper section of the mountain by most of the parties heading up the West Buttress route. Many tents and climbers could usually be found scattered about the snowy expanse. In those years, a medical research station run by Dr. Peter Hackett was located here, housed in a couple of large tents and supplied by helicopter. From the plateau, the route climbed a steep headwall, where there was fixed polypropylene rope to tie into, leading up onto the West Buttress ridge at 16,200 feet.

"We need to give the team a little more time to rest here," Harry said. "Why don't you, Gordie, and I ferry a load up to the ridge and then come back down and spend one more night here? That will give the rest of them time to recover and acclimatize." Gordie had accompanied us on our Mount Drum trip, and at age twelve, was the youngest member of our current climbing party, but also one of the strongest.

"Sounds good to me," I replied, stuffing sacks of food and cans of fuel into my pack. Later, as we inched our way up the steep headwall, the tents receded and became tiny colored specs on the vast, white plateau. We returned to the base camp that night, and the next day, we all moved up onto the ridge and dug platforms for a marginal tent camp that straddled the narrow ridge.

"Look at that view," Harry said, gazing out across a sea of clouds, with Mount Hunter and Mount Foraker piercing the cloud canopy and shining in the sun like islands rising out of a smoky ocean.

The ridgeline here was fairly exposed, and we spent a cold, uncomfortable night, struggling to keep the wind from blowing away the tents. At these latitudes in June, it was light almost twenty-four hours a day. I braced the tent wall against the wind with my back and watched the sun sink below the low cloud bank, casting a rose-pink alpenglow on the upper reaches of the Alaska Range. The full moon rose out of the clouds in the east and replaced the alpenglow with glittering moonlight.

"You don't see that everyday," I said to Gordie, as we listened to the wind shriek and threaten to tear apart the tent fabric. It was a hauntingly beautiful scene that more than made up for the sleepless night.

In the morning, the wind decreased in intensity, and we moved up along the hardened, icy ridge to safety of flatter, plateau-like terrain at 17,200 feet. "Hey, it looks like there's no other climbing party here," Harry said, as we trudged across the wide bowl of snow. "This is the final camp before the summit."

"Over here," I called to the rest of the team. I pointed to a large abandoned igloo and said, "Look, we can move right in."

The igloo was spacious enough to use as a kitchen and dining room. We pitched our tents safely behind protective snow walls that a previous expedition had left us. We had now been on the mountain for almost three weeks and had reached our final camp with only two days' worth of supplies left.

"We'll make our summit attempt early tomorrow," Harry said, "if the weather holds out. Try to get some sleep. Tomorrow will be a long day."

Sleep did not come easily to me at that elevation, and around 4:00 AM, we mobilized for the long haul up the headwall to Denali Pass, the Harper Glacier, and the summit snow field that led to the summit ridge. As soon as I stepped out of the tent, I knew we would not be able to summit that day. A lenticular (lens-shaped) cloud was starting to settle over the summit, and fingers of snow were blowing horizontally off the upper reaches of the mountain.

"That looks bad," I said to Harry, pointing at the lenticular cloud. "No way will we be able to summit today."

"I know, but its calm here in the basin, and there's always the chance that it will lift," he replied. "Let's start up the headwall to the pass and see what happens."

Approaching the top of Denali Pass at 18,200 feet, it became clear to everyone that the climb was now over. The wind was funneling directly over the top of the pass, and we had to shout to be heard over the freight train-like noise, but below the pass we were still completely sheltered.

"Well, that's it," Harry shouted over the roar of the wind. "We'll have to head back down now. We don't have enough supplies to wait out the weather."

"I'm just going to go and have a look over the edge of the headwall," I shouted back. "I want to see the Harper Glacier and the summit plateau. Go ahead and start down without me. I'll catch up."

"Okay, be careful," Harry said, as I untied from the rope.

Tethering my pack to the steep slope with a snow picket, I continued upward the last hundred yards to Denali Pass. The roaring of the wind became louder and louder as I approached the top of the pass. Cresting the steep slope, I began to feel the force of the wind but was able to crawl behind a rock outcrop near the top of the headwall, using it for protection. With my goggles on, I stood up to get a view of the Harper Glacier, and for the first time since jumping out of an airplane for parachute training, I was flying. I landed about thirty feet below the crest of the pass. The wind had blown me backward through the air, and when I flew below the ridgeline, I passed out of the wind stream and gravity pulled me abruptly onto the steep snow of the upper headwall. It happened so quickly that at first I had trouble figuring out what had happened, but it was such an unusual and thrilling sensation that I had to go up and do it again.

I don't know what speed that wind was blowing, but it was the coldest and most powerful wind I have ever experienced. The polar jet stream sometimes wanders and descends to encompass the summits of the Alaska Range, and I believe that it was the lower reaches of the jet stream I flew in that day.

American scientists became acutely aware of the power of the polar jet stream in 1944, during War World II, when over ninety United States B-29 Superfortress bombers participated in the first large-scale high-altitude bombing of Japan. The planes were flying at an altitude between twenty-seven-thousand and thirty-three-thousand feet. When they turned for a bombing run over Tokyo, the pilots were surprised to find their speed was 450 miles per hour, ninety miles per hour faster than the top speed of the aircraft, which resulted in a navigational error. Of the thousand bombs they dropped from that altitude, only a handful landed anywhere near their targets that day.

During the war, the Japanese had taken advantage of the jet stream to attack the mainland of the United States with *fusen bakudan,* "wind-ship bombs." From the fall of 1944 through the spring of 1945, they had launched more than nine thousand ninety-foot-diameter, hydrogen-filled balloons from the east coast of the main Japanese island, Honshu. The balloons had carried a payload of two incendiary devices and one anti-personnel bomb. The Japanese had hoped that the eastward flow of the jet stream would carry the balloons across the Pacific to land on the U.S. mainland. Over the years since the war, close to three hundred of the balloons have been found in the United States, although at the time, they caused very little damage. The most recent balloon was discovered in 1992 in Alaska, its payload long since rendered ineffective by the passage of time.

Following World War II, high-altitude aircraft and balloons documented the jet streams, which flow west to east in the upper northern hemisphere because of deflection by coriolis acceleration caused by rotation of the Earth. These streams of air can be three hundred miles wide and two miles thick, and they can travel for thousands of miles at speeds up to three hundred miles per hour. Though they generally move from west to east, the winds may loop north or south and rise and fall in altitude. When they dip down to caress the summits of the Alaska Range, it is impossible and foolhardy to continue climbing.

That morning, I soon caught up to Harry and the rest of the group, and by the time we reached the igloo, the ugly lenticular cloud had completely obscured the summit. We had missed our weather window, and with only limited supplies, needed to descend to the base camp. Over the next two days, we made our way back down the Kahiltna Glacier, through a snowstorm, and up the appropriately named Heartbreak Hill to base camp.

"We'll have to pack down a landing strip with our skis before we can be flown out," Harry said, pointing at the two feet of fresh snow gracing the glacier.

With the help of a few other climbing parties also waiting for a flight out, we made short work of it, and soon found ourselves back in the summer greenness of Talkeetna.

Harry was not done, however, with providing opportunities for me to climb McKinley.

"I need a guide to lead a group up the West Butt ... interested?" Harry asked me in the spring of 1984. "I have two European clients flying to Alaska in June. Gordie wants to be assistant guide."

"Sure, I can do that," I replied. "How old is Gordie now?"

"Fourteen, I think," Harry said.

Harry had recently purchased Genet Expeditions, one of the commercial climbing concessions guiding on Mount McKinley. Gordie, a Native Alaskan, was a veteran of our last McKinley expedition. Now, at the ripe old age of fourteen, he had been promoted to assistant guide, and he must have been the youngest person to guide commercially on the mountain. Even as a young teenager, Gordie was a great asset on an expedition team. He was strong, always able to carry more than his share of the load, had the patience and endurance of someone much older, and, most importantly, he was easygoing, uncomplaining, and never whined. I hoped that the clients would also be strong and give us an opportunity to climb the mountain in more of an alpine style (carrying fewer supplies and advancing steadily up the mountain, instead of making double carries between camps).

We met the clients, Claude and Roberto, in Talkeetna. They were somewhere in their early thirties, fit appearing, and able to speak English fluently. Neither had much mountaineering experience, but they were excited about being in Alaska and at the prospect of climbing McKinley. On a warm, beautiful summer day, Doug Geeting flew us all into the Alaska Range, leaving us on the ice and snow of the Kahiltna Glacier.

"I think our team is small enough and strong enough to try for single-load carries up the glacier instead of the usual double carries," I told the group, organizing base camp at Kahiltna International.

"Sure, I'll try that," Roberto replied.

"Yes, that sounds good to me," Claude added.

"You're the boss," Gordie said.

We made our way up the Kahiltna Glacier skiing with heavy packs and dragging loaded sleds. After four long days, we were above Kahiltna Pass and had stashed our skis for the return trip. At the end of the fifth day, we found ourselves on the plateau at 14,200 feet, pushing the boundary of how high we could go without stopping for acclimatization.

"The weather has been perfect so far, Gordie, but we should spend at least one rest day here to help acclimatize and sort gear for the upper mountain," I said.

After the rest, everyone felt strong and showed no signs of altitude illness, so on the seventh day, we headed up the fixed rope of the headwall with a week's worth of food and fuel. We bypassed the exposed camp on the ridge and continued all the way to the plateau at 17,200 feet.

"How's everyone feeling?" I asked, belaying the team to our high camp.

"Tired," was the universal response.

"Well, looks like we have the place to ourselves again, Gordie," I said. "And we're nicely provisioned with a week's worth of supplies for our summit bid."

"The weather's cooperating too, so far," he replied.

"No luxurious igloo to use this year," I pointed out. "We'll have to build our own snow walls to protect the tents."

The weather continued amazingly clear, and I decided to take advantage of it. After a few hours of sleep, we stirred at around 2:00 AM, melting snow for breakfast, collapsing the tents, and caching them with the extra gear. By 3:00 AM, we were headed up the steep headwall leading to Denali Pass. We crested the top of the pass in the bright morning sun, and there was no hurricane-force wind to lift me airborne this time. I was finally able to gaze upon the Harper Glacier and the Great Basin that those intrepid first climbers had crossed seventy-four years earlier.

Once Denali Pass was gained, the route proceeded up toward the rock outcrop known as Archdeacon's Tower and then onto a snowfield around the south side of the tower to a wide plateau. There, we actually descended in our slow, steady, high-altitude rhythm to what is known as the Football Field.

"Let's have a tea break here," I said, after belaying everyone to the base of Pig Hill at the end of the snowfield. We were at 19,500 feet, and even though the hill didn't look very steep, it seemed to take forever to plod up it to the start of the summit ridge.

"I really hate this hill," I confided to Gordie.

Once we reached the summit ridge, the pain of Pig Hill receded when an incredible vista opened up as the knife-edge ridge wound to the top. We had a perfectly clear, sky-blue summit day, although once we gained the ridge, the wind picked up and it became intensely cold. Before long, there we were on the summit with a few bamboo poles and flags flapping in the wind.

"Great job," I congratulated everyone as they arrived.

"Hey, we can look down on the summits of Huntington, Hunter, and Foraker," Gordie said.

"And look, there's the Cassin Ridge, the east fork of the Kahiltna, and across over there is the South Buttress," I said, pointing out the topography to Roberto and Claude. In the hazy distance, you could discern the curvature of the Earth, and behind us to the southwest; huge fingers of mare's tails reached out for us from a front moving in from the Gulf of Alaska.

"We can't stay long on the summit with this wind," I said. "Give me your cameras and I'll take your pictures."

"Let me get my flag out," Claude said.

"I have my country's flag also," Roberto chimed in.

After I took the traditional summit photos, we all turned around and began the long descent.

"I don't like the look of that sky," I said to Gordie, as we reached the plateau at 17,200 feet. The sky in the west had all the telltale signs of a major weather front moving in, and I was anxious to reach a lower altitude before it hit. After a two-hour nap in the snow, we loaded our packs and descended through the night to 14,200 feet.

"Let's rest here for a couple of hours," I suggested.

We slept for a few hours and regained strength with the lower altitude, so I decided to continue to push down the mountain while the weather held. Since we had already reached the summit, I had no desire to spend a week or more stormbound in a tent while waiting to be flown out to Talkeetna.

"We'll make good time once we reach our skis," I said to the rest of the team, as we plodded down toward Kahiltna Pass. "We can ski down the glacier and escape to Talkeetna before the front catches us. You two will have an extra week or so to tour Alaska," I pointed out to the Europeans.

After we reached the cache of sleds and skis, we redistributed the loads from packs to sleds and started skiing off down the glacier. It's not easy to ski when several people are roped together and carry heavy packs while trailing sleds, but I was still sorely disappointed to discover that the Europeans were not experienced enough skiers to accomplish the feat. After comically falling and tumbling down the glacier for a half hour, I faced reality. "This isn't working," I said. "Take off your skis, we're just going to have to walk."

By that stage, the fatigue of the rapid ascent and descent began to catch up with everyone, and our progress slowed.

"I don't think I can keep going like this," Roberto said, stumbling toward me on belay.

"Let's stop and camp," Claude said.

"I think we should push on to base camp," I said, undeterred by their exhaustion. "Otherwise we could end up trapped here for a week or more."

"You guys are doing great," Gordie added. "You can make it. It's not that far now," he lied.

"We'll take a short break here while I redistribute the load," I said with finality, as I started to unload some of the gear from their packs and sleds and pile it on my own.

"Hey, put some of that on my sled too," Gordie insisted. "I can carry more."

Our successful climb came to a sour ending as I pushed the Europeans beyond their endurance levels and the pile of gear on my sled grew larger and larger. I'm sure they have never forgiven me for it, but as we struggled up Heartbreak Hill to base camp, there was not a single whine of complaint from my fourteen-year-old assistant guide. We caught one of the last planes out that day before the weather closed down the mountain, and we arrived in Talkeetna, having made it to the summit and back down in ten days.

Chapter Eleven:
The Iditaski

In my dream, I'm lying face down in the snow, and something heavy is weighing me down, preventing me from rising. It's cold, and the ghostly light of the aurora borealis is shimmering overhead in the night sky. Sled dogs, no ... wolves are snapping silently at my face.

I wake up, relieved as usual to find myself in my own bed. It's that dream again, and it's all Joe Redington's fault.

In 1982, Joe Redington, "the father of the Iditarod sled dog race," was searching for a way to introduce more people to the history and adventure of the Iditarod Trail. He envisioned a cross-country ski race that would eventually attract as much attention as the world-famous Iditarod Dog Sled Race. I was one of thirty racers who answered his call in February 1983 and took part in the first Iditaski, which at the time was billed as the longest cross-country ski challenge in the world.

The Iditarod Trail was named for the abandoned gold town of Iditarod, situated near the Iditarod River in west central Alaska. Some parts of the trail had first been used for hundreds, if not thousands of years, by the Native Alaskans. Modern use of the trail peaked between the 1880s and the mid-1920s as miners traveled to the Nome area to delve for coal and gold. During summers, they took steamships from Seattle to Nome, which was located on the shores of Norton Sound, but from October to June, the sound was icebound, so people and supplies reached Nome only by dog sleds. By the end of the 1920s, bush planes began to replace dog sleds as the preferred means of transportation, and the trail fell into disrepair, although dogs continued to be used elsewhere in the state.

The arrival of the snow machine in the 1960s almost spelled the end for dog sledding in Alaska. The art was kept alive by a few hardy souls who raised and raced dogs, as well as the odd trapper living in the bush. Joe Redington was one of these intrepid dog mushers. He had moved to Alaska as a young man after serving in the Pacific Theater during World War II. In Alaska, he raised sled dogs and worked for the U.S. Air Force, using his dogs for search and rescue work. He and Dorothy Page (the president of the Wasilla-Knik Centennial Committee in 1966) organized the first Iditarod sled dog race in 1967 as a way to promote dog sledding. The twenty-five-mile race took place outside of Anchorage and was known as the Iditarod Trail Seppala Memorial Race. Redington was the force behind extending the race the thousand odd miles to Nome. The first true Iditarod Sled Dog Race took place in 1973.

It was meant to memorialize the delivery to Nome of diphtheria antitoxin by dog sled in 1925. The story has been featured in the animated Disney, *Balto*, as well as in many previous books and films. When diphtheria epidemic had threatened Nome, particularly Native Alaskans who had no immunity to the disease, in 1925, the closest supply of antitoxin serum was in Anchorage. The only two bush planes in the area had been dismantled for the winter. The governor of the Alaska Territory ordered the serum taken by train to Nenana, a town close to Fairbanks. From the train depot in Nenana, the serum was loaded on a dog sled and relayed over the next five-and-a-half-days from one musher to the next along the 674-mile trail, until it arrived in Nome on February 2. Twenty mushers and more than a hundred dogs were involved in the "wintertime race against death," (as it was called). A Norwegian musher, Gunnar Kaasen, and his lead dog, Balto, carried the serum on the last relay leg into Nome, and they thus became famous. Most Alaskans honor Leonard Seppala as the true hero of the race. He and his team, with his lead dog, Togo, carried the serum the furthest and negotiated the hardest stretch of trail. In 1978, the Iditarod Trail had been designated a National Historic Trail by an act of congress.

The first Iditaski was held in February 1983. The course started close by Cook Inlet and followed the Iditarod Trail for sixty miles, out to Rabbit Lake and back, making the total distance 120 miles. There were three checkpoints spaced twenty miles apart, where racers could stash food before the race and where all racers would be required to check in and have their mandatory gear inspected. All participants were responsible for their own survival and were required to carry a minimum amount of gear, including a stove with fuel, food, appropriate clothing, foam pad, sleeping bag, and bivy-sack (a waterproof covering for a sleeping bag) or tent.

I had done a considerable amount of cross-country skiing that winter and was fresh from winning the Hatcher Pass Mountain Man Ski Race the previous month. Compared to the Iditaski, that race was more of a sprint, consisting of a dash up and back down one of the peaks in Hatcher Pass. Since the Iditaski had never been run before, no one really knew what to expect, except that it would be long and, more than likely, very cold. Gig and Harry entered the race as well, and prior to the event, Gig and I occasionally did some training along the first twenty miles of the trail. I owned only one pair of skis in those days: metal-edged mountaineering skis, worn with a pair of heavy, leather double boots (a heavy leather outer boot combined with a lighter inner boot). This was a far cry from real cross-country racing equipment, but I figured the heavy boots would at least be' warm and keep my feet safe from frostbite.

"How are we going to carry all this gear in the race, Gig?" I asked.

"Harry says some racers are planning to pull sleds, but I think we should just use our packs," he answered.

Of course, we tried to load as lightly as possible and still have adequate gear for winter survival, but nonetheless, our packs weighed in at around forty pounds: light by gold-mining or mountaineering standards, but heavy for many hours of long-haul skiing. The day before the race, we each handed three small stuff sacks full of extra food and fuel to the race officials for placement at the various check points, and we made our last minute preparations for the race.

"Hey, I've got extra tickets for the Heart concert in Anchorage tonight," John said. "Want to go?"

"It's the night before the race," said Gig. "I'm not going."

"Well, will we just go to the concert and then come right home?" I asked.

"Of course," John assured me. I had always wanted to see the group perform live, particularly Nancy Wilson.

"All right, I'll go," I replied. "But we need to be home by eleven."

It goes without saying that after the concert we ended up at Chilkoot Charlie's, a popular downtown Anchorage watering hole. I tried to limit my carbo loading—drinking mostly orange juice and seltzer—but it was past 2:00 AM before we made it home.

"John, wake up," Gig said a few hours later. "It's time for the race."

The sharp pinpoints of the northern stars faded with the dawn as the thirty racers milled about at the start of the trail across from Knik Lake, overlooking the Susitna Flats on Cook Inlet. Not a breath of wind stirred the morning, but the sub-zero temperature still bit at my face. As the sun stabbed its yellow daggers over the Chugach Mountains from the south, I shouldered my pack. The racers started at one minute intervals, and I left somewhere in the middle of the pack. The cold fell from me as I settled into a comfortable skiing rhythm across frozen Knik Lake and headed down the Iditarod Trail northwest toward the Susitna River. The scraggly spruce trees stretched their snow covered arms skyward along this familiar portion of the trail, and I passed a few other racers as we wove our way through the fragrant conifer forests, across snow-encrusted tussocks and over frozen ponds toward the first checkpoint.

The checkpoints consisted of large, white, canvas tents with small woodstoves to provide heat for the race officials who would be staying there for the duration of the race. Their responsibilities included checking each racer as they passed through for the mandatory gear and coordinating by radio any rescue requests. Several snow machines and a small bush plane stood by, should the need arise for a rescue mission or evacuation. In addition, a large pot of water was kept simmering on the woodstove so racers could fill their water bottles and mix freeze-dried dinners without having to fire up their own stoves and melt snow.

With twenty miles of trail behind me at the first checkpoint, I still felt pretty good, so I had my gear checked off, filled my two insulated water bottles, and was on my way toward the Susitna River in less than fifteen minutes. This part of the trail was as wide as a single lane road and wound its way through mostly flat, wooded country, interspersed with small ponds and the occasional larger lake. I stopped frequently to drink and adjust clothing layers as the need arose. To stretch my water supply, I filled my plastic cup with powdered Tang and snow and then added hot water from the insulated bottles. I ate gorp and energy bars along the way and passed a few more racers as the short Alaskan daylight hurried to its end.

Above the southeast bank of the Susitna River lay the second way station, marking the forty-mile point, and I reached it just as the late afternoon dusk faded to dark. Inside the tent, I found the two lead racers eating. I stripped off layers of clothing in the heat of the tent. After having my gear once again checked off, I took time to eat a freeze-dried dinner before filling my water bottles from the pot on the stove.

"Should we camp here for the night or try to make it to Rabbit Lake?" I overheard one of the racers say to the other.

"I don't know. Let's rest for a while and then decide," the other one answered.

"I hear it will be at least thirty below tonight," one of the race officials announced to no one in particular.

"Well, I think I'll be on my way," I said, putting on my headlamp. "Thanks for the hot water." I shouldered my pack, strapped on the skis, and headed out into the Alaskan night, now in the lead.

The trail led down to the Susitna River and crossed over the frozen surface where the river was about a half mile wide. In the dark, I could faintly make out the outline of the forest as it rose along the far side of the river. A fresh dusting of snow covered the snow machine tracks that marked the trail. A multitude of old tracks crisscrossed the river, and I hoped I was following the right one as I set out across the wide expanse of ice. A hint of a breeze wafted down the river, dropping the chill factor as I skied. Once on the other side, the light of my headlamp flashed off a trail marker, and I followed the trail into the forest as it climbed the northwest bank and headed toward Rabbit Lake. A much narrower trail greeted me now, about the width of a dog sled or snow machine. In the dark forest the spruce trees gathered close, intertwining their fingers to form a roof over the trail. Every now and then, I followed the wrong set of snow machine tracks and hit a deadend in an impenetrable thicket of trees or brush, where I had to turn and double back. No doubt the trail would be more obvious in the daylight, and I wondered what the next racer would make of my meandering ski tracks.

The temperature kept falling during the night, and the snow developed that distinctive snapping crunch that it gets at temperatures below minus twenty degrees. Fortunately, once I entered the forest the river breeze disappeared, and the night was once again still and windless. The trail frequently broke out of the thick trees and crossed frozen swampland dotted with small ponds. For a few magic hours, the aurora borealis lit my solitary path through the dark. The lights shimmered in vast yellow-green and occasionally blue dancing curtains that hung in the frigid night sky.

The aurora is the visible result of the interaction of solar wind and the Earth's magnetic field. The solar wind consists of ionized particles, such as protons, electrons, ionized hydrogen, and ionized helium, which are ejected from the sun's corona and blown out across the solar system. The Earth's core generates a magnetic field, the magnetosphere, which surrounds the Earth. As the solar wind encounters this field, the charged particles stream around the planet, following the magnetic field lines to the poles. The solar particles strike atoms and molecules in the upper atmosphere and excite them to luminosity. The aurora borealis (as well as the aurora australis in the southern hemisphere) is the visible emission from these collisions. The colors produced depend on the type of atoms and molecules being energized. A yellow-green aurora is produced by oxygen atoms at close to sixty miles above the Earth's surface, while a rare, red color indicates oxygen much higher up in the atmosphere. Ionized nitrogen gives off a blue color, and neutral nitrogen produces a purplish-red aurora.

However, that night on the trail, I was not speculating about how the various colors of the aurora were formed, but I *was* starting to wonder where Rabbit Lake might be. Just as I began to think I had taken another wrong turn and should retrace my tracks, the trail exited through a small grove of trees and opened out once again onto a frozen lake. In the shimmering light of the aurora, I could make out the two tents marking the turnaround point along the shore.

"Hey, is this the Rabbit Lake check in?" I asked, after I reached the closest tent and poked my head in.

"Are you a racer?" a sleepy voice muttered from out of a sleeping bag.

"What time is it?" another voice asked.

"Two AM," the first voice responded. "We thought for sure we wouldn't see any racers until daylight at the earliest."

I shook a cloud of crystallized sweat off my hat and pullover and stepping into the dark tent, I said, "It's not much warmer inside the tent than outside. Your thermometer on the tree over there reads thirty degrees below zero."

"Sorry, we let the stove go out," an official said, and he clambered out of his sleeping bag and lit a gas lantern. "There won't be any hot water for a while," he added, lighting a pile of kindling in the woodstove.

"That's okay, I can melt snow for water," I said. I went outside and brought chunks of snow in and fired up my camp stove. "I wonder what freeze-dried delicacy I stashed here?" I muttered, rummaging through my stuff sack that I'd stationed at this tent before the race.

"Were you skiing with anyone?" an official asked from the comfort of his warm-looking down sleeping bag.

"No, I left the Susitna station alone and haven't seen anyone since then," I answered.

"We didn't think anyone would ski through the night," he said. "The race was planned so that people would camp out in the snow."

"I think most are," I answered, "but I'm sure others will ski through the night as well."

"You must be tired now," he said.

"Except for a couple of blisters on my heels, I don't feel too bad," I lied. I figured a short rest and a hot meal would fix me right up. I extracted every piece of clothing from my pack to fight the growing chill brought on by inactivity and sweat evaporation.

An hour later, I was grateful for the increasing warmth of the tent and my belly was full of hot turkey tetrazzini. "How about checking off my gear so I can get started back to Knik Lake?" I asked. "I think I've stayed here too long already, and if I don't get moving, I'll just fall asleep."

"Okay, good luck with the rest of the race," the official said in parting after he had checked my gear.

"At least I'll be able to follow my own tracks back to the Susitna," I said.

I shouldered my pack and stepped back out into the thirty-below darkness. Out bound now from Rabbit Lake, I skirted the shore and headed back into the conifer forest. Thirty minutes later, I met the next racer behind me who was headed to the turnaround point.

"You're already headed back?" he asked, as the beams of our headlamps illuminated the white fog of our breath. "How much farther to Rabbit Lake?"

"Not more than half an hour," I replied. "The tent will be warm for you, and there will be hot water on the stove."

Over the course of the next twenty miles, I encountered lumps and bumps in the snow that materialized into the sleeping-bag-clad forms of other racers who had bivouacked beside the trail for the night. About three hours out from Rabbit Lake, I met Gig skiing strongly toward me, his headlamp shimmering across a frozen pond.

"Hey, man, you're doing great. You're in the lead," Gig congratulated me, as we converged.

"Keep skiing, Gig. You're not too far from the turnaround point," I replied. After sharing a quick cup of hot Tang, we parted with encouraging words and continued traveling in opposite directions into the darkness.

I crossed the Susitna River just as day was breaking, and I entered the welcome warmth of the canvas tent at the check point. "You're skiing in from Rabbit Lake?" a racer asked, as he prepared to leave the checkpoint after camping there for the night.

"Yeah," I answered, "I'm on my way back now."

"How's the trail?" he asked.

"It's well traveled now," I replied. "You won't have any trouble following the tracks. Good luck."

Oh boy, beef stew for breakfast, I thought, opening a package of freeze-dried food and pouring hot water over it. But I discovered the thought of choking down another freeze dried dinner turned my stomach. I tried to force myself to eat it anyway.

"You should really try to eat more of that," the race official said. "You need it if you're going to keep skiing in this cold weather."

After only a few bites, I dumped the rest of the steaming reconstituted beef stew outside for the dogs, satisfying myself with some hot Tang. The warmth of the tent was enticing, and I stretched on the floor to ease the ache in my back.

"You're looking pretty tired," the official said. "Did you stop at all last night?"

"Nothing other than the hour I spent at Rabbit Lake," I answered. "Well, no sense lounging around here," I said, trying to get motivated.

"It should warm up today, once the sun makes it over the mountains," he said. "Good luck."

Back on the trail, I winced at the pain of heel blisters, which were made worse by the cross-country skiing gait, but after an hour or so of skiing, that pain merged with the discomfort caused by the pack and the ache of back and leg muscles, and I once again fell into the striding ski rhythm that carried me forward without conscious thought. The day wore on, and as the sun rose and slanted low in the southern sky, the temperature climbed. It felt like it was at least approaching a balmy zero degrees; not warm enough to have to think about changing wax on the bottom of my skis.

The end of a long straight section of the trail, somewhere around fifteen miles out from the Susitna, made for a good rest spot. I was definitely tired, and my skiing pace had started to slow down, so I stopped, took off my pack, and forced down some food. As I was sitting on my pack enjoying the early afternoon sunshine and gazing back down the trail from the direction I had just skied, I noticed a black speck bobbing in the distance. This speck slowly materialized into a skier, back bowed under the weight of a pack, coming steadily toward me. I soon was able to make out the same haggard face I had seen illuminated in my headlamp beam last night near Rabbit Lake. I thought about getting up and skiing off before he reached me, but ended up just sitting there munching from a bag of gorp.

"Have you seen the lead racer pass by?" he asked anxiously.

He didn't recognize me from our brief encounter last night, and I guess he thought no racer would just sit there and wait for another racer to catch them. "Yeah, I saw him pass by a few hours ago," I deadpanned. He let out a loud sigh, disappointment flooding his face as he stared down the empty trail disappearing into the distance. "No, just kidding. It's me," I said.

He looked to be about as tired as I felt, and we spent a few minutes talking about the race as he took a short water break.

"You tired?" I asked needlessly.

"No," he replied. "You?"

"No, I feel great," I lied. "Well, I suppose I should be moving on down the road."

"Yeah, the day's getting late," he said. "It will be dark soon."

Awkwardly, we both shouldered our packs at the same time and with him now in the lead, started to ski the remaining five miles to the last checkpoint station. His name was Mike Sallee, a former member of the U.S. Biathlon Team, and I discovered later that this was not the first time he had skied on the Iditarod trail.

In 1980, he skied the whole one-thousand-plus-mile trail for fun, in forty-five days.

The rest of that afternoon was a blur of tiredness, as I skied stride for stride behind Sallee until we reached the last checkpoint. I rummaged around in my stashed food bag to see if there was anything that looked appetizing, but I knew I couldn't eat another freeze-dried dinner. I grabbed a bag of chocolate pieces mixed with dried fruit and nuts and threw it into my pack. Mike had no intention of spending any extra time here, and as soon as he had his gear checked off and had filled his water bottles, he skied off on the last twenty-mile leg. I was on my way no more than five minutes behind him. Occasionally, I caught a glimpse of him from the top of a hill when the trail had a long straightaway.

Late afternoon approached, and the sun faded behind the mountains, allowing dusk to creep up on me with falling temperatures. *Wait a minute. This isn't the trail.* I was now on the part of the trail that I knew best, but while crossing a small lake, I became completely confused and had started skiing off in the wrong direction. *The trail is back that way. Look at your pace; it has slowed to a pitiful shuffle. You're tired now; try to eat a little more chocolate. I think I'm more exhausted now than I was that time on St. Elias.*

Darkness had fallen, and I once again broke out the headlamp. The sound of my skis on snow was nearing that twenty-below quality when I tripped and fell flat on my face. *Ah, this feels good. Maybe I can just lie here for awhile.* I lay in the trail, weighed down by my pack, happily eating some snow. My headlamp panned slowly along the side of the trail, and suddenly, wolves began jumping silently at my face from out of the woods. I lay there stupidly, said out loud, "You're not real," and went back to chewing the snow.

Struggling to stand, I found the pack was just too heavy now. Wriggling out of the shoulder straps, I rolled the pack off and then slowly stood up, but I was too weak to lift the pack back onto my shoulders. A quick handful of chocolate and fruit supplied a burst of energy that enabled me to drag the pack to a log, prop it up, and sling it onto my back. I could feel the sugar rush burn itself out in a matter of minutes, and in its wake followed an intense insulin-induced hypoglycemic low that brought the visions of the phantom wolves back to the trail.

"Well," I said to my ghostly companions, "this must be what they call hitting the wall. There's nothing left to do except shuffle onward into the night. I hope the finish line is near."

I had gone way beyond the "wall," and, after dragging myself up out of the snow, I shuffled forward as best I could, stopping occasionally to scarf down a handful of chocolate and converse with my ghostly companions. Energized by a burst of sugar in my blood, I surged forward for a few minutes but then gradually slowed to a crawl. This went on seemingly forever.

A far-off buzzing gradually drew closer to me, and as it intensified, I assumed I was being visited by a new hallucination. A blinding light raced toward me through the night, preceded by the screech of a chainsaw that grew louder and louder as it approached. *A train? A car with only one headlight? A drunken dog musher with a headlamp? An alien with a runaway chainsaw?* All these thoughts ran through my confused mind as the snow machine skidded to a stop in front of me.

"Hey, you're only a half mile from the finish line. Follow me and I'll lead you in," a helmeted figure said.

"Are you real?" I asked, reaching out to touch the cold metal of the machine.

Sure enough it was solid. He turned the snow machine around and started off down the trail. A surge of adrenaline or of relief flowed through me, and my mind cleared as I picked up the pace for the last push. The rider waited for me to catch up at the turns in the trail, and when the trail opened up onto the frozen expanse of Knik Lake, he gunned the machine and flew off across the lake in a spray of cold spindrift.

On the other side of the lake stood the finish line, bathed in brilliant white spotlights. As I approached closer, I could hear shouting from a crowd of people, but the lights prevented me from seeing them. It was a dream come true to glide under the banner marking the finish and drop the pack off my back, thirty-three hours and fifty-one minutes after starting out and nine minutes behind the winner, Mike Sallee.

This being Alaska, the finish line was located next to a bar, which was serving a free drink to the finishers of the race.

"Congratulations!" Joe Redington said, slapping me on the back. "You two really made this an exciting race. The next racer is more than eight hours behind you, so we all might as well go into the bar."

After I congratulated Mike Sallee on his win, we both shuffled off into the warm, cigarette-smoke-filled bar. Loud country music blared from a jukebox as Sallee and I waded through the curious crowd and bellied up to the bar to collect our free drinks. I wondered if I looked as tired as Sallee. He sat with his eyes glazing over and stared vacantly into the mirror hung behind the bar. Lines of fatigue were etched onto his face, and ice melted from his hat and slowly ran down his nose to drip onto the scarred wooden surface of the bar.

"Hey, Mike, are you going to enter the race next year?" someone asked him, as he stared at his reflection in the mirror.

"I'm too tired to think about it right now," he replied.

"I really had planned on people stopping and camping in the snow just like we do in the Iditarod," Joe Redington said. "Next year we'll have to make the race longer."

"For you two, drinks are on the house," the bartender smiled, wiping the pool of melting snow and ice off the counter. "What'll you have?"

"How about a cup of hot coffee?" Sallee asked me.

"I think all I can manage is some hot water," I replied.

"You look really bad," offered Peter (my old companion of Cordova fame from my first trip to Alaska) as a compliment.

"I think I feel worse," I answered, unwinding the ice encrusted scarf I had tied around my head to keep my ears from freezing. "Can you take me home, Pete?"

I'm not sure how I would have made it home if Peter and his lovely wife to be, Louisa, had not come to my rescue and met me at the finish. My house had become a way station and crash pad for any friends traveling through Alaska, and Peter and Louisa had been staying there for a couple of weeks while they searched for a place of their own.

Once he got me home, Peter helped me out of my boots, and we stared at my socks that were glued to my heels with congealed blood.

"That's going to hurt," Peter said.

"I think I'll try soaking them off in a hot bath," I said. I managed to painfully unglue them in the hot water, while massaging the cramps out of my legs, before falling into bed for an exhausted sleep.

The next day, I dragged my aching body out of bed, and found I could only fit my swollen feet into down booties and slowly shuffle along. In the afternoon, Peter and I collected Gig at the finish line. He had bivouacked in the snow for a few hours during the second night of the race. When he finished, he passed on his free drink, and we went right home to put him into the tub.

"Your blisters are much bigger than mine," he congratulated me. "They look like craters."

A few days later, Joe Redington presented me with two trophies: one for being first to the turnaround point at Rabbit Lake and one for placing second in the race. I still occasionally wake from the dream where wolves jump at me out of the snow as the aurora borealis dances ghost-like overhead.

Chapter Twelve:
The Talkeetna River

"We need to have one more trip before you leave the state for medical school," John said. "Why don't we go fishing for a few days on the Talkeetna River? Chris could drive down from Fairbanks with his kayak and meet us there." Chris was another childhood friend from New Hampshire, who had transplanted himself to Alaska and had just recently finished law school. John and I had grown up racing kayaks in New England and continued to kayak occasionally in Alaska, but Chris had become the most experienced whitewater kayaker, frequently boating on the Nenana and other rivers surrounding Fairbanks.

"Have you been on the river?" I asked.

"I flew over it last month on my way up north, and it looks like we could fly in and land on Stephen Lake in a float plane," John said. "From there it should only be about a three-day float down the river to Talkeetna. We could just relax and fish from our kayaks the whole way. The kings will be running."

"Sounds great," I said. "I could go for a relaxing three-day float. It's been a couple of years since I caught a king. What's the river like?"

"I didn't see anything significant from the helicopter," John answered. "It looked like mostly flat water."

And that's how John, Chris, and I found ourselves loading our gear into Cliff Hudson's float plane in the beginning of August 1983. John frequently criss-crossed the state in helicopters while managing exploration camps for ARCO. I had flown out of Talkeetna many times into the Alaska Range, en route to climbing expeditions, and had flown over the mouth of the Talkeetna River where it merges into the Susitna. There the Talkeetna was a large, braided, glacial river, which flowed slowly over a flat plain with the snow-covered Alaska Range towering to the northwest and the jagged Talkeetna Mountains to the east. I knew nothing about what the river was like closer to its source, but presumed that it must meander over the plains and between the foothills of the Talkeetna Mountains from Stephen Lake in a fashion similar to the lower portion of the river.

"Use these straps to lash your kayaks onto the pontoon struts," Cliff Hudson advised us. "It's only about fifty miles to the lake as the crow flies, and it won't take us long to get there."

"Make sure the straps are on tight," John said. "We don't want the kayaks falling off."

"You sure have a lot of gear for kayaking the Talkeetna," Cliff Hudson said, checking the stability of the kayaks attached to his pontoons.

"We're going to spend most of our time just fishing," we said.

John climbed into the copilot's seat, and Chris and I piled into the back with the gear. A few minutes later, the plane was airborne and winging its way up river toward Stephen Lake. From our cruising altitude we could see the sun glistening off the silver river as it curved this way and that across the heavily wooded plain. About twenty miles from Talkeetna, the ribbon of shiny gray water that was Sheep Creek joined the larger Talkeetna River from the south. We could see the green, forest-covered foothills of the Talkeetna Mountains clearly as we flew east.

A few minutes later, Cliff Hudson turned to us, and yelling over the roar of the engine, said, "I'll take you over the canyon so you can have a look at the water."

Canyon? I thought, struggling to see over the seats through the windshield of the plane.

"Yeah, the canyon is about twenty miles long," Cliff shouted. "They say it has the longest stretch of Class IV and Class V whitewater in the world."

Chris and I exchanged questioning glances and then strained our necks to see out the side windows. Far below us, I could make out whitewater rushing through a steep-walled canyon where the river cut through the foothills.

"There's the Sluice Box," Cliff yelled. "That's the longest rapid. I think it's twelve miles long."

How could we have lived and kayaked in Alaska for six years and never heard of this canyon? Looking down I saw a ribbon of white foam piercing the depths of the green wilderness.

"And there's the Toilet Bowl!" Cliff screamed. "They say that's the nastiest rapid."

"*Toilet Bowl?*" I mouthed silently to Chris over the noise of the plane.

I suppose we all thought about the water in the canyon for the duration of the flight. I had plenty of whitewater experience, but I knew we were not prepared for this kind of an expedition. We had no helmets, no wetsuits, and our boats would be stuffed full of camping gear and would not respond well in heavy whitewater. *Oh well, if worst comes to worst we can always portage around the big-*

gest water, I rationalized to myself. *Besides, most of the river will still be a flat float trip where we can do some fishing.*

The plane glided onto the smooth waters of Stephen Lake, and Cliff Hudson taxied to shore. We thanked him for the ride after unstrapping the kayaks from the pontoons and piling our small mountain of gear on the lake shore.

"Make sure you stop by the office when you're done, so I know you made it out safely," Cliff said, preparing to leave. "Have a good trip." The float plane taxied away from shore and, trailing glittering droplets of water, roared off into the late afternoon sunshine, leaving us surrounded by the silence of the Alaskan wilderness.

"Just a peaceful fishing trip floating down the placid Talkeetna," I said to John.

"Yeah, a relaxing float in the kayaks," Chris added.

"Well, I must have missed that part of the river when I flew over before," John replied. "Let's sort our gear and paddle to the far end of the lake where we can camp for the night."

Pulling out his evil-looking, matte-black, SWAT-team-style, pump-action twelve gauge shotgun with the folding metal stock that was apparently standard issue at the ARCO exploration camps, John said winking at us, "For close encounters of the bear kind." We knew there was a good chance we would see a grizzly or two along the river, feeding on the spawning kings.

"I hope the bears will be satisfied from gorging on fish and not mind sharing the river with us," I said.

Paddling across the flat water to the southern end, we found Prairie Creek exiting the lake and beginning its journey toward the silt-heavy Talkeetna River.

"There's a relatively flat spot," John said. "Let's break out the fishing gear and see if we can catch something to eat." Floating peacefully in our kayaks, we pulled a few artic grayling from the deep blue waters of the lake. We later grilled them over a campfire for dinner.

"It's about fifteen river miles to the Talkeetna," John said in the morning, as we began loading the boats with all the gear. "Let's stay together and keep an eye out for bears," he continued, placing the loaded shotgun between his legs and securing his spray skirt over the cockpit.

Prairie Creek was a shallow, clear-flowing stream that burbled pleasantly along, over a gravel bed. It wound its way gently downhill through dense alder stands and brush, curving frequently as it picked up speed.

"Hey, look at all the kings!" I exclaimed, paddling around the first bend.

The river was full of king salmon making their final pilgrimage to their birth waters. Where the water shoaled to a few inches over gravel banks, the dorsal fins of the three-to-four-foot fish stuck out of the river shark-like. Fish thudded into our boats and we could not help but strike fish with each stroke of our paddles. Brilliant red and white splotched, half-dead salmon flopped helplessly along the shore, and salmon corpses littered the banks of the stream. After we traveled a half mile, the air was permeated with the stench of rotting fish.

"Oh, that really stinks," Chris said.

These fish had spent the vast majority of their four-to-five-year lives at sea and had now returned to their birth river to lay eggs, spawn, and then die. How they are able to locate the exact stream of their birth remains a mystery, but fish biologists believe that salmon have an internal clock that enables them to monitor the length of daylight and thus determine their relative latitude. When spawning time draws near, this clock guides them close to their ancestral waters, and then their sense of smell helps them locate the exact stream.

After fighting their way upstream, sometimes for hundreds of miles, the salmon reach the spawning stream and seek out oxygen-rich, graveled riffles in the streambed. The female builds a redd (nest) by turning over on her side and slapping the gravel with her tail. This slapping attracts males, and both enter the dug out redd where the female releases her eggs and the male his milt (fish sperm). Once the eggs are fertilized, the female covers the redd with gravel and may repeat the process four or five more times in different spots. She can lay over a thousand eggs each time. Once done spawning, salmon guard their redds for a week or so before they die.

Incubating under a layer of ice and snow, the tiny eggs lie buried in the gravel all winter. Toward late winter, the eggs hatch into alevin that receive nourishment from the still attached yolk sacs. For three to four months, these alevin grow buried in the gravel before they emerge as fry. The small fry, now recognizable as fish, live in the stream for over a year while they feed on insects, unhatched salmon eggs, and each other. When they grow to a certain size, they are called smolts and undergo a process (called smoltification) by which juvenile salmon change from freshwater fish into saltwater fish. These changing fish are drawn downstream to an estuary environment, where further physiological and behavioral modifications transform them from solitary freshwater dwellers into the schooling saltwater fish that we are most familiar with. It is during this downstream trip that they build their "smell record" for the future return spawning run. During their ocean life, they live in schools and feed off smaller fish. They return to their birth waters to spawn after four to five years, thus completing the circle of their lives.

"Hey, look at those half-eaten fish on the bank over there," John said. "A bear had to have done that. I wonder why we haven't seen any yet with all these fish laying around."

"Don't tempt fate," I answered.

Sure enough, right around the next bend, a grizzly bear awaited us, wading on all fours in the shallows with salmon strewn behind him all over the gravel bank. We floated the kayaks as far away from the bear as possible as we passed. John retrieved his SWAT-team shotgun and called to the bear to let him know we were there. The bear squinted at us and slowly ambled out of the water to sit and munch a half-eaten king. He hardly looked up at us as we paddled by less than twenty feet away across the shallow stream.

"Man, those bears sure look big when you're sitting in a kayak at water level," I commented. "I'm glad you brought your gun."

Scientists have recently come to appreciate how much these bears are an integral part of the salmon-spawning stream ecosystems. The bears are seeking to put on a substantial layer of fat to see them through their winter hibernation, and thus, they rarely eat a whole salmon, preferring to eat only those portions rich in fat. Trying to eat as much as possible and avoid confrontations with other bears, they scatter and carry salmon for a considerable distance into the surrounding vicinity, effectively distributing nutrients from the sea about the immediate watershed area. Not only do these nutrients fertilize the forest, but they help to support the myriad insects, birds, and small mammals that inhabit the streamside environment. The State of Washington is currently experimenting with dropping dead salmon from helicopters along rivers that bears no longer inhabit to try to improve the health of the local ecosystem.

We saw plenty of evidence of bear activity on our fifteen-mile journey down Prairie Creek, including half-eaten fish and large paw prints covering sandy portions of the gravel bars, but we encountered no more grizzlies. Later that day, the current flushed us out of the fish-laden, clear water of Prairie Creek into the swift, gray, silty glacier water of the Talkeetna River.

"Whoa, this water is really cold," I said, splashing the silty water on my face.

"Its glacial source is not that far upstream," John replied.

While Prairie Creek had been a shallow, pleasant float, where we constantly had run aground, the Talkeetna proved to be the opposite. It was much wider and deeper, and we could feel it gathering strength for its plunge through the canyon. Over the next few miles we encountered easy Class II and Class III rapids.

"Hey, that was a great little overflow," I yelled, pulling into an eddy behind a boulder at the end of one series.

"Let's stop here for the night on this island so we don't inadvertently enter the canyon today," Chris suggested, after plunging through the rapid.

Beaching the boats on a small, sandy island in the middle of the river, half covered with alders, we scouted for a suitable campsite. "No bear sign on the island," I said. "That's good. This beach right here will do."

After unloading the kayaks and pitching the tents, we started a small bonfire to warm up. "Once the sun goes behind the hills, it gets cold down here on the water," John said.

"I don't think the canyon is that far from here," Chris said, as we all settled around the fire. "I brought a little something special along," he added, pulling a bottle out of one of his waterproof kayak floatation storage bags.

"Oh yeah, a bottle of Bailey's Irish Cream," John said.

"When we enter the canyon, we need to be careful," Chris said. "Let's plan to stop and scout each rapid before we run them."

"I'll drink to that," I added, grabbing the bottle of Bailey's. "If the rapids are really continuous like Cliff said, it won't take long to run those twenty canyon miles. It also might make it hard to stop and scout them."

"We'll see what the day brings," John said, as I handed him the bottle and we settled in to enjoy the late evening Alaska twilight.

In the morning, we shook off the chill and, after packing camp into the boats, headed off downstream. It was about ten river miles from the end of Prairie Creek to the beginning of the canyon, and there was no doubt where the canyon starts: the valley walls abruptly closed in on the river and the roar of thrashing water filled the air.

"Pull off over there," Chris yelled, bracing into an eddy backwash. "We can scout the first rapid from that ledge."

The first rapid consisted of an impressive river-wide ledge with crashing foam and boiling whitewater that disappeared into the horizon line as the river turned rightward into a narrow slot canyon.

"Looks like we can make it river left," John said, pointing at a possible line.

"Yeah, I think you're right," Chris agreed. "I'll go first and we can regroup in that eddy down there in the middle just past that monster hole."

And so we began our descent into the canyon with Chris leading the way. This was big, powerful water, and I was soon soaked from plunging through standing waves. *If only I had a wetsuit or at least a paddling jacket*, I thought to myself. The whitewater was more or less continuous in the first few miles, and resting places proved to be far and few between.

It happened somewhere around mile five of the canyon. One second I was bracing against a standing wave, and the next second I was sitting upside down in the icy, dark, glacial water. Automatically I went into roll mode. Reaching for the water surface at the front of my kayak, I leveraged the flat of the paddle blade against the water and rolled with my hips. *One failed roll.* I didn't even get a breath of air. Regroup. Get the right position. And roll! *Two failed rolls. Shit! I hate it when the boat is full of gear. No worries, third times a charm.* Bam! I smashed into an underwater rock with my right shoulder, lost my grip on the paddle, and ripped my spray skirt off the cockpit of the boat. I got out as water rushed into the boat, and immediately I was fighting for air in the midst of a whitewater hell. One second I was underwater, the next at the surface, and the next careening off rocks, trying to keep myself feetfirst downriver. Time was measured in pounding heartbeats between hastily gulped breaths of air at the surface, as the icy, swirling darkness continued to grasp at me.

"Grab the stern loop!" John screamed, fighting to approach in his yellow plastic kayak. I didn't need to be told twice. I managed to grab the stern of his boat and worked my hands down to the stern loop, but my fingers were too numb to grasp the rope. Before the boat could escape me, I thrust my right hand through the loop and twisted it tight around my wrist.

"Hang on, I'm going to try to ferry to shore," John yelled. Paddling madly upstream and angling his boat ever so slightly toward the southern shore of the canyon, he managed to slowly drag me across the river until we bumped up against rocks lining the bank. Bouncing off rock after rock, we finally were able to scoot behind a large boulder, and the eddy wash pushed us to shore.

"Th-th-thanks for saving my life, a-again," I shivered, dragging my sorry ass out of the river like a drowned rat. There were only a few boulder-strewn feet of shore between the wall of the canyon and the roaring river, but I was able to drag John's kayak half out of the water onto a rock to prevent it from floating away downstream.

"Your boat is gone," John said.

"I s-s-see that," I said. The first law of bailing from your kayak is to never let go of your boat. "I couldn't roll, and then I hit a rock, and that was it," I explained lamely.

"Chris tried for the boat, but it was full of water and he couldn't control it," John said. "There he is now, in that eddy below us on the other side of the river."

"I'll have to walk out," I concluded. "At least to the bottom of the canyon, and then maybe we can tie the boats together like a raft and I could ride on the back."

"You won't be able to walk along the river in the floor of the canyon," John said. "You'll have to climb out."

"I know," I replied. "It doesn't look that bad; maybe a couple hundred feet at the most. Once over that rock band, it looks to be more of a steep scramble than real rock climbing."

"Still, you don't want to fall," he pointed out.

"It should only be about fifteen miles to the bottom of the canyon," I said. "That should take me five or six hours, depending on how bad the bushwhacking is. You guys will probably be out of the canyon in an hour or two."

"We'll meet at the junction of Iron Creek," John said. "It flows into the Talkeetna just after the river leaves the canyon." I had a vague recollection of seeing a river entering from the south through the side window of the plane as we flew over. "Here, take this," he said, handing me the shotgun. "You should take these matches, too. Do you want to take some food?"

"Just give me that granola bar," I answered. "Chris can't hang out in that eddy forever. It will only be a few hours to the end of the canyon. I can eat when I meet you there."

"Okay, good luck," he said, clapping me on the back. "See you at the bottom."

"Hey, can I trade you for your sneakers?" I asked. "I don't think these wetsuit booties will be very good for climbing."

"Sure, no problem," he replied.

John hunkered down in his kayak, and I pushed him off the rock back into the swift current where he paddled over to Chris's eddy. Having nearly drowned in the rapids of the canyon, I felt almost happy not to be headed back down it in a kayak. I stashed the plastic bag of matches in the pocket of my still-dripping polypropylene pullover, slung the shotgun over my shoulder, and started scaling the rock of the canyon wall. After a relatively easy vertical section of rock, the slope eased off and became dotted with small bushes, grasses, and loose rock. *This isn't so bad. Still, like he said, you don't want to fall. Be careful.* Close to the top of the slope, I turned and gave my two friends a thumbs-up wave and watched as the bright red and yellow kayaks peeled out of the eddy and disappeared through the whitewater around a bend in the canyon.

Okay, now I need to make some good time. Let's see, it's about noon so I should be to the end of the canyon late afternoon or early evening. Just in time for dinner. At the top of the canyon wall there was an up-sloping bench of land following the general contours of the canyon. There was no trail, but the trees and brush were not too dense, and I was able to travel at a good walking pace. I had few opportunities to view the water in the canyon, and I never caught sight of the kayaks again that afternoon.

Four or five hours later, the terrain changed as the canyon neared its end and the bench descended toward the river where thick brush and alders crowded together to hinder my progress. The roar of the river became progressively louder, and finally, I broke through a screen of alders and found myself on what appeared to be a trail. A hundred yards later, I learned exactly what kind of trail I was on. A familiar fishy odor wafted from the brush, and soon, I came across the putrid remains of half-eaten salmon scattered haphazardly under bushes and along the trail. I was on a game trail frequented by grizzlies that feasted on the salmon bounty from the nearby river. Unslinging the shotgun from my shoulder, I double checked that a round was chambered and that the safety was off. Having no pots and pans to bang together to make noise, I started loudly singing my new mantra, "Please let me stay at the top of the food chain!"

The game trail wound its way in spurts along the river bank, frequently disappearing into an impenetrable wall of brush, only to pick up again a hundred yards further downstream. After an hour or so of starting at every rustle of leaves and snapping of twigs, certain that a bear waited around each bend to challenge me for food chain supremacy, I discovered that the trail broke out of the thick growth along the river and ran into a fast, clear-flowing river swirling its waters into the siltiness of the Talkeetna.

This has to be Iron Creek, I made it! I eagerly looked downstream and then upstream, expecting to see the familiar yellow and red kayaks pulled up on shore along side the tents with John and Chris cooking dinner, waiting to exchange tales of the day's adventures.

"All right, this is not funny, guys. Come on out," I called loudly. Only the constant din of the two rivers answered me. *Well, they must have stopped a little bit upstream.* I followed the Talkeetna as best I could upstream until it entered the canyon, and confirmed what I already knew: no one was here. I slowly made my way back to the confluence of the rivers and searched the banks for any messages or signs of recent human visitation. Nothing. *How could they not be here? It should only have taken them a few hours to finish the canyon. I must have been bushwhacking for at least six or seven hours.* Disappointment and despair gnawed at my gut as the worst possibilities flooded my mind. *There's no way they could have missed Iron Creek, and there's no way they would have left me here. That means they're still in the canyon, and either they lost their boats like I did and are walking out, or perhaps they needed to portage around some of the rapids. Portaging in that canyon could take hours. Or, maybe they're dead.*

I gathered wood for a fire and settled in for a long, hungry, lonely night. August in that part of Alaska was marked by the arrival of dusk around 9:00 PM, followed by a gray blanket of darkness that rose from the depths of the valleys and slowly consumed the surrounding mountains, and then the sky. The temperature during the sun-filled day might approach 80 degrees, but at night descended to the low 40s. I built a fire in front of a large rock, and I curled up between them. The heat reflected off the rock warmed my backside as I snuggled into the pebbly sand of the riverbank, using my life vest as a pillow. While I waited for the first hints of dawn, I took what comfort I could from the cold metal of the shotgun cradled in my arms and dozed off intermittently, feeding the fire whenever the cold awakened me.

Dawn came early, and I was up and about as soon as it was light enough to see. I decided to backtrack up the canyon a ways to see if I could find any sign of them. After two hours of trying to hug the canyon rim and walk back upstream, I acknowledged the futility of the endeavor. Given the lay of the land, there was no way to keep much of the river in sight, and so, I returned to the mouth of Iron Creek in the late morning. The way I saw it, I now had two options: I could sit here without food and hope that they would eventually show up, or I could walk out to Talkeetna and fly back in with Cliff Hudson to search for them. The second option seemed the obvious choice. I found a flat, white rock, and, using the fire-blackened end of a stick, I wrote a message in case the two of them found their way to Iron Creek:

Walking out to Talkeetna to get help

John

I figured the whole trip we had planned down river was about eighty river miles, and I had covered thirty to thirty-five by boat and foot to the end of the canyon. The remaining forty to fifty miles should only take two or three days, depending on how hard the bushwhacking was. *Without a map, you will have to follow the river to Talkeetna,* I told myself. *No cutting across country if you don't know where you are. But first you need to get across Iron Creek.*

The first obstacle was staring me in the face. At its mouth, Iron Creek was twenty to thirty yards wide and looked fast and deep. The last thing I wanted to do was swim that river and end up in the glacial waters of the Talkeetna again. I knew I would just have to walk upstream and find a crossing. A mile or so upstream the river narrowed but still required swimming through rapids to reach the other side. *You're wasting time here,* I thought. *You need to be on your way to Talkeetna, so just get in the water, you wimp.* I hoped I was far enough upstream not to get swept into the Talkeetna. Jumping from boulder to boulder as far as I could across the river, I eased into the icy current, holding the shotgun over my head with one hand while stroking out as best I could with the other. I fended rocks off with my feet as I was rushed downstream, and I made my way to the opposite shore after a few minutes in the cold, wild, sluice ride. It wasn't so bad. There was still plenty of river to spare, and the shotgun was more or less dry.

After a half-mile walk downstream, I was staring at the prior night's campsite across Iron Creek. There was no sign of Chris or John, so I turned west and started following the Talkeetna. Winding first this way and then that, the river slowly worked its way out of the foothills of the Talkeetna Mountains. Occasionally, I came across game trails that sped my pace along, until the trails eventually petered out. Sometimes I was able to cross a hill or ridgeline and cut off a loop of river, but frequently this led me into thicker stands of trees and brush that only slowed down my overall progress. There were small, clear streams flowing into the Talkeetna that provided me with drinking water throughout the day. When darkness began to close in, I foraged firewood from a pile of driftwood by the bank of the river. Placing myself between a rock and a nice roaring bonfire, I hunkered down for another hungry night, and a conversation with myself.

I wonder how many miles I made today? Tomorrow will be better with an earlier start, but I still can't waste any time foraging for food. I need to make it to Talkeetna as soon as possible. That's okay; I've been hungry before. At least I didn't see any bears today, and it's still not raining.

I awoke shivering in the dawn, the fire long since having gone out. After slaking my thirst in a nearby stream, I continued the downstream journey. The foothills receded, and the river widened and began to braid into multiple channels. The forest and undergrowth thickened and seemed to bar my way like an evil adversary. The thick stands of alders along the riverbank made streamside travel almost impossible, and it was not much better bushwhacking along the nearby bench above the river.

I was so hungry now, I hoped I *would* see a bear. *I'll show him top of the food chain*, I thought.

Suddenly I stumbled into a forest of devil's club; now I would have to go back down to the river. Devil's club is a native plant that grows in dense clusters, five to eight feet tall, and is covered with dagger-like thorns along its stem. Even its palm-like leaves sport thorns along the underside, and it much deserves its scientific name, *Oplopanax horridus*.

I didn't realize devil's club grew this far north in Alaska, but leave it to me to find a huge patch of it in the forest. The Native Alaskans have used it for hundreds of years as a medicinal plant, and recently there has been some excitement that the plant may be of value in treating diseases as diverse as tuberculosis and diabetes. I was far from excited at having found it and turned back to struggle along the riverbank.

A few times during the day, I heard the far off buzz of a small plane flying high overhead—much too high to be able to spot me along the river. When the river divided into more than one channel, I was sometimes able to make good time along a sandbar, but invariably the braids coalesced and I was forced back into the vegetation that crowded the bank. Forward progress was frustratingly slow, but toward dusk I was rewarded with the sight of the next major river obstacle, Sheep Creek. This glacial river flowed from the south to join the Talkeetna River about twenty miles northeast of the town of Talkeetna. *Only twenty miles to go now, but Sheep Creek is almost as wide as the Talkeetna here. How am I ever going to get across?*

I walked out on a long sandbar that extended into the Talkeetna just above the mouth of Sheep Creek. The bar was littered with tangled piles of driftwood and logs left high and dry by the river. *It's going to be dark in an hour or so*, I thought. *I might as well stop here for the night. If only I could tie a couple of these logs together, I could make a raft of sorts and float down the rest of the river. That would certainly be a lot easier than swimming Sheep Creek and struggling through the bush. Yeah, but if it falls apart or sinks, you'll end up swimming in the Talkeetna again.*

After piling up enough firewood to last the night, I went back into the woods to search for vines that I could use to lash logs together. Using a sharp rock to cut a few thin, flexible alder saplings and some woody creepers, I experimented with tying a couple of branches together and thought, *You know, this might actually work.* But I didn't know how long it would hold together. I hoped it would at least get me across Sheep Creek. I just needed to move a couple of logs together at the river's edge. Using a rock as a fulcrum and a long branch as a lever, I managed to muscle two suitable logs to the waters edge before darkness called a halt to the building project. I would have to finish the rest in the morning. *Now for the fire.* I thought. *Maybe if I torch all the wood on the sandbar somebody would see it and investigate. No, probably not a good idea, I might burn down the forest.* So, I settled for my usual driftwood fire and took comfort in the knowledge that I would make it to Talkeetna the next day, either by river or by foot.

The lonely dark of night slowly gave way to the gray dawn, and when it was light enough to see, I gathered more saplings and vines and began to bind the two logs together. Before the makeshift raft was finished, a faint buzzing sound caused me to search the skies overhead for a small plane. The sound became progressively louder, but no plane came into view. The noise suddenly got louder, and it was now coming unmistakably from downstream. I stared in disbelief as an outboard-powered aluminum skiff roared around the bend in the river, heading upstream. *It's a boat!* Frantically waving both arms over my head, I tried to yell to them over the clamor of the engine. The boat slowed, hugging the opposite bank of the river from where I stood on the sandbar, and the two men in the craft stared at me from across the water.

"Hey, I need some help here!" I shouted to them, waving my arms.

They looked at each other and held a short conversation as they approached the sandbar, but kept the boat in the middle of the river. I suppose I must have been an unexpected sight, staring at them with wild eyes, dressed in a spray skirt and life jacket, and waving a twelve-gauge, SWAT-team shotgun over my head.

"What happened?" one of them shouted.

"I lost my kayak and my two friends in the canyon upstream three days ago, and I've been walking out to get help since then," I explained. "Do you think you could give me a ride downstream to Talkeetna?"

"That thing's not loaded, is it?" the other asked as the boat floated by on the current.

I ejected all the shells into the sand and said, "Not now."

Gunning the engine, they landed next to me on the sandbar. "Hey, thanks man," I said, shaking their hands. "I really need to get back to Talkeetna to find a plane and see if I can locate my friends."

"No problem," one replied. "We're glad to help out."

"It's just that you looked a little wild at first," the other added.

"Well, that's because I haven't eaten in three days," I blurted out. "Say, you wouldn't happen to have any extra food, would you?"

One of them pushed their cooler over to me and said, "Sure, eat whatever you want here."

The two of them were from Anchorage and had come to fish for salmon on the tributaries of the Talkeetna. It was pure luck they had decided to cruise a little further upstream than usual that day. I devoured most of their lunch while the boat headed downriver at high speed. In less than an hour, I was standing at the town boat launch, only one mile from Talkeetna.

"Hop in the truck and I'll give you a ride into town," the captain said.

"I'll never be able to thank you enough for your help," I said sincerely. "Can you drop me off at Cliff Hudson's?"

"I was starting to wonder about you guys. You're a day overdue," Cliff Hudson said, as I walked into his office. "I was just thinking of flying upriver to have a look for you."

"Actually, Cliff, I had a little problem out there," I began. "I lost my boat three days ago in the canyon, and I haven't seen my two friends since then. They were supposed to meet me at the bottom of the canyon, but didn't show. Over the past three days, I've been walking out to get help to go back and find them."

"Here's $20. Go and get yourself some food at the Fairview while I fuel the plane and then we'll go have a look," he said.

After my second meal in an hour, I found myself flying back upriver at an altitude of a few hundred feet. "There's where I camped last night," I yelled at Cliff over the engine noise, pointing to the sandbar marking the junction of Sheep Creek and the Talkeetna.

The plane continued upstream, following the curves of the river, and soon we flew over the mouth of Iron Creek and then over the lower portion of the canyon. "Look, there!" Cliff yelled, pointing at the telltale bright red, yellow, and blue of three kayaks stuck together in the middle of a huge logjam that spanned the river.

"That doesn't look good," I said, as the plane circled lower over the canyon. Huge torrents of whitewater pored over and through the mad tangle of logs, and spray shot high over the bows of the trapped boats. There was no doubt that it would be certain death for any kayaker caught in that logjam.

"I don't see any evidence of bodies in the boats or any sign of your friends along the shore here," Cliff said.

The day had been an emotional roller coaster with the excitement of my fortuitous rescue by boat followed by the hopeful searching from the plane, but everything seemed to come crashing down at the sight of those three ensnared boats.

"Maybe they escaped the river before their boats were trapped in the logjam," I said over the roar of the engine, trying to keep the despair out of my voice. "We might have missed seeing them in the dense brush along the river."

"We'll fly to the top of the canyon and then back down the river," Cliff answered.

The plane banked slowly at the top of the canyon and headed back downstream at a lower altitude. The depressing sight of the three kayaks again greeted me, and soon the canyon was behind us. There was no sign of John or Chris on the silent flight back to Talkeetna.

Taxiing to a stop in front of his hanger, Cliff shut down the engine. "Thanks for helping me search for them," I said miserably.

"Don't give up hope yet," Cliff replied. "It's not easy to spot a person from that altitude, particularly with the vegetation along the river. I'll call the State Police from the office and see if they can send their helicopter to search for them."

Two hours later, I was showered in dust as the State Police rescue helicopter landed at the dirt airstrip, and a flight-suited officer jumped out and walked over to me. There was a crew of four: pilot, copilot, and two rescue personnel. I gave them the quick version of the history of the trip along with a description of John and Chris.

"I can show you exactly where the boats are trapped and help search from the helicopter," I said.

"I'm sorry, but there's no room for you in the chopper, especially if we find them. You'll just have to wait here," the officer informed me.

The helicopter lifted off and disappeared over the trees as I sat on the hood of my truck watching helplessly. I hated waiting. I would rather have been still walking through the devil's club. At least I was doing something then.

An hour dragged by, and then my stomach dropped as a faint stutter became the unmistakable approach of a helicopter. The rotor-blown dust obscured my vision as the rescue helicopter landed. My heart was in my throat as I waited for the dust to clear and for the craft to be shut down. Were there more than four people in there? I couldn't really tell.

The door popped open on the opposite side of the chopper, and I could make out the flight-suited legs of one of the officers as he jumped to the ground. These were followed by two sets of legs clad only in shorts and spray skirts, and then John and Chris were hobbling toward me from around the front of the helicopter.

"Man, that was a long three days," I said, clapping them on the back. "What happened to you?"

"Take us to get something to eat, and we'll tell you all about it," John answered.

"Hey, your feet are a mess," I said to John, looking down at his swollen, red, bloody feet. "Why are you barefoot?"

"Your stupid wetsuit booties were sucked off in the whitewater when I lost my boat, and I had to walk out barefoot," he explained.

Over another meal at the Fairview Inn, we traded stories about the last three days. After I climbed out of the canyon, they continued down through the rapids.

They decided to portage around one particularly nasty spot, which took hours, carrying their boats and gear up and over the steep north canyon wall and then back down to the river.

"It was a portage from hell and took up most of the day," John said. "I lost my kayak soon after that," he continued. "Chris tried to rescue me, but ended up losing his boat as well."

"We both managed to drag ourselves out of the river, but it was on the north side of the canyon—the opposite side from you," Chris added. No boats, no gear, no food, no gun, no matches with which to build a fire, and for John, no shoes.

"We made our way slowly up and along the north rim of the canyon," John continued.

"From the rim we saw all three kayaks trapped in a huge logjam," Chris said.

"I know. I saw them when I flew over with Cliff earlier today," I said. "No telling if that logjam would have been visible from river level in a kayak," I added. "Hitting that would have been certain death."

Their walk out was similar to mine, only slower, and for John, much more painful without shoes. They walked during the day, as I had, for as long as it was light. Without the luxury of a fire, they huddled together for warmth and shivered the nights away.

"Today, we were being shadowed by a grizzly and retreated to the end of a sand spit sticking into the river," Chris said.

"We thought we would have to try to swim across the river to escape the bear when the helicopter shot around the bend at river level," John continued. After circling the joyous, waving pair, the helicopter landed on the spit and plucked them from their ordeal, returning them to the world.

"The worst part for me was not knowing whether you were dead or alive," I confessed. "I need to settle up with Cliff Hudson, and then let's go home to Wasilla."

The next day, Chris returned to Talkeetna and chartered a helicopter to fly him back into the canyon to try to salvage the boats. Hanging off a skid as the helicopter hovered over the foaming logjam, he was able to snare all three boats with a cable and pull them out of the river. Not only did he salvage all the boats, but he retrieved all the gear stored in them as well. All we ended up losing were the three paddles, my wetsuit booties, a few meals, some sleep, and a little bit of pride. All in all, not bad, considering that we could easily have lost all our lives.

The Talkeetna Canyon has recently become a popular destination for kayakers from around the world. There are now several kayak and raft guiding operations working out of Talkeetna, and I hear the canyon can be crowded with boaters.

Chris has gone back and kayaked the canyon with raft support a few times over the years, but I plan to keep my canyon memories as they are.

A week after wandering out of the Talkeetna Mountain wilderness, I loaded all my worldly possessions into the truck, and with Denali as my copilot, left Alaska, bound for medical school in Boston, Massachusetts, and for a different life. But that adventure is a whole other story.

I had no idea what challenges awaited me on the other side of the country, but I knew that my Alaskan experiences would provide me with the confidence and determination to meet those challenges, and that the bonds of friendship I had forged in Alaska would continue to sustain me and last a lifetime.

About the Author

After graduating from Bowdoin College in Brunswick, Maine, John McGoldrick heeded the siren call of adventure and moved to Alaska. He lived there from 1977 to 1983, when he returned to New England to attend medical school at Tufts University School of Medicine in Boston, Massachusetts. He completed his emergency-medicine residency in Denver, Colorado, where he was able to continue his rock climbing and mountaineering pursuits.

John sold the house he built in Alaska, bought a sailboat with the proceeds, and now enjoys sailing the coast of Maine, where he lives with his wife and two children. He plays classical guitar and is a fourth-degree black belt in Shotokan karate. While practicing emergency medicine, he wrote a number of papers in medical journals as well as chapters in a medical textbook. In addition to being an emergency physician, he home schools his two children, aged ten and thirteen, when he's not off adventuring with his family.

Sources

Bodett, Tom. *As Far as You Can Go Without a Passport: The View From the End of the Road: Comments and Comic Pieces*. Cambridge, MA: Perseus Books, 1986

Boxberger, Daniel. "Ethnicity and Labor in the Puget Sound Fishing Industry, 18801935." *Ethnology* 33, no. 2 (1994): 179–182.

Browne, Belmore. *The Conquest of Mount McKinley*. Seattle: The Mountaineers Books, 2001. First published 1913 by G.P. Putman's Sons, The Knickerbocker Press.

Bull, Stephen. *Encyclopedia of Military Technology and Innovation*. Westport, CT: Greenwood Press. 2004.

Cherici, Peter, and Bradford Washburn. *The Dishonorable Dr. Cook: Debunking the Notorious Mount McKinley Hoax*. Seattle: The Mountaineers Books, 2001.

Clark, Henry. *History of Alaska*. New York: Macmillan, 1930.

Cook, Frederick. *To the Top of the Continent*. Seattle: The Mountaineers Books, 2001. First published 1908 by Doubleday, Page & Co.

Dillehay, Thomas. "Lost World: Rewriting Prehistory—How New Science is Tracing America's Ice Age Mariners." *American Antiquity* 70, no. 1 (2005): 202–205.

Dixon, James, William Manely, And Craig Lee. "The Emerging Archaeology of Glaciers and Ice Patches: Examples from Alaska's Wrangell-St. Elias National Park and Preserve." *American Antiquity* 70, no.1 (2005): 129–132.

Evans, David, and James Claiborne, eds. *The Physiology of Fishes, Third Edition (Marine Biology)*. Boca Raton, FL: CRC Press, 2006.

Freeman, Otis, ed. *Geography of the Pacific*. New York: John Wiley & Sons, 1951.

Fukuyama, Frances. *The End of History and the Last Man*. New York: Free Press, 1992.

Gende, Scott, and Thomas Quinn. "The Fish and the Forest." *Scientific American* 295, no.2 (August, 2006): 84–88.

Gough, Barry. *The Northwest Coast: British Navigation, Trade, and Discoveries to 1812*. Vancouver: University of British Columbia Press, 1992.

Grosvenor, Melville Bell, Merle Severy, and Edwards Park. *Great Adventures With National Geographic: Exploring Land, Sea, and Sky*. Washington DC: National Geographic Society, 1963.

Higginson, Ella. *Alaska the Great Country*. New York: Macmillan, 1908.

Hornbein, Thomas, and Robert Schoene. *High Altitude (Lung Biology in Health and Disease)*. New York: Information Healthcare, 2001.

Hutchinson, Kevin Don. *World War II in the North Pacific: Chronology and Fact Book*. Westport, CT: Greenwood Press, 1994.

Kerski, Joseph. "Investigating Glaciation with U.S.G.S. Resources." *Focus* Spring 2000: 8

King, Cuchlaine. *An Introduction to Oceanography*. New York: McGraw-Hill, 1963.

Klein, Herbert and Daniel Schiffner. "The Current Debate about the Origins of the Paleoindians of America." *Journal of Social History* 37, no.2 (2003): 483–486.

Lance, Edward, and Bart Geets. *Climates and Weather Explained*. New York: Routledge. 1997.

McArdle, William, Frank Katch, and Victor Katch. *Essentials of Exercise Physiology*. New York: Lippincott, Williams, & Wilkins, third edition, 2005.

Mozée, Yuonne. *Walter Harper*. Seattle: The Mountaineers Books. 2001.

Murphy, Brendan, and Damian Nance. "How Do Supercontinents Assemble? One Theory Prefers an Accordion Model; Another Has the Continents Travel the Globe to Reunite." *American Scientist* July–Aug. 2004: 324–328.

Posadas, Barbara. *The Filipino Americans.* Westport, CT: Greenwood Press, 1999.

Radostite, Otto, et al. *Veterinary Medicine: A Textbook of the Diseases of Cattle, Sheep, Pigs, Goats and Horses.* Philadelphia: W. B. Saunders, 2000.

Redfern, Martin. *The Earth: A Very Short Introduction.* Oxford, England: Oxford University Press, 2003.

Rick, Torben, Jon Erlandson, and Rene Vellanoweth. "Paleocoastal Marine Fishing of the Pacific Coast of the Americas: Perspectives from Daisy Cove, California." *American Antiquity* 66, no.4 (2001): 595–598.

Starr, Frederick, ed. *Russia's American Colony.* Durham, NC: Duke University Press, 1987.

Stuck, Hudson. *The Ascent of Denali.* Seattle: The Mountaineers Books. First published 1914 by Charles Scribner's Sons.

Turner, Christy. "Three Ounces of Sea Shells and One Fish Bone Do Not a Coastal Migration Make." *American Antiquity* 68, no.2 (2003): 391–395.

Waterman, Jonathan. *A Most Hostile Mountain.* New York: Henry Holt and Company, 1997.

978-0-595-41644-8
0-595-41644-6

Breinigsville, PA USA
12 December 2009
229090BV00001B/120/A